Banking on Knowledge

It is not often that a group of such distinguished contributors is brought together to comment on a fascinating new development in the global community. This important and timely book presents new and challenging material, and makes a significant contribution in an area of growing interest among scholars and policy-makers.

Professor Don Abelson, University of Western Ontario, Canada

This study provides invaluable insights into the links between international institutions and national think tanks in promoting local 'ownership' of programmes for development and socio-economic change. The World Bank emerges as an active player, providing support for national reformers even under adverse domestic conditions.

Professor William Wallace, London School of Economics, UK

Banking on Knowledge is one of the first studies of the way in which the World Bank is reinventing itself as the 'Knowledge Bank'. The book addresses how international organisations and governments are developing partnerships with think tanks, research institutes and other knowledge institutions in the hope of informing and improving policies for reform and development around the world.

The book focuses on the recently established Global Development Network (GDN). The GDN is a new and ambitious initiative and possibly the largest worldwide non-governmental enterprise aimed at producing knowledge as a public good on a global scale.

The contributions to *Banking on Knowledge* are from an internationally acclaimed group of experts, including an original and groundbreaking piece by Joseph Stiglitz, former chief economist and vice president of the World Bank. Subjects covered include:

- the changing policy emphasis in the World Bank as it develops alliances with non-governmental actors and promotes civil society;
- first-hand accounts of the making of this new global network amid the plethora of existing political, commercial and non-governmental networks;
- detailed case studies of the problems faced by think tanks and other know-ledge institutions across the world; and
- whether knowledge, information and data are successfully used by experts to influence policy.

Since the papers in this volume were first presented, the GDN has continued to develop as a new type of global institution that knits together policy institutes around the world, helping them to generate, share and apply new knowledge about pressing development issues.

Timely, original and provocative, this book is essential reading for students, researchers, policy makers and professionals with an interest in the future of the World Bank, the strategies of think tanks and the changing nature of development.

Diane Stone is reader in the Department of Politics and International Relations at the University of Warwick. Her previous books include *Capturing the Political Imagination* and (as co-editor) *Think Tanks Across Nations*.

Routledge/Warwick Studies in Globalisation
Edited by Richard Higgott
*Published in association with the Centre for the Study of
Globalisation and Regionalisation, University of Warwick*

What is globalisation and does it matter? How can we measure it? What are its
policy implications? The Centre for the Study of Globalisation and Regionalisation at the University of Warwick is an international site for the study of key
questions such as these in the theory and practice of globalisation and regionalisation. Its agenda is avowedly interdisciplinary. The work of the Centre will be
showcased in this new series.

This series comprises two strands:

Warwick Studies in Globalisation addresses the needs of students and teachers, and
the titles will be published in hardback and paperback. Titles include:

Globalisation and the Asia-Pacific
Contested Territories
Edited by Kris Olds, Peter Dicken, Philip F. Kelly, Lily Kong and Henry Wai-chung Yeung

Regulating the Global Information Society
Edited by Christopher T. Marsden

Routledge/Warwick Studies in Globalisation is a forum for innovative new research
intended for a high-level specialist readership, and the titles will be available in
hardback only. Titles include:

1 Non-State Actors and Authority in the Global System
Edited by Richard Higgott, Geoffrey Underhill and Andreas Bieler

2 Globalisation and Enlargement of the European Union
Austrian and Swedish Social Forces in the Struggle over Membership
Andreas Bieler

Banking on Knowledge

The genesis of the Global
Development Network

Edited by Diane Stone

Generating Local Knowledge

London and New York

First published 2000
by Routledge
11 New Fetter Lane, London EC4P 4EE

Simultaneously published in the USA and Canada
by Routledge
29 West 35th Street, New York, NY 10001

Routledge is an imprint of the Taylor & Francis Group

Typeset in Baskerville by Taylor & Francis Books Ltd
Printed and bound in Great Britain by Biddles Ltd, Guildford
and King's Lynn

British Library Cataloguing in Publication Data
A catalogue record for this book is available from the
British Library

Library of Congress Cataloging-in-Publication Data
Banking on knowledge : the genesis of the Global Development Network /
Diane Stone, editor.
Includes bibliographical references and index.
1. Economic development–Research. 2. Communication
in economic development. I. Stone, Diane, 1964–
HD77.B36 2000
338.9'007'2–dc21   00–055329

ISBN 0–415–24847–7 (hbk)
ISBN 0–415–24848–5 (pbk)

Contents

Contributors

Simon James is a consultant on public administration reform. He worked previously for the Organisation for Economic Co-operation and Development in Paris, and before that in the United Kingdom Cabinet Office and the Department for Education and Employment. He is the author of *British Cabinet Government* (second edition 1999) and *British Government: A Reader in Policy-making* (1997), both published by Routledge.

Erik Johnson is a knowledge management officer in the World Bank Institute, where he is involved in the development and management of the Global Development Network (GDN). Mr Johnson has worked for other political and economic development institutions in a number of capacities: as a board member, executive director, staff member and consultant. As director of policy studies and evaluation for the Center for International Private Enterprise, his responsibilities included needs assessments, program development, and evaluation of projects to support indigenous non-profit institutions involved in economic reform and building democracy. Mr Johnson has published numerous articles on think tanks and public policy. He has an MA in public and international affairs from the University of Pittsburgh and a BS in management from Keene State College.

Kao Kim Hourn was educated in the United States and is now the executive director and senior research fellow of the Cambodian Institute for Cooperation and Peace (CICP), a leading policy-oriented think tank in Cambodia, and a member of the ASEAN Institutes of Strategic and International Studies. He also serves as a member of the Supreme National Economic Council (SNEC) of Cambodia with the rank of minister. Recent articles have been published in *Panorama* (2000).

Ivan Krastev is a political scientist and director of the Centre for Liberal Strategies in Sofia. At present, he is fellow in the Institute for Advanced Studies, Berlin. He has been a former fellow at Collegium Budapest, the Institute for Advanced Studies in Budapest and the Woodrow Wilson Center for International Scholars in Washington, and a visiting fellow of St Anthony's College, Oxford.

Stella Ladi is a graduate of the University of Athens and a doctoral student at the University of York in Great Britain, where she also completed her MA in public administration and public policy. Her research topic is 'Globalisation, policy transfer and think tanks'. She is also an affiliated researcher of the research institute ELIAMEP in Athens.

Evert Lindquist is director of the School of Public Administration at the University of Victoria in Canada. He previously worked at the University of Toronto. He is the author of numerous articles on think tanks and central government agencies and has been chair of the Research Committee of the Institute of Public Administration of Canada.

Oleg Manaev is a founder and director of the Independent Institute of Socio-Economic and Political Studies, the first think tank in Belarus, founded in February 1992. In June 1997, he founded and chaired the Belarusian Think Tanks (BTT), a non-governmental and non-profit national association that unites eighteen leading independent research and analytical centres from the capital and most regions of the country. Dr Manaev is also professor in the Department of Social Communication at the Belarusian State University. He has edited and contributed to a dozen books and published over one hundred scholarly articles on the media, democracy and think tanks, as well as various publications in the mass media.

Helen E.S. Nesadurai is a doctoral candidate in the Department of Politics and International Studies. She holds a British Chevening Scholarship and the Chevening Scheme's ASEM (Asia–Europe Meeting) Award for Malaysia. Prior to coming to the Centre for the Study of Globalisation and Regionalisation at the University of Warwick, she was with the Institute of Strategic and International Studies (ISIS), in Malaysia where her most recent research focused on how Southeast Asian countries related to wider processes of Asia-Pacific economic cooperation. Her current research interests centre on the institutionalisation of regional cooperation. Her PhD dissertation examines the political dynamics of regional institution building in ASEAN and the relationship between institutional design and progress on regional economic cooperation using the ASEAN free trade area as a case study. She holds an MSc in development economics from the University of Oxford.

Knut G. Nustad received his education from the University of Oslo (BA) and Cambridge University (MPhil, PhD). His thesis in social anthropology examined one of the largest urban development projects ever undertaken in South Africa, with a focus on the consequences of addressing poverty and inequality as development issues. His latest work has continued to be involved with the discourse of development and on the transformation of politics into policy.

Gabriel Ortiz de Zevallos is an economist with a master's degree in public administration from Harvard University. He is currently executive director of the APOYO Institute and member of the board of the Peruvian Consortium for Economic and Social Research (CIES). Publications include 'Think tanks in Peru' (in McGann and Weaver (eds), Transaction Press, 2000), co-editor of 'Implementacion de Politicas Publicas en el Peru' (Instituto APOYO, 1995), and editor of 'Economia Politica de las Reformas Institucionales: los Casos de Educacion, Salud y Pensiones' (Inter-American Development Bank, 1999). He has been professor in the Economics Department of the Pontificia Universidad Catolica del Peru.

Alejandro Salas is a political scientist with a master's degree in public policy and administration from the Institute of Social Studies in The Hague, Netherlands. He is project coordinator of the Civil Society Task Forces Initiative at the APOYO Institute. He has professional experience in the Social Development Ministry in Mexico and the Executive Committee of the Partido Revolucionario Institucional (PRI). Additionally, he has been professor in the Political Science Graduate Program of the Pontificia Universidad Catolica del Peru.

Ole J. Sending is a research fellow at the Norwegian Institute of International Affairs and a PhD student at the Department of Administration and Organization Theory at the University of Bergen, Norway. His background is in political science, economics, sociology and economic history. Mr Sending's PhD project examines how knowledge and expert advice influences, and is used by, political actors in international negotiations in the UN. He uses the International Conference on Population and Development held in Cairo in 1994 and the World Summit for Social Development held in Copenhagen in 1995 as cases.

Joseph Stiglitz is a professor of economics at Stanford University (on leave) and a senior fellow at the Brookings Institution in Washington. From 1997 to 2000, he was chief economist and vice president of the World Bank. He served on the US President's Council of Economic Advisers from 1993 to 1997. He is the author of numerous publications.

Diane Stone is reader in Politics and International Studies and an associate of the Centre for Studies in Globalisation and Regionalisation at the University of Warwick. She is working on her fourth book, which will address the transnationalisation of think tanks, especially their interactions with international organisations, and a further book on global governance and policy. Recent articles are to be found in *Global Society* (2000), *Governance* (2000), *Politics* (1999) and *Policy and Politics* (1998). Other research interests include knowledge institutions, the political economy of higher education, conceptual developments in the study of policy networks, and the political process of policy transfer.

Ratna M. Sudarshan is a senior economist at the National Council of Applied Economic Research, New Delhi. She has previously worked as research and planning officer at the South Asia office of IDRC, project coordinator at the Institute of Social Studies Trust and lecturer in economics at the University of Delhi. She has a master's degree in economics from the University of Delhi and University of Cambridge. Recent publications include a book co-edited with Maitreyi Krishnaraj and Abusaleh Shariff, *Gender, Population and Development* (Oxford University Press, Delhi, 1998).

Prologue

'An idea whose time has come' is a well-worn phrase but very apt in reference to the Global Development Network (GDN). The GDN seeks to build the capacity in developing countries to undertake socio-economic research that informs and influences policy. The idea has found wide appeal in both the research community in the developing world and in the member countries of the Organisation for Economic Co-operation and Development (OECD). The foundation has been laid for a truly powerful and vibrant interaction between the resources of the rich and the ideas of the poor.

Characterizing an evolving global institution is not easy. However, three features stand out. First, the GDN has a history. It builds on a decade-long effort to establish regional research networks, such as the African Economic Research Consortium and the Economic Research Forum for the Arab Countries, Iran and Turkey, throughout the developing world. Second, it serves its constituents. The activities to be supported by the GDN and its governance structure are being determined via an open, worldwide debate. And third, the GDN is part of the electronic age. Surveys have revealed that research and policy institutes throughout the developing world are linked to the Internet and are regular users of e-mail. The GDN is therefore implementing many of its activities, including the discussion of governance, through electronic communication.

This volume focuses on one important aspect of the GDN's mission – to find ways to ensure that high-quality research moves out of the lecture hall and into the corridors of power. It draws on some of the papers presented at the launch of the GDN in Bonn in December 1999. The title of that conference – 'Bridging Knowledge and Policy' – captures well the content of this volume.

The second annual conference, to be held in Tokyo in December 2000, will focus on another aspect of the GDN's mandate – its multidisciplinary approach to development – and is titled 'Beyond Economics'.

Lyn Squire
Director
Global Development Network Secretariat
World Bank
23 June 2000

Foreword

The notion that effective policy decisions must be based on sound policy ideas would win general consensus in any country. Most people would also agree that sound policy ideas must be grounded in rigorous and objective research. However, the claim that policy-oriented research conducted outside government would add value and give enhanced legitimacy to the policy-making process would, at best, probably win just a few supporters. One of the goals of the Global Development Network (GDN) is precisely to change the perceived role and potential contribution of think tanks and research centres in the formulation, monitoring and lobbying for policy options in the developing world and transition economies. The stated mission of the GDN is to generate and share knowledge related to development and transition, to facilitate networking and to create global products that will build research capacity and help researchers to transfer knowledge to policy makers. It can be argued that the GDN is one of history's largest worldwide non-governmental enterprises to be aimed at producing a public good that is available from anywhere around the planet, a good that will prove vital for the future of humankind: knowledge.

The collective decision to create the GDN was based on a set of shared beliefs, an opportunity and bold ambition. What are those beliefs? First, while in centuries past, improvement in human welfare was predicated on advances in agricultural yields and later technological and scientific progress, it is becoming increasingly evident that the future of our well-being will predominantly rest on the availability and judicious use of knowledge defined in the broadest sense. Second, the old notion that knowledge confers power and temporarily bestows a competitive edge, while still valid to a degree, is being superseded by the realisation that the greater gains can accrue when knowledge is shared. Nowhere is this proposition easier to defend than in the field of policy formulation in the pursuit of development. The third belief could be paraphrased with the transplanted and somewhat provocative view that policy making is too important to be left to policy makers alone. Although in most cases this statement would need to be qualified to travel unchallenged, the basic underlying tenet is that in no human society is 'good' knowledge for development exclusively in the hands of policy circles. Otherwise, why pursue democratic principles, encourage political plurality or foster public debate on policy options? Failure to falsify this belief would, by default, constitute enough legitimisation for the emergence and vibrancy of think tanks and research centres in any forward-looking society. Indeed, human beings are all in the fight for development together, and on the same side.

A number of unprecedented factors have recently converged to create an opportunity potentially to enhance human welfare around the world with a degree of effectiveness that was impossible to attain hitherto. Consider that knowledge in general, and research-based knowledge in particular, is more widely distributed worldwide today than at any other period in history. In most countries, this has given rise to local capacity to tackle key societal challenges with the help of advanced global knowledge in the hands of indigenous researchers who are also intimately familiar with their immediate environment. The multitude and diversity of geographical and historical experiences in facing development challenges do not constitute an obstacle as much as they provide a wealth of knowledge and wisdom that bodes well for rapid advances in welfare gains around the world. The potential benefits of these two factors will be easier to capture thanks to the formidable recent developments in information and communications technologies. The widespread availability of Internet access and electronic messaging, among various forms of communication and data transfer, has already created what could be referred to as the global policy forum. As a result, it will be increasingly difficult for anyone in the world to claim ignorance as an excuse for making uninformed policy decisions. Furthermore, such remarkable advances will undoubtedly lead to the advent of a policy-related information society that could have a profound effect on the way people get informed and build their opinions, thus setting the table for a state of 'continuous democracy' in policy making.

The bold ambition underlying the creation of the GDN is to forge the biggest ever solidarity chain based on knowledge by making its generation and sharing a worldwide, long-lasting and collective enterprise. And yes, the world has the means to achieve it. In this instance, the notion of solidarity has many advantages, among which I would like to mention two. The very idea of generating knowledge in a global context and applying it while adapting it locally constitutes a cost-effective approach that will benefit everyone. Moreover, the diversity of legitimate and accepted sources of policy ideas and options emerging from all corners of the world will put to rest the often heard criticism that a few global institutions impose their views on the developing world without distinction or compromise. The resulting stronger sense of ownership and the feeling that solutions to local policy challenges are home-grown could lead to wider acceptance of policy reforms.

The thirteen chapters of this book are a fair indication of the nascent architecture that will pave the way in the quest for new policy ideas and ways to share them nationally and globally. Johnson and Stone outline the rationale underlying the GDN and its early development. Stiglitz demonstrates the need to scan knowledge globally and reinvent it locally, while Nustad and Sending explain how knowledge can be conceived more broadly as an effective tool for development. These authors give evidence of the considerable potential that think tanks have in their quest for participation in policy debate and partnership with other stakeholders. In the following section, the local partnerships of knowledge institutions are explored in greater detail by Manaev, Sudarshan, Ortiz de Zevallos and Salas. In the third part of the book, Kao, James and Krastev address the daunting task faced by think tanks around the world, namely how to influence policy making while maintaining institutional autonomy and scientific rigour. In the last section, three sets of authors, Nesadurai and Stone, Ladi, and Lindquist undertake a successful attempt to unravel the treacherous nexus of knowledge, policy and power, an effort that illustrates the conceptual battles that lie ahead on the road to a knowledge-based world.

Where do we go from here? While everyone will have a glimpse of what can be accomplished from reading these chapters, I would venture to guess and perhaps hope that nobody really knows, and it would perhaps be for the better because, with the GDN and similar initiatives, the future might hold pleasant surprises for all of humanity.

Diery Seck
Executive Director
Secretariat for Institutional Support for Economic Research in Africa
Dakar, Senegal
2 June 2000

Acknowledgements

In one of the many planning meetings that took place in the World Bank Institute (WBI) to launch the Global Development Network, the idea for this book was first floated. Many people inside and outside the WBI played a small or large part in its development. I am particularly indebted to Ishac Diwan who provided me with the opportunity to learn about the 'Knowledge Bank' and to participate in the launch of the network as a member of the GDN secretariat.

Alongside Erik Johnson, Haleh Bridi and Susan Wilder, other people in the WBI involved in the GDN include Chris Duggan, Mona Yafi, Maxine Alonso Pineda, Mariana Todorova, Karen Sirker and Hana Salah. In addition, Ron Kim, David Ellerman, Lawrence MacDonald, Wolfgang Reinicke and Salah Brahimi, who were based elsewhere in the World Bank, were also very helpful during my time in Washington. Kent Weaver from the Brookings Institution and Jim McGann also provided insight and alternative viewpoints that informed my thinking about the themes in this volume.

The three anonymous referees, and especially Don Abelson and William Wallace, provided thoughtful advice, sound criticism and strong encouragement to proceed with this project. I was in the fortunate position to be on study-leave from the University of Warwick during the first of half of 2000. Consequently, this volume rapidly took shape from February through May 2000 while I was based as a visiting fellow in the political science program of the Research School of Social Sciences at the Australian National University. I am grateful to the director of the school, Ian McAllister, and the staff, visitors and graduate students in the program who made it such a pleasant and productive stay. Lorraine Elliott, Tomoko Akami, Anna George and Toni Makkai reminded me that there was much more to life than the GDN.

In the desire to produce this book in time for the second GDN conference, all the contributors in the volume must be thanked for meeting my demands and deadlines for drafts with great equanimity. Additionally, Craig Fowlie and Milon Nagi at Routledge were very cooperative and flexible in the quick production of the book. Finally, I am very thankful to Richard Higgott for tolerating in good humour my long absences in the USA and Australia.

Diane Stone
8 June 2000

List of abbreviations

ADF	Asian Development Forum
APEC	Asia Pacific Economic Cooperation
ASEAN	Association of South East Asian Nations
ASEAN–ISIS	ASEAN Institutes of Strategic and International Studies
CASE	Center for Social and Economic Research [Poland]
CEE	Central and Eastern Europe
CEN	Canadian Environmental Network
CDRI	Cambodia Development Resource Institute
CGIAR	Consultative Group on International Agricultural Research
CICP	Cambodian Institute for Cooperation and Peace
CIDA	Canadian International Development Agency
CIPE	Center for International Private Enterprise [USA]
CLS	Centre for Liberal Strategies
DAN	Development Analysis Network
DEC	Development Economics Vice Presidency of the World Bank
EDI	Economic Development Institute [now WBI]
EU	European Union
GDN	Global Development Network
IDF	International Dialogues Foundation [Netherlands]
IEA	International Economics Association
IISEPS	Independent Institute of Socio-Economic and Political Studies [Belarus]
IMF	International Monetary Fund
IPCRI	Israel/Palestine Center for Research and Information
LFMI	Lithuanian Free Market Institute
MDF	Mediterranean Development Forum
MedPIN	Mediterranean Policy Institute Network
MENA	Middle East/North Africa
NATO	North Atlantic Treaty Organisation
NCAER	National Council of Applied Economic Research [India]
NGO	non-governmental organisation
NIRA	National Institute of Research Advancement [Japan]
ODC	Overseas Development Council [USA]

OECD	Organisation for Economic Co-operation and Development
OSCE	Organization for Security and Co-operation in Europe
PAFTAD	Pacific Trade and Development Conference
PBEC	Pacific Basin Economic Council
PECC	Pacific Economic Cooperation Council
PRS	Policy Research Secretariat [Canada]
PSI	Policy Studies Institute [UK]
SARDC	Southern African Regional Documentation Centres
SEAF	South East Asian Forum
SEA–RED	South East Asian Roundtables on Economic Development
SEWA	Self Employed Women's Association (India)
SIGMA	Support for Improvement and Management in Central and Eastern European countries
SISERA	Secretariat for Institutional Support for Economic Research in Africa
TACIS	Technical Assistance to Commonwealth of Independent States
UNDP	United Nations Development Programme
USAID	United States Agency for International Development
WBI	World Bank Institute
WTO	World Trade Organization

Part I

The GDN and knowledge for development

1 The genesis of the GDN

Erik Johnson and Diane Stone

In December 1999, the Global Development Network (GDN) – an association of research institutes and think tanks – was launched by the World Bank in cooperation with the United Nations, the governments of Japan, Germany and Switzerland, a group of regional research networks, and a number of other international development institutions. This initiative is designed to enhance the quality and availability of policy-oriented research, strengthen the institutions that undertake this work and offer networking opportunities in order to address better the causes and possible solutions to poverty and meet the challenges of development. The GDN seeks to support the work of think tanks, research institutes and development researchers by providing better information about and access to resources such as research funds and professional development programmes. It also helps to coordinate and disseminate research efforts and build capacity for institutes and individuals in developing countries. Another important role of the GDN is the multi-disciplinary concern to forge political, sociological, economic, anthropological and other research to inform policy making at a national level as well as in international organisations.

The GDN has a longer history than that marked by the first GDN conference in 1999 – GDN99. It was pre-dated by a number of regional meetings of think tanks, consultative discussions and initiatives designed to generate new research. Accordingly, the first section of this introductory chapter outlines the gestation of the network prior to GDN99, while the second section focuses on the planning and activities surrounding the GDN99 conference in Bonn, Germany. The final section addresses issues surrounding the future development of the GDN. The chapters that follow were first prepared for the inaugural meeting of the GDN. Therefore, they represent much of the conceptual underpinning of the initiative and the first in-depth examination of the core issues and debates it seeks to address.

The World Bank has not been alone in initiating dialogues with research institutes and think tanks. A number of international organisations have engaged with institutes for years, albeit on a less systematic basis than that represented by the GDN. Nevertheless, the GDN represents a valuable study of a number of developments. First, it provides insight into the changing emphases within the World Bank as it seeks ways to implement the principles behind its

'Comprehensive Development Framework' and in its moves to become the 'knowledge bank' (see Wolfensohn 1999). Second, the GDN is a medium through which to gain first-hand accounts of the making of a new global network. This may reflect more generally on our understanding of other partnerships and private regimes that are emerging to facilitate the delivery of goods and services at global and regional levels (see, for example, Cutler *et al.* 1999; Reinicke 1998). Third, the GDN provides a lens through which to observe the manner in which knowledge, information and data are used by the development community to inform policy and the extent to which these attempts are successful or not with governments and international organisations. Finally, this book addresses the ways in which these organisations, or their researchers, are embedded in or distant from civil society. The degree to which think tanks and research institutes engage in partnerships with other local organisations has significant impact on how global modes of knowledge are made local and the converse, of the local informing the global.

The origins of the GDN

Think tanks, research institutes or policy analysis centres have been in existence for most of the past century. Research centres based in universities or elsewhere have had a long, albeit mixed, history in developing countries. Think tanks were first apparent in North America and Western Europe (see Smith 1991; Day 2000; Sherrington 2000). The think tank form spread to other regions of the world in the post-Second World War era, especially in Asia and Latin America from the 1970s (on Asia, see Langford and Brownsey 1991). Considerable growth took place in Eastern and Central Europe after 1989 (Quigley 1995). As noted on the GDN website:

> In the past decade, the number and activities of these institutions – many of which are independent – has increased dramatically, driven in part by democratization, and in part by the sheer complexity of 'second generation' (beyond adjustment) reform issues. Increasingly, they are playing a role in bridging the gap between development knowledge and policymaking, areas in which governments no longer have a monopoly or even a comparative advantage.
>
> (http://www.gdnet.org/about.htm)

The proliferation of think tanks is reflected in the number of international directories and reference guides that have been published to keep track of organisational developments (see Chipman 1987; Day 1993; National Institute for Research Advancement). This dramatic growth has awakened the interest of international organisations in their potential uses in informing policy, aiding development and promoting civil society.

The Global Development Network concords with the bureaucratic imperatives and public rhetoric expounded by the World Bank. It has undergone significant changes in its public representation under the presidency of James Wolfensohn and former senior vice-president and chief economist Joseph Stiglitz. This is epitomised by the Comprehensive Development Framework, which highlighted the need to put 'countries in the driver's seat' as well as the need to engage civil society in development programmes. A strong theme running through the World Bank in the late 1990s was the emphasis on 'social capital' (see Dasgupta and Serageldin 1999; and for a critique, Fine 1999). 'In this context, think tanks constitute crucial civil society institutions that transcend government changes and offer a consistent source of knowledge for quality improvement of locally generated economic policies' (EDI 1998). More specifically, the 1999 *World Development Report* stressed the importance of knowledge in development processes. In concert with these trends, the World Bank has engaged with think tanks and research institutes (both inside and outside government) to draw them into partnerships in the formulation, delivery and evaluation of policy through knowledge development.

The regional meetings

The GDN has its origins in efforts to develop research capacity in Africa and the Middle East in the early 1990s. These meetings began building the base for a global network of such institutions, the GDN itself. The first meetings and capacity-building initiatives grew out of the now defunct Mediterranean Policy Institute Network (MedPIN). MedPIN began in 1996 as an effort to achieve economies of scale in addressing regional policy issues (that is, private provision of infrastructure) by coordinating a group of leading think tanks from each MENA country, with the World Bank Institute (then called the Economic Development Institute) as the sponsoring partner. Soon after its founding, MedPIN was subsumed into the newly founded Mediterranean Development Forum (MDF), transforming itself into a core group of partner institutions that act as the organising committee for the MDF's regional meetings.[1] The MDF provides a platform for leading MENA experts, high-level government officials and civil society representatives to meet and engage in a dialogue to set the region's development agenda. Meetings have been held in Morocco (1997 and 1998) and Egypt (2000). The idea of a regional 'development forum' has also caught on in Asia, where the Asia Development Forum held its second meeting in June 2000 in Singapore, and in Africa, where the first meeting took place in Ethiopia in October 1999. While each of these forums has been a multi-partner event, the World Bank Institute has been the leading organiser in MENA and Asia, while the United Nations Economic Commission for Africa has taken the lead in that region. Furthermore, the role of think tanks has been institutionalised only in the MENA process, whereas the Asian and African initiatives include think tanks only as one of many constituencies.

Before their transition into MDF partners, the MedPIN group convened one meeting in cooperation with the Center for International Private Enterprise (CIPE), a private, non-profit foundation based in the United States. Based on a model developed by CIPE for the Central European region, a workshop was organised in 1997 in Cairo to focus specifically on capacity building for think tanks. Building on the success of this meeting, CIPE and the World Bank Institute worked in partnership to convene four more regional think tank meetings in Moscow (1997), Bucharest (1998), Beirut (1999), and Harare (1999), drawing together the directors of leading think tanks from each region. The objectives were twofold: first, to build the institutional capacity of think tanks in core areas of their operations (that is, strategic planning, communications, evaluation and advocacy) so that institutes could more effectively translate their ideas into practice; and, second, to encourage and enhance their role as effective representatives of civil society in national policy debates.

The regional research networks and competitions

In tandem with institutional capacity building were efforts to promote research. The World Bank, in partnership with other leading development institutions, was instrumental in the founding of regional research networks in Africa (African Economic Research Consortium) and the Middle East and North Africa (Economic Research Forum). However, early efforts were sporadic. In 1998, a more systematic approach to capacity building was developed through the Development Economics Vice-Presidency (DEC) headed by Joseph Stiglitz. DEC sought partnerships with similar networks in other regions with the goal of forming a global research network. In Latin America and Eastern Europe, DEC entered into partnerships with existing networks. In Russia, East Asia and South Asia, DEC played a more active role in the establishment and support of new regional institutions. These seven regional research networks are:

- Africa Economic Research Consortium.
- Center for Economic Research and Graduate Education (Eastern Europe).
- East Asian Development Network.
- Economic Education and Research Consortium (Russia).
- Economic Research Forum (Middle East and North Africa).
- Latin American and Caribbean Economic Association.
- South Asian Network of Economic Institutes.

With funding from the World Bank's Development Grant Facility, the first activity of the regional research networks was to establish regional research competitions. Since June 1998, these competitions have disbursed more than $10 million to the regional networks to support the generation of new development research. The general approach is the same in each region: an open, competitive allocation of research funds based on the priorities determined by each region.[2] The main objectives of the regional research competitions are to build local research capacity and broaden the domestic market for policy-relevant research. Three outcomes are anticipated: first, by sharing information, knowledge and analytical tools, a cross-fertilisation will take place; second, a self-regulating research community will develop; and third, a level of independence and credibility will be gained by local researchers.

The consultative meeting

In June 1998, representatives of twenty-two think tanks from countries in the developing world participated in a consultative meeting held at the World Bank in Washington to develop specific proposals for a new initiative in capacity building for knowledge institutions. The launching of this new initiative was part of the ongoing efforts by the World Bank Institute to create a unified strategy to help clients to build their knowledge capacity for national and regional development. The WBI also sought to expand and deepen its impact and outreach substantially by shifting from the 'retailing' of training programmes to 'wholesaling' them to partners such as locally based knowledge institutions. The remainder of this section paraphrases parts of the report written subsequent to this meeting (EDI 1998).

Vinod Thomas (then director of the EDI) emphasised two reasons behind the World Bank's support of knowledge institutions. First, they are fast becoming influential voices in the policy circles of developing countries and as such are playing an increasing role in bridging the gap between knowledge and power centres. Second, as the World Bank embarks on a major effort to deepen and restructure its development knowledge base, from research to training and information management, it will be in a unique position to supply the kind of products that think tanks need most. At the same time, the World Bank would benefit greatly from the contributions of these important development players, both by weaving the voices of local policy analysts into its emerging knowledge management system and by expanding existing communication channels between bank staff and the outside world.

The participants at the consultative meeting endorsed the idea of the GDN. However, for this initiative to be successful and driven by the think tanks, they argued that it needed to be based on the principles of ownership, sustainability, credibility and autonomy. Underpinning all of these principles is a commitment to local participation.

Ownership

Think tanks in developing countries face difficult challenges in persuading policy makers to use local policy advice rather than consulting with experts from the World Bank and other international organisations. Rehman Sobhan of the Centre for Policy Dialogue in Bangladesh stated that 'governments have been so intellectually colonised over the last twenty years that the notion that any policies can in fact originate from a domestic political discourse and establishments is beyond their thinking'. This situation is illustrated by the irony embedded in the fact that local researchers often feel that only by becoming World Bank junior consultants can they have a chance at being heard by their own governments. In the same vein, Fred Opio of the Economic Policy Research Centre in Uganda pointed out the difficulties often encountered in getting policy makers to accept reforms that are designed locally, while World Bank reforms, which frequently ignore local realities and conditions, are embraced readily.

Sustainability

Participants articulated three sustainability dimensions. First, in most cases, policy reform based on advice with an international origin tends to result in a 'brain drain' of researchers and an erosion of local professional skills, or 'de-capacity building'. Second, economic policy reforms that originate in international institutions like the World Bank are less sustainable, having been disconnected from domestic political institutions and processes. Third, the main sources of think tank funding – foundations and other donors – cannot be expected to continue to support them indefinitely, as their number has grown dramatically in the last twenty years, and particularly since 1989.

Credibility

Participants offered three main reasons why think tanks lack credibility with policy makers in their own countries. First, the financial constraints affecting think tanks in developing countries are a major source of uncertainty, which undermines their credibility. To illustrate this point, Sadikou Alao, president of the Research Group on the Democratic, Economic and Social Development of Africa based in Benin, explained that the recent drastic reduction in the government's financial support for policy research in his country has led to a significant decrease in the quantity and quality of such research, which in turn has undermined its credibility. The result is that policy makers have become reluctant to embrace locally designed policy reforms. Second, with the increasing constraints affecting their traditional funding sources, think tanks are often forced to find alternative sources, which in some cases are seen as undermining their credibility. In this connection, many participants questioned whether having the World Bank as a partner engaged in knowledge development would help or hinder their credibility. On the one hand, in countries where the World Bank's standing is relatively weak, think tanks that receive its financing often face challenges in getting their products accepted. On the other hand, in countries where the World Bank is viewed as a reputable institution, think tanks frequently see the Bank's support as a way of bolstering their credibility. Third, think tanks often face major difficulties in generating output that is accepted by all stakeholders. According to Appollinaire Ndorukwigira of the African Capacity Building Foun-dation in Zimbabwe, credibility is related not only to the quality of policy advice but also to the extent to which think tanks themselves create effective relationships with government, the private sector and civil society.

Autonomy

A fundamental goal of think tanks is the protection of their independence as they pursue their research objectives. A number of factors affect the ability of a think tank to maintain its independence, including financial sustainability and credibility. Think tank survival depends on funding from a myriad of sources, which sometimes exert significant influence on their research priorities and outcomes as well as on administrative matters. Many participants expressed their concern that the acceptance of funding and support from governments, business groups and international organisations such as the World Bank may interfere with their autonomy. Additionally, as donors have cut their unrestricted core funding in favour of support earmarked for specific activities, think tanks are facing increasing difficulties in setting their own agendas. Ashok Lahiri of the National Institute of Public Finance and Policy in India recommended increasing 'south–south' exchange programmes in training, research and capacity building as a way of furthering the autonomy of think tanks.

The main outcome of the consultative meeting was a commitment by the participants to create a global network of institutes and organise an international conference. As a follow-up to the consultative meeting, a special session on the role of think tanks in policy making was also organised for the October 1998 annual meeting of the World Bank. Furthermore, World Bank representatives carried the momentum of the meeting forward by involving themselves in two related, yet independently organised, initiatives.

The Barcelona meeting

In July 1998, an international workshop was convened with the object of compiling an analysis and international reference guide on think tanks. While this meeting was initiated independently of World Bank activities, the timing was right for the organisers to attract sponsorship from the bank. The organisers were Jim McGann, an independent consultant based in Pennsylvania, and Kent Weaver, senior fellow at the Brookings Institution in Washington. Both have published on the role of think tanks (see, *inter alia*, Weaver 1989; McGann 1995).

The papers prepared for the workshop have been assembled into a publication (McGann and Weaver 2000). This was more of a scholarly exercise than that represented by previous World Bank meetings. Nevertheless, the editors were responding to what they regarded as a general perception of the need for expert knowledge in policy, that is:

> Policymakers need understandable, reliable, accessible, and useful information about the societies they govern. They also need to know how current policies are working, as well as possible alternatives and their likely costs and consequences
>
> (*ibid.*)

Their book represents one of the first attempts to map systematically the extent of the development of public policy research organisations around the world, investigating the role that these organisations play in the policy formulation process and civil societies. A considerable amount of literature has been generated on think tanks in developed countries (see Marsh 1980 on Australia; Lindquist 1989 on Canada; Gellner 1995 on Germany; Gaffney 1991 on Britain and France; Abelson 1996 on the USA). However, little material has been comparative or addressed think tanks in developing countries (but see Telgarsky and Ueno 1997; Johnson 1997; Stone *et al.* 1998).

The meeting convened by the secretary-general of the United Nations

In May 1999, the United Nations secretary-general, Kofi Annan, convened a closed meeting to ask for the assistance of think tanks in providing analyses to guide UN policy making (ODC 1999). The secretary-general met the leaders of twenty-seven independent policy research organisations from around the world to engage their best thinking on the policy challenges and research needs of the UN and its specialised agencies. There were two broad reasons for the meeting. First, the UN wished to identify how its research requirements converged with or could be met by the ongoing research agendas and work of the independent research community. Second, the UN sought to initiate a working dialogue with these organisations and investigate possibilities for partnerships.

Like many governments and other international organisations, the UN is confronted by the exploding numbers of non-governmental organisations (NGOs) and the avalanche of information. Research institutes represent useful intermediaries to shape, channel and coordinate UN relations with other non-state actors. Instituting active and productive relationships with all such groups involves more resources and time than the UN can devote to determining which NGOs have goals consonant with its own, those that perform in a reliable and effective manner, and in avoiding misusing or being misused by NGOs. The UN meeting identified a role for the research community to act as a 'quality check system' for evaluating NGO–UN interaction. Possible roles identified included:

- communication and translating global values and agreements to regional and local audiences;
- reviewing international agreements and recommending the formulation of national and regional policy options;
- convening and building alliances between NGOs and civil society; and
- training and teaching fledgling NGOs in organizational management, planning and advocacy.

(*ibid.*: 7)

The UN meeting saw a number of recommendations emerging from participants, such as establishing an on-line database of think tanks; the designation of an accessible focal point for the research community at the UN; and convening civil society meetings for the secretary-general and other UN officials. Participants also resolved to coordinate their activities with the GDN.

Summary

The activities prior to the official launch of the Global Development Network in December 1999 provided the impetus as well as the necessary rationale for a more coherent and ambitious exercise. A select number of individuals involved in these UN and Barcelona meetings had already crossed paths in the regional research networks and regional meetings throughout 1998 and 1999. Such inter-actions had at least four beneficial outcomes. First, it helped to build inter-personal relations and cross-cutting networks in the research institute and think tank community. Second, the meetings began to generate awareness and wider support in the donor community. Third, a common perspective, impetus and growing consensus was built around the idea of, and need for, a global network of think tanks and research institutes. Finally, think tanks in developing countries began to share professional experiences in a way that had previously not existed, thereby realising many of their common problems and possible solutions.

Launching the Global Development Network

Until the first planning meeting of the Global Development Network in May 1999, the loose strands that were soon to become the GDN had yet to come together under a common roof. Convened by Joseph Stiglitz and jointly organ-ised by the Development Economics Vice-Presidency (DEC) and WBI, participants in this meeting included the leaders of each of the seven regional research networks as well as a number of potential sponsors and partners. These included the International Economics Association (IEA), the United Nations Development Programme (UNDP), the National Science Foundation and CIPE in the USA, and NIRA in Japan. In addition to endorsing the idea of a Global Development Network of research and policy institutes, the meeting arrived at three conclusions: first, to launch a survey of research institute needs throughout the developing world; second, to undertake a global research project involving all seven networks; and, third, to begin preparing for the launch of the GDN.

Preparing for the launch

Following the May 1999 planning meeting, the group of GDN partners began to consolidate. In addition to the commitment of the regional networks to organise a global initiative, sponsors began to offer their support. The German govern-ment offered to host the launch event in Bonn and finance the largest portion of the budget. This decision was largely fuelled by the government's current strategy to make Bonn an international centre for development research. This intention was outlined by all leading German representatives at GDN99, including the German president, the minister of economic cooperation and development, and the mayor of Bonn. The Japanese and Swiss governments were also keen to support the creation of the GDN.

In addition to government backing, the GDN idea also attracted a number of organisations with a specific interest in think tanks. The Center for International Private Enterprise (CIPE), a partner in each of the regional meetings, was the first to come on board. The CIPE has been financing economic reform-oriented think tanks since its creation in 1984. The Japanese institute NIRA, which publishes a global directory of think tanks and analyses Japanese and global think tank trends, also saw its interests represented in the GDN. In Africa, the Secretariat for Institutional Support for Economic Research in Africa (SISERA) saw an opportunity for African institutes to forge valuable global contacts. In Eastern Europe, Freedom House sought to bring the group of think tanks it supported through the USAID-funded Democracy Network into the GDN fold.

Motivated by a variety of different causes, a number of UN agencies also lent their valuable support to the GDN, including the United Nations Development Programme, the United Nations Children's Fund and the United Nations University in Tokyo. In the corporate sector, Sun Microsystems and Deutsche Telekom provided essential computer hardware and Internet connectivity at GDN99.

The GDN secretariat

The GDN secretariat took shape during 1998–99. Two departments of the World Bank united to comprise the secretariat: Development Economics (DEC) and the World Bank Institute. Most of the work in organising the launch in Bonn centred in the World Bank Institute with the Division of Economic Policy for Poverty Reduction (WBIEP). Ishac Diwan, manager of WBIEP, was the leader of the WBI side of the secretariat. Mariana Todorova began as the task manager for the GDN in the WBI until becoming the World Bank resident representative to Sri Lanka, at which point Middle East and North Africa regional coordinator Haleh Bridi stepped into the role. Susan Wilder worked in the secretariat from the beginning, while both of the authors began working in WBIEP in mid-1999.

A number of individuals in DEC were also actively involved. Lyn Squire, director of research, coordinated with the WBI on key elements of the launch. DEC took the lead on GDN activities such as the regional research competitions, the global survey and the global research project.

The global survey was conducted jointly by DEC and IEA in an effort to gauge the interest of research institutes in a variety of potential products that could be offered by the GDN, including annual conferences, training, a scholarly journal and various electronic tools. In total, 500 research institutes were canvassed throughout the developing world. The preferences revealed in the survey suggest that the GDN should strive for a two-pronged strategy: limited participation in well-designed activities with high marginal costs per participant on the one hand, and widespread provision of on-line services with low marginal costs on the other hand (Global Development Network 1999).

Global research project

The global research project (GRP) began in late 1999. The first theme of the GRP is to focus on a comprehensive explanation of economic growth. It was modelled on a study already under way in Africa and includes four thematic papers for each region, and a series of review meetings and consultations, the first of which was in Cairo in October 1999. More than forty researchers from all parts of the developing world had an opportunity to exchange views and receive input from some of the world's foremost economists and political scientists, including Joseph Stiglitz, François Bourguignon and Robert Bates. Organised by the IEA, a second workshop was convened in Prague in June 2000 to allow a final, independent, review of the thematic papers. The effort demonstrates a key element of the GDN: that is, the incorporation of training and mentoring within specific research activities.

The second phase of the project moves to country studies against the framework of the thematic papers. A workshop in Nairobi in December 1999 brought together sixty authors from thirty African countries to work with a group of resource people in developing the research strategy. This constitutes one of the most intensive research efforts ever undertaken in Africa. It is intended that this approach will subsequently be extended to other regions.

The first electronic discussion[3]

Following the release of the call for papers and invitations to attend the GDN launch, it became clear to the secretariat that demand for attendance would outstrip the capacity of the event. Partially in response to this situation, but also as a means of building momentum towards the launch, an on-line discussion was initiated. The on-line discussion is a tool that the World Bank has begun to use with greater frequency as a way of expanding the timeline of a single event and shaping its content and impact by involving participants and non-participants in consultations before and after the conference. Beginning in November 1999 and ending a week before the launch in December, the GDN electronic discussion focused on four themes.

The first week addressed the ways in which the market for policy research operated; the political constraints and controls that think tanks sometimes encountered; the format in which these organisations communicated with government; and scope for policy impact and influence. For many respondents, that the research agendas and the products of think tanks are market-driven is an acceptable and uncontroversial reality. For others, however, funding dependence distorts research agendas to fit donor priorities. In particular, some contributors argued that foreign sources of funding produced research output oriented to the financing institution's objectives rather than for domestic consumption. One strong and unanticipated theme that emerged concerned the role of consultants in the development process and a perception of conflict and competition rather than collaboration with think tanks. Some contributors suggested that consultancy work diminished the status of substantive research undertaken by institutes and think tanks. In other cases, the use of foreign consultants was viewed as undermining the development of local capacity and undervaluing endogenous knowledge. Whatever the case, there is relatively little examination of the role of development consultancy firms in the development process and transition countries to match the work that has addressed think tanks to date (but see Nesseth 1999; Wedel 1998).

The second week of the discussion revealed both cautious and positive statements about the ways in which think tanks and research institutes could engage with NGOs and community groups to promote people's participation in policy making. A number of messages expressed a sense that think tanks could not perform this kind of role unless civil society is well established with legal protections, an independent media, a viable middle class and a political regime supportive of civil rights. Authoritarian and illiberal regimes, civil war, poverty or endemic corruption can quell civil society voices. On a more optimistic note, a few contributors reported how rewarding involvement with local groups could be once the effort had been made to engage with and seek the participation of NGOs, academics and ordinary people. Although not a straightforward process, the time taken to explain initiatives and a genuine objective to seek societal input meant that local knowledge and experience aided and improved project implementation.

The last two weeks of the discussion focused more on potential GDN roles and the ways in which it would develop. Potential was seen in the way in which the GDN could help to build capacity and strengthen national research institutions, disseminate knowledge, provide avenues for exchange and establish new partnerships to 'creatively match' or 'melt the ice' between institutes, donors and policy makers. Paralleling themes developed in the chapters by Stiglitz, Krastev and Ladi, one clear message was that 'one-size policy approaches', 'desktop models' or 'world standard research methodology' could not be applied universally to countries but that in the transfer of ideas and policy, more scope was required for the use of local knowledge.

To a large extent, many of the contributors addressed the issues and concerns covered in the June 1998 consultation, the regional meetings and the Barcelona workshop. The discussion was varied. By no means was there a consensus on the policy roles of think tanks or their place in civil society. Similarly, resolution and agreement on the role of the GDN, its future course and governance structure was neither sought nor found through the discussion. What the discussion did achieve was to facilitate a process whereby conference participants and non-participants could outline and reinforce some of the key themes to be addressed in Bonn and begin an open process of defining the role of the GDN.

The launch of the GDN

In December 1999, the Global Development Network was launched with an inaugural conference in Bonn entitled 'Global Development Network 1999: Bridging Knowledge and Policy'. GDN99 was attended by more than 600 researchers, think tank representatives, donors and policy makers. Participants came from eighty-five countries and included representatives from more than 250 research institutes and think tanks. This was one of the largest gatherings of knowledge institutions working on development issues ever held.

To help to establish the credibility of the GDN as an asset to policy making, government officials were invited to speak at the plenary sessions. Speakers included high-level ministers from Uganda, Zimbabwe, Bulgaria, Senegal, Columbia and the Philippines. The president and senior vice-president of the World Bank also spoke, and the UN secretary-general sent a video message. The panel sessions were broken down into three themes. First, cutting-edge development research, primarily from the field of economics, was featured in almost half the sessions. Each of these sessions included not only top researchers but also at least one policy maker with the task of testing the policy relevance of research proposals. Second, key issues related to the 'business of think tanks' were addressed by the directors of some of the world's leading institutions as well as by experts in the field of think tank/NGO management, policy analysis and political science. Finally, a number of open and closed sessions were devoted to mapping out the future programmes, funding and governance structure of the GDN. One of the more successful activities was the 'knowledge marketplace' – an extended midday break where *ad hoc* podium presentations were staged along-side the exhibition booths of agencies and institutions. This structure provided a unique opportunity for substantive exchanges as well as free-form networking among think tank scholars, donors, policy makers and policy practitioners.

While GDN99 was successful on many counts, reservations were expressed by some of the participants in Bonn and in later electronic discussions. There was a notable dominance of economists at the meeting rather than a more representa-tive mix of development researchers and practitioners. Yet another concern was a perceived lack of consultation with some donors who were engaged in similar programmes with research institutes and think tanks. In other words, the GDN was regarded by some as a competitor that might 'squeeze out' existing networks. One of the more strident criticisms concerned the general direction of the GDN under the influence of the World Bank. In a back-to-the-office report filed by one of the Scandinavian participants, the following was stated:

> The institutions around which the GDN is built represent a rather technical form of neo-liberal analysis. At a time when development research sees the emergence of a 'new institutionalism' that draws on social and environ-mental sciences and the humanities, GDN appears to represent a die-hard commitment to a brand of macro-economics cut from the Washington consensus cloth of ten years ago. This approach represents itself as politically

neutral, but in actuality many of the GDN's core think tanks work very closely with some rather questionable regimes.

(Gould 1999)

These criticisms and concerns cannot be dismissed lightly. Inevitably, there will be ideological differences; invariably, there are different perspectives on the most appropriate course for development and transition. Insufficient liaison and consultation with interested parties and existing networks may have caused some insecurity. Institutionalising governance arrangements, creating clear lines of communication and building accountability structures were discussed in Bonn but could not be agreed upon. Such difficulties are to be expected at the beginning of any new global initiative, especially one with such a diverse range of participation. In fact, division and diversity may be inherent in the GDN as a site of political contention and where there are many countervailing views. Instead of seeking to promote a common identity, difference may be the dominant reality.

Nevertheless, the Bonn conference did establish and advance the Global Development Network on a number of fronts. First, GDN99 began a participatory process of consultation on the future of the GDN, launching three committees to recommend a governance structure, future products and a web strategy for the GDN. Second, the identity of the GDN began to be shaped, and broader public awareness was built. Third, GDN99 created new global linkages and a model for future networking and sharing of experience. Finally, donor support was generated for core and new GDN activities, including the next conference, the GDN web site and development awards.

In addition to its offer, through Finance Minister Miyazawa, to host the second GDN meeting in Tokyo, the Japanese government also announced its sponsorship of the Global Development Awards. These awards are designed to encourage research on development, especially in developing countries. Prizes of $125,000 will be awarded to the most outstanding research on development and the most innovative development project.[4] It is expected that the competition will be run on an annual basis, with the winners being announced at the GDN's annual conference.

The future of the network

At the time of writing, the GDN is barely six months old. The months leading up to the second conference in Tokyo in mid-December 2000 include a number of activities that will significantly shape the future of the initiative. At this stage, the GDN is more of a process than an organisation (Giszpenc and Squire 2000). Under the guidance of the World Bank – where the secretariat continues to be based – committees have examined the key issues of GDN operations. In addition, public consultations have been held to ensure a steady flow of stakeholder input and friendly criticism of the GDN process. The following elements constituted the day-to-day operations and consultative process of GDN.

GDN committees

During the Bonn meeting, three high-level committees were formed to make decisions regarding the future of the GDN. First, the Governance Committee is responsible for deciding how the GDN should be structured and governed, examining issues such as legal structure, board composition, membership and secretariat location. This body will also draft a constitution for the GDN and select an executive committee, which will act as a provisional board of directors for the GDN before a legal structure can be decided on. Second, the Products Committee will be examining the global market for knowledge products that could potentially be offered by the GDN, beginning with the ten products suggested in Bonn (see below). Three working groups have been formed to examine these and other products in the areas of research funding, professional development and networking. Finally, the Web Strategy Advisory Group will decide how the GDN will operate 'virtually' through the use of the Internet.

On-line discussions

In order to open the work of the committees to broader public participation, the GDN web site will post all documents produced by the committees while also initiating on-line discussions to feed into its deliberations. These open-feedback mechanisms are likely to become a permanent feature of the GDN. Two such discussions have already been completed since GDN99, one on governance and the other on web strategies.

The governance discussion took place for five weeks in January and February 2000, leading up to the first Governance Committee meeting in March 2000.[5] The discussion generated considerable comment, with many people expressing different views concerning GDN membership, objectives and roles, and some of it critical of GDN aspirations. Even within the group of World Bank coordinators of the GDN, there were and remain different perspectives on the direction of GDN development. While electronic discussions cannot be used as a mechanism for decision making, they have certainly set the agenda for the work of the Governance Committee. This first discussion highlighted some of the most difficult challenges to be met in the formation of the GDN and provided some strong views on which direction the initiative should take.

Immediately after the governance discussion had concluded, an electronic consultation on the role and direction of the GDN's web site, GDNet, was launched.[6] Participation in this discussion included not only those from previous discussions but also a number of experienced web strategists from leading development web sites. Key themes that emerged from the discussion included the need to ensure maximum access to technology for developing countries, use of peer review and quality control systems, and increasing access to developing country publications and systems for quickly and easily linking policy makers with global experts. There was also a strong sense that the open and participatory process of the GDN should largely be conducted over the Internet.

The GDN products

The ten GDN products presented in Bonn have since begun to move in two concurrent directions. First, the annual conference, development awards, regional research competitions and global research project have begun to mesh into an integrated programme supporting and globally recognising locally generated development knowledge. Quality research is rewarded by both regional and global research grants and global awards, while the annual conference serves to showcase these works. In most of these efforts, the GDN serves as a mobiliser of resources and a facilitator, with most of the implementation being undertaken by the regional research networks. Less progress has been made on products such as training, scholarships and staff exchanges.

In all areas, the GDN is acting not as a provider of services but as a market analyst. Information produced by the GDN such as the survey can be used by the GDN community to educate donors and other providers about the efficiency of their products and the manner in which grant processes, funding regimes, scholarships and so forth correspond to the needs of research institutes. The information will also be used to help the governing body (when established) to decide on future directions for the GDN and to inform the donor community. The intention is to use the occasion of the annual conference to present a GDN programme to the donor community for consideration.

Local knowledge and global networks

The Global Development Network is not the first network of think tanks and research institutes to come into existence. Research networks and partnerships have a long history. International networks of think tanks have coalesced around common areas of interest and policy themes as well as around ideology. An early example of an international network coalesced around the institutes of international affairs in Europe and the USA that formed after the Versailles settlement. They maintained lines of communication until such efforts tapered off in the years before the Second World War (Wallace 1994). Similarly, the Institute of Pacific Relations, founded in 1925, is one of the pioneering non-governmental think tank organisations of the Asia-Pacific region. With national branches in the USA, the UK, Australia, Canada, Japan, China and Russia, the IPR was a key institutional advocate of Wilsonian internationalism during the interwar years (Akami 1998).

Today, numerous networks are apparent. Groups such as the Council for the Development of Social Science Research in Africa (CODESRIA), the Southern African Regional Documentation Centres (SARDC) and SISERA have been working to network African institutes together on issues of common concern. Since 1997, the Japan Center for International Exchange has convened 'Global ThinkNet' meetings to promote policy-oriented dialogues through think tanks between Japan and other countries or regions. Other Japanese institutes, including the NIRA (as a sponsor of the GDN) and the Nomura Research Institute have helped to develop regional and international research networks.

Think tank and research networks are particularly noticeable at the regional level. In many cases, such networks are a reflection of shared historical conditions, ties of language and ethnicity, and similar or trans-border policy problems. For example, institutes in the post-communist transition countries of Eastern and Central Europe have shared experiences with privatisation and political reform and can learn from policy innovations in neighbouring countries. The enormous growth in the number of think tanks in this part of the world (see Struyk 1999) has propelled think tank networking. The recently established 'Transition Policy Network' is a group of think tanks working cooperatively to provide technical assistance in the transition countries of Central and Eastern Europe (CEE) and the newly independent states (NIS) (www.urban.org/TPN). Chapter 8 by Ivan Krastev and Chapter 10 by Helen Nesadurai and Diane Stone develop the idea of regional and global networking in greater detail. Regional networks are usually composed of a smaller number of think tanks, and individual directors and scholars are familiar with each other. As a consequence, they tend to be stronger than international networks. International networks can be more diffuse, with a greater number of actors. Common identity, consensus and collective action are more difficult to engineer.

Not only have research networks, research institutes and think tanks been engaged in global public policy networks for years, but transnational coordination is often feasible when networks are created in specific policy fields. An examination of networks such as the Consultative Group on International Agricultural Research (CGIAR), the World Commission on Dams and the Global Water Partnership reveals that institutes are one set of key actors drawing together local knowledge and contributing valuable information and expertise (Reinicke 1999/2000). The transnational character of many policy problems establishes a dynamic for research collaboration, the sharing of information and cooperation on other activities that pull think tanks into the global domain to meet the demands of governments and international organisations for information, analysis and other knowledge services. At the same time, these institutes gain access to ideas, information and policy models and approaches that can be adopted and modified for local policy development. Similarly, institutes are drawn into transnational networks of NGOs and activists in specific policy areas such as protection of the Amazonian forests or human rights or land mine clearance.

The GDN is distinct from many of these other networks in that it is more ambitious and a consciously *global* network of research institutes, think tanks and development specialists. While it is still evolving, numerous suggestions have emerged concerning the manner in which the GDN might operate as a network. For example, one suggestion that emerged in the electronic discussions is that the GDN might become a 'network of networks'. Another trajectory is that the GDN will evolve to incorporate a wider range of knowledge institutions. The organisational foundations for the GDN have been built on think tanks and research institutes. However, there is a wider universe of knowledge institutions. These include training organisations, further and higher education institutions, foundations, consultancy firms and professional associations. It is a constellation of knowledge organisations with which research institutes and think tanks are interdependent and with which they have developed an intricate pattern of relations. Moreover, these connections are as likely to be international as national in composition.

The emergence of the GDN is symptomatic of globalisation and the manner in which advances in communications and information technology, and the lower costs of travel, have enabled actors with common research and policy interests to interact internationally on a regular basis. Yet these networks are also symptomatic of the role of knowledge and expertise in global governance and evidence of strong sources of demand for policy-relevant research. In other words, as part of the global knowledge industry, the generation and dissemination of high-quality research allows research institutes and think tanks collectively to exert their presence and some influence through their involvement in 'global public policy networks' (*ibid.*; also Cusimano 1999). It is a theme that Stella Ladi pursues in her chapter on 'policy transfer networks'. At the same time, the 'knowledge' conveyed by think tanks must be based on solid empirical research and analysis. Some parts of the developing world still have a long way to go in generating research that is both high-quality and policy-relevant.

Policy influence cannot be guaranteed through the inherent persuasiveness of ideas or on the assumption that policy research will gradually seep into the consciousness of politicians, bureaucrats and other decision makers. The belief that reason will prevail is frequently proved wrong. The idea that think tanks need to 'build bridges' between knowledge and policy is a partial recognition of the problem of research informing decision making. However, such rationalistic views of the role of 'science' or knowledge in the policy process ignore many intervening social and political factors. This problem is pursued by Knut Nustad and Ole Sending in Chapter 3 and in the Conclusion.

The question of how to ensure effective utilisation of knowledge in development remains difficult. It is an ongoing and unresolved debate in the think tank and research institute community, where strong differences often emerge concerning the role of advocacy in presenting research findings. The issue of influence is more complicated and complex than this as the chapters by Simon James and Evert Lindquist indicate. One implicit theme in the chapters by Ivan Krastev and Kao Kim Hourn is that the influence of, or at least the opportunities for, intellectuals and their organisations is greater in the more fluid political contexts of economic reconstruction and political transition.

A global network is an ambitious vehicle through which to share knowledge. Chapter 2 by Joseph Stiglitz addresses the wider objectives and aspirations for the GDN as a mechanism for learning and the diffusion of policy knowledge within the development community, but he also stresses the value of local knowledge. In different ways, the chapters by Ratna Sudarshan in India, Gabriel Ortiz de Zevallos and Alejandro Salas in Peru and Oleg Manaev in Belarus address the dynamics of local knowledge production. The civil society interactions and knowledge partnerships built by think tanks strengthen their knowledge base and establish a wider social platform for their engagement with both national and local decision makers. It is at this level of governance and economic reform, rather than in the relatively elite and rarefied domains of global networks, that the GDN faces some of its greatest challenges.

Notes

The authors would like to acknowledge the assistance of Mariana Todorova, David Ellerman and Lyn Squire in writing this chapter.

1   One of the main reasons for the shift from MedPIN to MDF was the movement of MedPIN's WBI partner David Ellerman from MENA regional coordinator to advisor to Senior Vice-President Joseph Stiglitz. As the leading figure behind the MDF, Ishac Diwan, manager of the Economic Policy for Poverty Reduction Division of the WBI, built on Ellerman's activities in the MENA region and eventually expanded this work to the global level by becoming one of the driving forces behind the Global Development Network.
2   The World Bank provided a total of $2.4 million to the seven regional networks in 1998 and $3.2 million in 1999.
3   This discussion was moderated by Diane Stone. An archive can be found on the world wide web at http://www.worldbank.org/devforum/forum_gdn.html
4   In addition to the larger prizes, medals of $10,000 (first place) and $5,000 (second place) will be awarded in five thematic areas, to be determined each year.
5   Go to http://www.worldbank.org/devforum/forum_gdn.html for an archive of this discussion, which was moderated by Lyn Squire during January and February 2000.
6   This discussion took place from mid-February until the end of April 2000. The moderator was Erik Johnson. An archive of this discussion can be found at http://www.worldbank.org/devforum/forum_gdn.html

References

Abelson, D. (1996) *American Think Tanks and their Role in US Foreign Policy*, New York: St Martin's Press.

Akami, Tomoko (1998) 'Post-League Wilsonian internationalism and the Institute of Pacific Relations, 1925–1945', *Journal of Shibusawa Studies* 11 (October): 3–35.

Carrothers, T. (1999) *Aiding Democracy Abroad: The Learning Curve*, Washington: Carnegie Endowment for International Peace.

Chipman, J. (1987) *Survey of International Relations Institutes in the Developing World*, London: International Institute for Strategic Studies.

Cusimano, M. K. (ed.) (1999) *Beyond Sovereignty: Issues for a Global Agenda*, Boston: Bedford.

Cutler, A. C., Haufler, V. and Porter, T. (1999) 'Private authority and international affairs', in A. C. Cutler, V. Haufler. and T. Porter (eds) *Private Authority and International Affairs*, Albany: State University of New York Press.

Dasgupta, P. and Serageldin, I. (1999) *Social Capital: A Multifaceted Perspective*, Washington: World Bank.

Day, A. J. (1993) *Think Tanks: An International Directory*, Harlow, Essex: Longman.

Day, A. (2000) 'Think tanks in Western Europe' in J. G. McGann and R. K. Weaver (eds) *Think Tanks and Civil Societies: Catalysts for Ideas and Action*, Somerset, NJ: Transaction Press.

Economic Development Institute (EDI) (1998) 'Capacity building for knowledge institutions', Global Development Network Initiative, Washington: Economic Development Institute of the World Bank.

Fine, B. (1999) 'The developmental state is dead – long live social capital?' *Development and Change* 30(1): 1–19.

Gaffney, J. (1991) 'Political think tanks in the UK and ministerial cabinets in France', *West European Politics* 14(1): 1–17.

Gellner, W. (1995) *Ideenagenturen für Politik und Öffentlichkeit. Think Tanks in den USA und in Deutschland*, Opladen: Westdeutscher Verlag.

Giszpenc, N. and Squire, L. (2000) 'Back to the future: global technology for local development', *Foreign Policy*, Washington: Carnegie Endowment for International Peace.

Global Development Network (1999) 'Researching the researchers' [http://www.gdnet.org-/pdfs/SurveyResultsp1b.PDF].

Gould, J. (1999) 'The Global Development Network Conference', memo to Finnida, December.

Johnson, E. (1997) *Improving Public Policy in the Middle East and North Africa: Institution Building for Think Tanks*, Washington: Center for International Private Enterprise.

Langford, J. W. and Brownsey, K. L. (eds) (1991) *Think Tanks and Governance in the Asia Pacific Region*, Halifax, Nova Scotia: Institute for Research on Public Policy.

Lindquist, E. (1989) 'Behind the myth of think tanks: the organization and relevance of Canadian policy institutes', unpublished doctoral thesis, University of California, Berkeley.

Marsh, I. (1980) *An Australian Think Tank?* Sydney: University of New South Wales Press.

McGann, J. (1995) *The Competition for Dollars, Scholars and Influence in the Public Policy Research Industry*, New York: University Press of America.

McGann, J. and Weaver, R. K. (eds) (2000) *Think Tanks and Civil Societies: Catalysts for Ideas and Action*, Somerset, NJ: Transaction Press.

National Institute for Research Advancement [http://www.nira.go.jp].

Nesseth, H. (1999) 'Constructing authority in the global political economy: global consultancy and financial liberalization in Indonesia', paper prepared for the annual meeting of the International Studies Association, Washington. February 16–20.

Overseas Development Council (ODC) (1999) 'Dialogue with think tanks: a report of a meeting with the United Nations secretary-general', 4–5 May, United Nations Headquarters, New York.

Quigley, K. F. F. (1995) 'The beginnings of public debate: think tanks in Eastern Europe', *NIRA Review*, Autumn [www.nira.go.jp/publ/review/].

Reinicke, W. H. (1998) *Global Public Policy: Governing Without Government?* Washington: Brookings Institution Press.

Reinicke, W. H. (1999/2000) 'The other World Wide Web: global public policy networks', *Foreign Policy*, Winter.

Sherrington, P. (2000) 'Shaping the policy agenda: think tank activity in the European Union', *Global Society* 14(2): 173–89.

Smith, J. A. (1991) *The Idea Brokers: Think Tanks and the Rise of the New Policy Elite*, New York: Free Press.

Stone, D., Denham, A. and Garnett, M. (eds) (1998) *Think Tanks Across Nations: A Comparative Approach*, Manchester: Manchester University Press.

Struyk, R. J. (1999) *Reconstructive Critics: Think Tanks in Post-Soviet Bloc Democracies*, Washington: Urban Institute Press.

Telgarsky, J. and Ueno, M. (eds) (1997) *Think Tanks in a Democratic Society: An Alternative Voice*, Washington: Urban Institute Press.

Wallace, W. (1994) 'Between two worlds: think tanks and foreign policy', in C. Hill and P. Beshoff (eds) *Two Worlds of International Relations: Academics, Practitioners and the Trade in Ideas*, London: Routledge and London School of Economics, 139–63.

Weaver, R. K. (1989) 'The changing world of think tanks', *PS: Political Science and Politics* 22(3): 563–78.

Wedel, J. (1998) *Collision and Collusion: The Strange Case of Western Aid to Eastern Europe*, New York: St Martin's Press.

Wolfensohn, J. (1999) 'A proposal for a comprehensive development framework', presentation to the board, management and staff of the World Bank Group [http://www.worldbank.org/cdf/cdf-text.htm].

World Bank (1999) *Knowledge for Development: World Development Report 1998/99*, New York: Oxford University Press.

2 Scan globally, reinvent locally

Knowledge infrastructure and the localisation of knowledge

Joseph Stiglitz

The importance of the Global Development Network

It was a great pleasure for me to help to inaugurate the Global Development Network (GDN). In my remarks at GDN99 in Bonn, I sought to do two things: first, to explain why I think the GDN is so important and why the World Bank has taken such an active role as a catalyst in promoting it; and second, to develop some of the thinking that lies behind the creation of this new institution.

Towards a new relationship between developing and developed countries

It has been just over fifty years since the beginning of the end of colonialism and just a decade since the end of the Cold War. Yet old ways of interacting persist, and it takes time for the evolution of new modes of behavior, new bases for relationships founded on equality and respect.

I realise that it has become unfashionable to refer back to the dark days of colonialism, and yet, as we attempt to develop institutions to meet the challenges of this new century, our success in doing so will depend, I believe, on understanding the histories, how we – the developed and developing countries, and the economies in transition – came to be where we are today. Colonialism served to eviscerate existing institutions in the affected countries, which is almost all of the developing world. It tried to graft on to existing cultures foreign institutions and ideas, but in a process of imposition, in which control and authority lay outside and not within, it is not surprising that the graft did not take hold. What was left in its place was a void – the old was destroyed, but nothing really viable had been created in its stead. Worse still, in all too many countries, they were left without the human capital required to create an alternative, let alone to adapt to the rapid changes that have marked the latter half of the twentieth century. And too many countries were robbed of the dignity and self-confidence with which to address these imposing challenges, which would have placed strains even on societies in far better positions.

The colonial mentality has evolved. While no one today speaks, like Kipling, of the 'white man's burden,' I have too often sensed a paternalism that is but a close cousin. Gone are the days of gunboat diplomacy, forced signing of unfair trade treaties, the Opium Wars, or forcing Egypt into being a protectorate because of bad debts. But no one would claim that the playing field – in international trade negotiations, debt restructuring or any of the multitude of other arenas in which the developed and developing countries interact – is a level one. Economic power relations play out with potentially no less disastrous consequences for developing countries. This point was brought home forcefully by the terms and conditions imposed on the countries receiving bail-outs in the East Asia crisis, which, as Martin Feldstein pointed out, went far beyond what was required to address the concerns of the crisis. Democratic processes were undermined as countries were forced to sign agreements changing the basic mandates of central banks, and previously negotiated trade agreements were overturned as new-found bargaining powers based on the weakened positions of the affected countries were exploited.

So long as the Cold War persisted, there was neither time nor opportunity to address these fundamental issues. That conflict – a battle of competing ideologies, values, economic systems – was all-consuming. And the impact of that conflict on the developing countries was profound. Too often, they took the view that the enemy of their colonial enemy was their friend and embraced their socialist ideology. They saw some of the successes of the USSR, its rapid emergence from feudalism to a world superpower, and underestimated the costs that it had imposed and overestimated the underlying strengths. The end of the Cold War, the failure of the Communist system, thus forced the developing world to re-examine fundamental beliefs.

Meanwhile, the world was changing rapidly. A new generation of leaders was emerging in the developing world, partially freed from the scars of colonialism, highly trained, with a new sense of self-confidence. Globalisation brought prospects of integration into the world economy – with access to technology, markets and capital. Global competition offered the prospect of a new relationship between developing countries and multinationals, with more of the surplus accruing to the developing world.

But many of the ways of interacting between the developed and the developing world did not take full cognisance of these changes. Conditionality, while ostensibly based on freely negotiated terms of agreement, went far beyond what could be justified by fiduciary responsibility and democratic accountability on the part of the developed countries and the international financial institutions. With the end of the all-consuming Cold War, there ensued a new emphasis on democracy and democratic processes, and it came to be recognised that the way conditionality worked in practice often undermined these democratic processes and institutions. New perspectives on development focused on development as a transformation of society, a change in minds and mindsets, and it came to be recognised that such transformations could not be imposed; indeed, the attempt to do so could often be counterproductive. Thus the subsequent econometric results suggesting that conditionality was ineffective in promoting development came as no surprise (see World Bank 1998b). In response to these changes, the

World Bank evolved a new framework for thinking about development that was both more comprehensive in its approach and more inclusive in its involvement. At its center was, as President Wolfensohn expressed it, 'putting the country in the driver's seat.' [1]

This brings me to why I think the GDN is so important. If the developing countries are really to be 'in the driver's seat,' they have to have the capacity to analyse the often difficult economic issues they face. Local researchers, combining the knowledge of local conditions – including knowledge of local political and social structures (with the learning derived from global experiences) – provide the best prospects for deriving policies that both engender broad-based support and are effective. That is why locally based research institutions are so important.

I have, on several occasions, also spoken of the importance of democratic institutions for successful development. To be sure, we should value democratic institutions as an end in themselves, not just as a means to more successful development. But the lessons of the past century have been clear: authoritarian regimes have caused untold human suffering. Amartya Sen has argued forcefully that even famines can be checked by democratic processes; it is not the shortage of food but its distribution, and democratic processes would simply not tolerate such outcomes. Think tanks, policy institutes, play a vital role in promoting the informed public discussion that is absolutely essential for meaningful democratic processes and the generation of a political consensus. These institutions, and the associated institutions of a free and vibrant press and independent universities, provide an important check on the abuse of power – including abuses of majorities against minorities and the widespread corruption that has been shown not only to have a corrosive effect on society but also to undermine development efforts (World Bank 1997; Transparency International and IBRD 1998).

This past century has seen the battle between two ideologies, but the end of the Cold War does not mark the end of ideology. Ideological battles continue to be fought, sometimes on a grand scale, more often on a minor scale. Recent discussion of capital market liberalisation is illustrative of the former. Many strongly advocated this, in spite of the absence of evidence suggesting that, for most developing countries, it would promote their growth or investment; indeed, there was some evidence to suggest that it would not do so, and that it would in fact increase the risks they faced – risks that they were ill-prepared to undertake and that would inevitably increase the extent of poverty in their countries. Unfortunately, the predictions of the critics of capital market liberalisation have been more than borne out. How can we explain the strong advocacy of a major change in the international economic architecture other than by ideology and/or capture by certain special interests? But the strongest antidote to both is science – theory and evidence. 'Science' – at least the word – can be abused; as the word has undertaken positive overtones, ideologies have claimed to find justification for their tenets in 'science.' Yet the foundations of the scientific method have managed to withstand such abuses, whatever form they take.

We in the ideas business should never forget the power of ideas. Keynes put this forcefully when he wrote:

> Practical men, who believe themselves to be quite exempt from any intellectual influences, are usually the slaves of some defunct economist. Madmen in authority, who hear voices in the air, are distilling their frenzy from some academic scribbler of a few years back.
>
> (1936: 383)[2]

The scribblers of America's Declaration of Independence surely did not know either the power or the reach of their ideas when they wrote, 'All men are created equal ....' They may have had in mind 'all property-owning white males are created equal ....' But the force of the idea came from its appeal to deep principles, and once articulated, it took on a life of its own – a life that brought within its embrace first blacks, then women. And that same force lives on: it does not stop at America's border. The same force of argument that led the American colonists to declare their independence from Britain doomed colonialism more generally. And today, its reach has been broadened to attack neo-colonialist mentalities and economic imperialism. Indeed, as an economist, I find it remarkable how often the force of the arguments can overcome the logic of self-interest and become an important agent for reform and change.

Recent discussions of transparency arising from the East Asia crisis help to illustrate what is at issue. Originally, in a thinly veiled attempt to explain how the Western banks could have engaged in such bad lending practices (every loan needs both a borrower and a lender, and the lender is fully as much at fault for a bad loan as the borrower), Western bankers and their governments contended that the underlying problem behind the crisis was a lack of transparency. For the international institutions and Western governments that had pushed premature financial and capital market liberalisation, this was an attempt to evade responsibility for their misguided policy advice. But the concept of transparency took on a life of its own, spreading its potentially disinfecting sunlight to areas that were far from the original intentions – a demand for transparency on the part of the hedge funds and offshore banks, and ultimately on governments, central banks and the international financial institutions themselves. This demand for transparency is now joining forces with basic concepts of equality in demands for a re-examination of the very process of governance of the international institutions.

I have lauded the virtues of the kind of think tanks and research institutions that are gathered here today. It is my hope, and the World Bank's hope, that by bringing these institutions together into a global development network they will add strength to each other not only through the exchange of knowledge but also through a common understanding of the importance that they play in promoting sustainable, democratic and equitable development. Let me be clear: in many parts of the world, substantial obstacles confront these institutions – from the ubiquitous financial constraints to the shortage of those with the requisite skills, both in research and in articulating key ideas in ways that allow their widespread dissemination and facilitate public debate. But in too many countries, there are further, artificially created, barriers – hostile governments, trying to suppress democratic debate, worried about the consequences of public scrutiny of their actions. And here, I believe, is one arena where, standing together, we can exert international social pressure: there are basic core standards to which all countries need to adhere, institutional principles that constitute the *sine qua non* of meaningful democratic debate. The basic human rights of a free press and free speech can be undermined by the exertion of economic pressures, which is why these institutions need to be independent of the government with assured independent sources of funding, and why the individuals within the institutions need to be protected by academic freedom.

We should not be surprised at either the vehemence or the subtlety with which these institutions and the individuals in them may be attacked, or at attempts to undermine their credibility, especially by governments whose political legitimacy is questioned. And the same holds true at the international level, and perhaps more so. For we must recognise that while international institutions can take or promote actions that have huge effects on the economic fortunes of millions and the political fortunes of many, their governance has a certain lack of representativeness along many dimensions – the developing countries and their billions of people are underrepresented; while the voice of financial interests is heard loudly and with clarity, it is not clear that other voices – the workers, who risk losing their jobs or seeing real wages plummet as a result of misguided policies, or the small businesses forced into bankruptcy by what in any other context would be viewed as usurious interest rates – are heard at all.

In nation-states, some governments derive their legitimacy not only through the electoral process but also by their ability to build a national consensus – a consensus based on trying to find a shared sense of values, a broad sense of equity and a common understanding of the underlying economic processes. In such cases, the success of the policies adopted – including a sense of equitable sharing of the fruits of growth or the pain of contraction – is often a prerequisite for the maintenance of that legitimacy. By contrast, policies based on ideologies not widely shared, especially when those ideologies are seen to serve the self-interest of special interests and to result in inequitable burden sharing, undermine the credibility of the institution, and when the institution's effectiveness in part depends on its credibility, then there is a downward vicious circle. No wonder then that such institutions find open discussion and public debate about the appropriateness of policies – even months or years later – an anathema.

Today, no one is upset at the debate over whether Roosevelt's New Deal policies had much impact in bringing the US economy out of its depression; such understanding is essential if we are to craft policies designed to address economic downturns in the future. But in the international community today, there are still many who are greatly upset at the prospect of revisiting the question of the appropriate response in the global financial crises of 1997 and 1998. The argument seems to be: the emperor may have no clothes, but to mention this risks global economic instability! I, at least, have greater faith in our global economic architecture than that.

But this does raise some fundamental issues: when the governance of any public institution is subject to questioning, when there is a lack of representative-ness, a failure to establish consensus, a reliance on ideology rather than science, and especially an ideology closely linked to the interests that are disproportion-ately represented in its governance, clear evidence of a lack of equitable burden sharing, and a record of failure – it is time to rethink basic premises. Many insti-tutions are learning to become learning institutions, adapting to changing circumstances. At the World Bank, this is precisely the course that President Wolfensohn set five years ago. I raise these issues here, not because this is neces-sarily the appropriate forum for their discussion but because I believe that research institutes and think tanks have a vital role in raising these questions and demanding answers that are responsive to the perspectives and concerns of the developing world.

More generally, the world is embarking on an experiment – a closely integrated global economy that is striving for global governance without global govern-ment. If this experiment is to be successful, it will be based on a process of global consensus building in which institutions and individuals that are coming here this week for the first time, in the Global Development Network, will be pivotal.

Epistemological foundations: knowledge infrastructure and the GDN

Let me now move on to the second topic, concerning the nature of knowledge and the role of knowledge in development. The World Bank's initiative in fostering the GDN is part of the idea of the Bank as a 'knowledge bank.' We have come to appreciate the transformative power of knowledge in development (World Bank 1998a). Yet we must be wary of simple analogies between a 'knowl-edge bank' and a 'money bank.'

Disembodied knowledge has the characteristics of a public good – non-rivalrous and, once public, non-excludable – while money is the quintessential private good (Stiglitz 1995; Economic Report of the President 1997).[3] Thomas Jefferson, the third president of the United States, described knowledge in the following way: 'He who receives an idea from me, receives instruction himself without lessening mine; as he who lights his taper at mine, receives light without darkening me' (1984). In doing so, Jefferson anticipated the modern concept of a public good.[4] Thus disembodied knowledge for development is indeed a global public good and, like other public goods, it would be undersupplied if left entirely to private initiative.

The Internet has in practice brought knowledge access closer to the ideal of a global public good. The communication revolution has made great strides in facilitating communication within countries and has also enhanced the ability of developing and transitional countries to tap into the global pool of (codified) knowledge. The Internet should prove to be a tool of immense power in sharing knowledge within our network of GDN institutes.

Today, developing countries face both great risks and great opportunities. Internet growth has been most rapid in the United States, and not surprisingly, slowest in the less developed countries. The enhanced ability to share and acquire knowledge in the advanced industrialised countries may increase the knowledge gap, resulting in the less developed countries becoming even more disadvantaged.

At the same time, they can tap into a larger knowledge pool than they ever had access to before. Today, a child anywhere in the world who has access to the Internet has a modern 'Alexandrian Library' at her fingertips. It is too soon to see how these opportunities and forces – for convergence or divergence – will play out, whether the knowledge gap between developed and developing countries will be widened or narrowed. But it is clear that it is incumbent upon the developing and transitional countries to do everything they can to enhance their ability to tap into the reservoir of global knowledge. The GDN partners are local nodes in that emerging global knowledge infrastructure.

Knowledge has a number of characteristics that differentiate it from ordinary goods. We have already noted several of these, including the global public goods nature of knowledge. The peculiar characteristics of knowledge make it incumbent on us to think anew how we can promote the transformative power of knowledge effectively. In particular, what is the role of local knowledge institutions such as the policy and research institutes of the GDN in the broad process of democratic social learning?

I see a role far more subtle than just the technology-driven visions of 'downloading' global knowledge – as useful as that may be. I want to argue three main theses:

1   the overwhelming variety and complexity of human societies requires the *localisation of knowledge*;
2   practical know-how is largely *tacit knowledge* that needs to be learned by horizontal methods of twinning, apprenticeship and seconding; and
3   each society, through its knowledge institutions, should take an *active role* ('in the driver's seat') in the local learning process.

That is, one size of 'clothing' does not fit all societies. A society learns to be a 'tailor' partly by apprenticeship – it is hard to write down all that needs to be known about tailoring in a book, and even were it possible to do so, it may not be the most efficient way by which information can be transmitted from one individual to another – and a society should be its own 'tailor' to find the best fit.

General versus local knowledge

We will analyse knowledge along two dimensions, the general–local dimension and the explicit–implicit dimension. Global public knowledge exemplifies knowledge that is general and explicit. As we move along these dimensions, we will see the different roles of central as well as local knowledge institutions. We start with the general–local dimension.

Money 'travels' better than knowledge. General knowledge is knowledge that holds across countries, cultures and times; local knowledge takes account of the specifics of place, people and time. 'Every man is mortal' is general knowledge, while 'drive on the left' is best practice in London but not in New York. A 'best practice' might work well in some countries but fail miserably when recommended in other contexts.

In questions of institutional development, it is very difficult to know *a priori* just how general is a 'best practice.' Robert Cole studied the diffusion in industry of quality circles and Japanese-style quality methods. The process of local adaptation was so extensive and creative that it amounted to a local reinvention of the 'global best practice.'

> The significance of this point of view is that contrary to the simplistic use of the term by many economists, there is, in principle, no such thing as diffusion of best practice. At best, there is only the diffusion of best practices, practices that evolve in the course of their diffusion. Contrary to popular wisdom, there are times when it pays to reinvent the wheel.
>
> (Cole 1989: 117)

Donald Schön, in a study of social learning, concluded that 'Every alleged example of local implementation of central policy, if it results in significant social transformation, is in fact a process of local social discovery' (1971: 161). Prudent counsel is to scan globally for best practices but to test them locally, since local adaptation often amounts to reinventing the 'best practice' in the new context. The knowledge bank can 'scan globally'; the GDN partners have to 'reinvent locally.'

Many 'visiting economists' have painfully discovered that the 'devil is in the [local] details' (see Seers 1962). It is the local component of knowledge that requires adaptation – which in turn requires the active participation of those who know and understand the institutional environment. Local adaptation cannot be done by the passive recipients of 'development knowledge'; it must be done by the 'doers of development' in the course of their activities (quoted from President Mkapa of Tanzania in Wolfensohn 1999b).

There are two points here: the necessity that knowledge be made applicable locally and that the adaptation be done by the local 'doers of development' (not given as a gift or imposed as a condition from the outside). It is by local selection, assimilation and adaptation of knowledge that local doers 'make it their own.' Even by taking a machine or device apart and putting it back together again, one can 'make it one's own' even if there is little adaptation or redesign. Those of us who have been teachers are familiar with this principle: successful teaching requires active learning.

In the context of development, where what is involved is 'social learning' and adaptation, more is entailed: it is not just a matter of being 'open' or 'closed' to outside knowledge; it is a matter of being open to outside knowledge in a way that reaffirms one's autonomy. For Gandhi, this was intellectual *swaraj* (self-rule or autonomy):

> I do not want my house to be walled in on all sides and my windows to be stuffed. I want the cultures of all lands to be blown about my house as freely as possible. But I refuse to be blown off my feet.
>
> (Mahatma Gandhi, quoted in Datta 1961: 120)

Only by remaining 'on one's feet' from an intellectual standpoint can the local doers have the self-confidence to select, assimilate and adapt the external knowledge – instead of being overwhelmed and rendered intellectually dependent and subservient.

Considerable effort is required to adapt development knowledge to local conditions and culture. The research institutes and policy institutes ('think tanks') of the GDN are examples of local knowledge institutions that can play that important role. In the developed countries and increasingly in developing countries, think tanks have proliferated and have become important agents for the introduction and adaptation of new policy initiatives.[5] Think tanks or research institutions are no less necessary for transplanting social innovations to new contexts. The Japanese use a metaphor based on the gardening technique called *nemawashi* of slowly preparing and wrapping each root of a tree in order to transplant it.[6] The chances of a successful transplant are much greater than if the tree is simply pulled up in one place and planted in another.

Development institutions have sometimes tried a 'faster' transplant method. After a quick trip to a country, the standard wisdom (in earlier days, typically the Washington consensus) is conveyed, often with little attempt even to nuance it to the economic, political and social situations of the country. Frequently, the policy advice would be backed up by conditions on policy-based lending to motivate the country to implement the best-practice recipes – indeed, given the lack of broad-based buy-in, and often the unsuitability of the advice to the country's situation, conditionality was the only way of having the advice followed. Occasionally, in an attempt to achieve broader-based support, experts might come in to give a longer senior policy seminar to local government officials; the experts then return home hoping that their sound advice will take root. Yet this policy reform process is designed to promote neither active learning nor lasting institutional change. As these reforms were externally imposed rather than actively appropriated by the country, there was often little 'ownership' of the reforms. Compliance might be only perfunctory; the 'quick' transplant might soon wither and die.

Here is an illustration. Foreign advisors would never have the power of an occupying army. Yet the US Army in postwar Japan showed the limitations of trying to change institutions by imposing new laws and statutes:

> When SCAP [Supreme Commander for the Allied Powers] broke up the Mitsui and Mitsubishi trading companies into hundreds of fragments – 213 successor companies in all – ... the employees loyally rallied round the new

fragments formed by their old section or subsection chiefs ... who in turn adhered to the companies organised by their old division chiefs ... and director, and all of them recombined as soon as they could. Within five years, like droplets of mercury coalescing into ever bigger drops on contact with each other, both the Mitsubishi and the Mitsui trading companies were substantially reconstituted as before. Two hundred thirteen became two again. Their staffs had been held together by personal relations in the meantime.

(Cohen 1987: 358)

Those personal relationships and social habits are part of the 'invisible root structure' – the social embeddedness of institutions – that requires more subtle methods of transformation than just issuing decrees or passing new laws. By the same token, Japan was 'given' anti-trust laws that were similar to those that have worked so effectively in the United States; yet these laws never really took root, with an evolving competitive structure far different from that of the USA.

Local policy and research institutes can be seen as *nemawashi* organisations that carefully adapt and prepare a transplanted policy initiative to survive and perhaps thrive in the local environment. It takes longer, but the roots are better prepared for the local soil. The political process of changing policies and implementing new ideas is usually rather messy and in need of 'high maintenance' support. Officials or parliamentarians constantly need more information and advice – more 'back-up,' more thinking about how best to adapt the policies to local circumstances – in order to carry out the policy reforms. As a result of this process of adaptation, which often involves reinventing the idea, perhaps by finding and emphasising local antecedents, the government officials see the policy reform not as a foreign imposition but as a local product that addresses their needs and which they can sponsor.

Advisors from developed countries or international organisations may not always fully appreciate these problems. The 'knowledge business' has its own political economy. Those who are legitimated in their expertise, prestige and privileges by the 'universality' of their messages are disinclined to recognise limitations or subtleties in the local applicability of their technical expertise.[7] Novel complexity, genuine uncertainty, conflict of values, unique circumstances and structural instabilities are all downplayed or ignored, since they might diminish the perceived potency of the expertise and undercut the client's faith in that potency. On the other side, the client may want the security and comfort of being in the hands of the professional expert who will solve the perplexing problems (see Schön 1983). These are some of the strong institutional forces to underappreciate the subtleties of local knowledge, to hamper the growth of autonomous client ownership and to stymie the development of indigenous local knowledge institutions.

Codified versus tacit knowledge

We now move to the explicit–implicit or codified–tacit dimension of knowledge. Explicit or codified knowledge is knowledge that can be spoken, written or codified to be saved on a computer disk or transmitted over a telephone line. But we know more than we can say. We know how to ride a bike, how to recognise a face, and how to tell a grammatical sentence in our native language, but we would be hard put to turn this knowledge into explicit or codified knowledge to archive in a database for dissemination over the Internet. Michael Polanyi (1962) pioneered the distinction between tacit (or personal) and explicit knowledge in the philosophy of science, and the distinction has since proved important to an understanding of problems in the transfer of technologies, not to mention the 'transfer' of institutions.[8]

A technology is sometimes identified with blueprints and instruction books.

> But in fact technology consists of complex 'bundles' of information – both codified and tacit – as well as physical capital. Because tacit information is not readily transferable among firms and countries, technological blueprints do not contain inherent performance characteristics (such as set productivity levels). Instead, these blueprints have to be translated into specifications and procedures that are specific to particular applications – an uncertain creative process that can result in highly variable levels of performance.
>
> (Bell and Pavitt 1995: 74)

The same holds *a fortiori* for 'social technologies' or institutions. In a codified description of a 'best practice' case study, the uncodified tacit knowledge is often 'the rest of the iceberg.'[9] Some tacit knowledge might be transformed into codified knowledge (see Nonaka and Takeuchi 1995) so that it could be transferred by conventional methods, but the remaining tacit knowledge needs to be transmitted by special methods such as apprenticeship, secondment, imitation, study tours, cross-training, twinning relations and guided learning by doing. These methods of transferring tacit knowledge will be called 'horizontal' methods of knowledge transfer – in contrast to 'vertical' methods, where knowledge can be codified, transmitted to a central repository or library and then accessed by interested parties.

We have seen two reasons why the theory of 'downloading the best practice' fails: the best practice needs to be localised, and much of the best practice may be in the form of practical know-how that cannot be 'downloaded.' But there is still an important role for international development agencies (global knowledge): even concerning that tacit dimension of the best practice, the central agency may know who knows *x* without knowing *x* itself. It is 'second-order' knowledge of where the practical knowledge is; it is a 'pointer' to the practical knowledge. A central agency can fruitfully play a match-making, facilitating and brokering role in horizontal learning, but not a direct training role. In particular, the knowledge bank is in a good position to 'scan globally' to identify good practices, and then it can play a *brokerage role* to facilitate a horizontal learning process between developing countries facing problems and the countries with successful practices.[10] It can perform another role: certifying the quality of the messengers and messages; in a noisy world, with many alternative theories vying for center stage, there needs to be some way of sorting through the cacophony, establishing credibility.

The various methods of horizontal learning differ substantially from those employed in traditional classroom settings, where what goes on is 'vertical' teaching and training in explicit codified knowledge:

- Study tours arranged by local knowledge institutes allow people to 'see how it is done' in nearby societies. The Marshall Plan for the postwar reconstruction of Europe involved many horizontal techniques such as study tours for business leaders ('business to business') and government officials.
- Cross-training is being 'shown how to do it' by those who have already 'done it,' particularly in nearby societies. It is the implicit knowledge alternative to being explicitly 'told how to do it' by an international expert.
- Twinning and secondments pair together similar organisations or institutions for a horizontal transfer of know-how.
- Foreign direct investment might also be viewed as a method of horizontal learning. For instance, a major source of learning about lean production methods and their adaptation to American culture was Japanese direct investment in production facilities in the United States.

Due to the tacit component in practical development knowledge, few of the real reasons for success might be captured in the codified knowledge of the best-practice case study. In addition, there would be much variation due to *Rashomon* effects, academic predilections and ideological precepts in the best-practice case studies.

> The architect of social change can never have a reliable blueprint. Not only is each house he builds different from any other that was built before, but it necessarily uses new construction materials and even experiments with untested principles of stress and structure. Therefore what can be most usefully conveyed by the builders of one house is an understanding of the experience that made it at all possible to build under these trying circumstances.
>
> (Hirschman 1970: 243; quoted in Scott 1998: 328)

For instance, in one World Bank Institute program, local institutes arranged for government officials, law makers and business people from an African country to learn directly and horizontally from a nearby East Asian country that had faced similar economic and ethnic problems not too long ago – all of which was undoubtedly more effective than seminars based on codified case studies taken as blueprints.

Summary of knowledge dimensions

The general versus local dimension and the codified versus tacit dimension can be used to generate a 2×2 grid (see Figure 2.1).

	Codified knowledge	Tacit knowledge
General knowledge	Global public goods. Generally applicable and 'downloadable,' i.e., can be transferred by conventional vertical teaching methods – but 'rediscovery' improves ownership.	General tacit knowledge (e.g., implicit grammatical rules of English) could be learned by horizontal methods (e.g., natural language learning) or might be (partly) codified and taught.
Local knowledge	Localised explicit knowledge. Even if hypothetically available from center, should be locally 'reinvented' to have ownership	'The hard stuff.' Combines horizontal learning and local reinvention.

Figure 2.1 The dimensions of knowledge

Active social learning and the negative effects of passive learning

My third thesis is that the knowledge institutes and policy makers of developing countries should play an active role in reappropriating and adapting knowledge for development (even if the center could through some sort of 'flexible speciali-sation' make a local adaptation and transmit it to the locality).

The contrasting 'standard view' (usually held implicitly rather than espoused explicitly) sees a central authority transmitting universal messages and best-practice formulas along a transmission belt to passive clients, who are encouraged by aid and constrained by conditionality to 'get the message.' Rather than encouraging clients to develop their analytical and research capacities, the process of imposing conditions undermines both the incentives to acquire those capacities and a client's confidence in their ability to use them. Rather than involving large segments of a society in a process of discussing change – thereby changing their ways of thinking – excessive conditionality reinforces traditional hierarchical relationships. Rather than empowering those who could serve as catalysts for change within such a society, it demonstrates their impotence. Rather than promoting the kind of open dialogue that is central to democracy, it argues at best that such dialogue is unnecessary, at worst that it is counterproductive.

That standard view of delivering knowledge for development leads to an impairment in the self-confidence, self-esteem and self-efficacy of the client (Lane 1991; Bandura 1995). The message behind the 'main messages' is that the clients are unable to take charge of their own learning process and to find out these things in their own way. They need to be 'helped' – to be shown the way. New forms of intellectual colonialism are masked as 'quality control.' But these ways in which the standard methodology 'shows them the way' only reinforce the client's passivity and perceived lack of self-efficacy.

In addition to lacking self-confidence about the efficacy of their actions, a party might lack self-confidence in their own intelligence, judgment and other cognitive skills. In an extreme state of dependency, they might be like a marionette not only in their 'actions' but also in their opinions, views and 'knowledge.' This cognitive aspect of dependence is clearly very relevant to understanding the detrimental effects of passive learning and tutelage.

The cognitively dependent recipients of the main messages will also often play a role in perpetuating the dynamics of stifling critical reason in favor of bureaucratic 'reason' in the development agencies. As such countries have become cognitively dependent, they might be distressed if they should hear the 'authorities' arguing among themselves about 'development knowledge' and development strategies. They are accustomed to being told the 'best practices' to follow, so it weakens their faith in the prestigious authorities if there is any public disagreement. How can the patient have faith in 'warring doctors'? Thus the complaints (real or imagined) of the cognitively dependent client are used as arguments in international agencies to keep any real debate about development strategies well behind the closed doors of the major development organisations. (To be sure, there may be other reasons for the international agencies wishing to stifle open discussion: public scrutiny of failed policies in the developed countries could not only undermine the support for these agencies but also induce more accountability and improved governance, weakening their current sense of autonomy. And there is a real risk that such public scrutiny could force changes in their policies and practices.)

The obvious corollary of the traditional mode of operation is that there will be very little learning in the sense of correcting mistakes at the level of the development agency. Once there is a public commitment of the agency to a certain view, then the agency's prestige and 'brand name' is on the line. Any untoward consequences of a policy *must* be due to flawed implementation on the part of the client. Criticism from outside the agency can usually be ignored, and criticism from within the agency must be suppressed because it would weaken the franchise value of the brand name and 'confuse' the client. But note that in defending their own autonomy, they undermine the autonomy of the very countries they are supposed to help; even the language used to defend the 'no debate' position is one that connotes an aura of benevolent paternalism – but one that demonstrates a complete lack of faith in the country to make its own decisions.

Social learning, consensus building and other democratic processes

We now turn to the positive virtues of active learning and to the broader vision of democratic processes as active social learning writ large.

George Bernard Shaw insightfully quipped: 'if you teach a man anything he will never learn it' (1962: 174). Ortega y Gasset wisely suggested: 'He who wants to teach a truth should place us in the position to discover it ourselves' (1961: 67). Thus if a global knowledge-based institution wants a country to learn a 'truth' about development, then it should help the local knowledge institutes and policy makers to carry out the requisite research, experimentation and social dialogue to learn it themselves – to make it a 'local social discovery.' Creating this local knowledge infrastructure and practice entails 'learning how to learn', that is, creating the capacity to close the knowledge gap, an essential part of a successful development strategy (Stiglitz 1987). This process of autonomous social learning is not a 'feel-good frill'; it is a key part of developing local democracy.

Social learning and effective change cannot be imposed from outside. Indeed, the attempt to impose change from the outside is as likely to engender resistance and barriers to change as it is to facilitate change. At the heart of development is a transformation in ways of thinking, and individuals cannot be forced to change how they think. They can be induced to take certain actions, or even to utter certain words, but they cannot be forced to change their hearts and minds. To impose a model without a self-directed local learning process would be to 'short-circuit' and bypass the active learning capacity of the local policy makers and to promote a state of passivity, dependence and tutelage.

This process of encouraging autonomous local social learning is closely connected to the whole process of promoting democracy. Some social thinkers – John Dewey perhaps foremost among them – have emphasised that active social learning writ large provides a social philosophy for democracy as government by discussion and consensus building.

> To foster conditions that widen the horizon of others and give them command of their own powers, so that they can find their own happiness in their own fashion, is the way of 'social' action.
>
> (Dewey 1957: 270)

> For all alike, in short, the chief thing is the discovery and promotion of those activities and active relationships in which the capacities of all concerned are effectively evoked, exercised, and put to the test ... This cooperation must be the root principle of the morals of democracy.
>
> (Dewey and Tufts 1908: 303–4)

Beyond technocratic development models

Predominant currents of development thinking in the past have usually been more narrowly technical – at least in economics. It has been almost an article of faith that if certain technical allocation issues were solved, economic development would inevitably follow. The problem of development was seen as a technocratic problem of increasing capital investment and allocating resources more efficiently, not as a process of democratic social learning.

As an illustration, consider two of my predecessors as chief economist: Hollis Chenery in the 1970s and Anne Krueger in the 1980s. The two came at the development problem from very different perspectives: Chenery from the planning perspective, Krueger emphasising the need to 'get prices right' and to leave markets to work their magic. But both approaches saw development as a technical problem requiring technical solutions: better planning algorithms, better trade and pricing policies, better macroeconomic frameworks. Neither approach reached deep down into society, and neither emphasised the participatory nature of the development transformation.

Poland has in recent years implemented particularly effective policies for its post-socialist transition, and India has likewise found an effective development path. In spite of many changes in government, those countries have stayed on course. The reason for their effectiveness is not just some technical 'correctness' of the policies but the ownership that the countries have for policies arrived at through their own participative processes of democratic discussion, consensus building and *swaraj*. Outside agents, including donors, can encourage ownership through persuasion – that is, through presenting evidence, both theoretical and empirical, that particular strategies and policies are more likely to bring success than other approaches. But the degree of ownership is likely to be even greater when the strategies and policies are developed by those within the country itself, when the country itself is in the driver's seat.

Consensus building and democracy

Inside a country, the ability to resolve disputes in a 'democracy-friendly'[11] manner is an important part of social and organisational capital. Reforms often bring advantage to some groups while disadvantaging others. There is likely to be greater acceptance of reforms – a greater participation in the transformation process – if there is a sense of equity, of fairness, about the development process, a sense of ownership derived from participation, and if there has been an effort at consensus formation. Numerous examples (such as Ghana) have shown the importance of consensus formation for instance in achieving macroeconomic stability. By contrast, a decision to, say, eliminate food subsidies that is imposed from outside through an agreement between the ruling elite and an international agency is unlikely to be helpful in achieving a consensus – and thus in promoting a successful transformation.

Charles Lindblom (1990) contrasts the technocratic model for governing society with the alternative model of a self-guiding democratic society based on the use of 'reflective intelligence' (Dewey), the competition of ideas and government by discussion. To see the distinction quickly, Lindblom suggests, 'compare Marx with Franklin Roosevelt or Jan Tinbergen with Saul Alinsky' (*ibid.*: 216). In the technocratic (Marx–Tinbergen) model, the 'correct solutions' are already defined but may be unknown. If 'scientific' techniques could uncover those answers – even localised answers – independent of any political process, then the answers could be whispered into the ear of the prince and disseminated from central authority to passive citizens. After severely criticising technocratic development paradigms, Hirschman counsels 'a little more "reverence for life," a little less strait-jacketing of the future, a little more allowance for the unexpected – and a little less wishful thinking' (Hirschman 1970: 239; quoted in Scott 1998: 345).

In the model of a self-guiding democratic society, preferences and self-determined actions are endogenously transformed in the social/political process. Social 'democracy-friendly' dialogue – led by local knowledge institutions as in the GDN – builds consensus; it does not 'discover' or 'impose' consensus. Those who participate in the consensus-building process then have an 'ownership' of the resulting policies, and thus *that* policy knowledge will be transformative.

Concluding remarks

We are embarking here on an enterprise of potentially immense importance – creating a new global institution, the Global Development Network, devoted to enhancing democratic governance at the local, national, regional and global levels, to promoting dialogue, and to strengthening the processes of consensus building. Underlying all these efforts is the pursuit of knowledge – global knowledge about general principles, local knowledge about how those general principles play out in the multitude of local contexts over our vast globe – knowledge based on well-constructed theories and meticulous analysis of the empirical evidence. I believe that it is only through such open discussion and active research that we will break free from the chains of ignorance, the traps of poverty, the grip of elites and the blinders of ideology and self-interest in our quest for a more democratic, equitable and sustainable transformation of societies.

Notes

1   The notion of the 'country in the driver's seat' is one of the central themes in the Comprehensive Development Framework (CDF) outlined in Wolfensohn (1997; 1998; 1999a,b) and in Stiglitz (1998).

2   In the same vein, the early nineteenth-century poet Heinrich Heine (1797–1856) pointedly remarked:

> mark this, ye proud men of action: ye are nothing but unconscious hodmen of the men of thought who, often in humblest stillness, have appointed you your inevitable work.
>
> > (Heine 1959: 106; a 'hodman' carries stone, bricks or
> > mortar for a mason or bricklayer)

3   While the public good properties of knowledge had long been noted (Arrow 1962), early articulations of knowledge as a public good (in the sense defined by Samuelson 1954) include that of Stiglitz (1977) and Romer (1986). For an early textbook discussion, see Stiglitz (1986).

4   As did St Augustine (AD 354–430), who said in one of his sermons:

> The words I am uttering penetrate your senses, so that every hearer holds them, yet withholds them from no other … All of you hear all of it, though each takes all individually. I have no worry that, by giving all to one, the others are deprived. I hope, instead, that everyone will consume everything; so that,

denying no other ear or mind, you take all to yourselves, yet leave all to all others.

(quoted in Wills 1999: 145)

5 The literature on think tanks has burgeoned over the past decade. See, *inter alia*, Smith (1991), Langford and Brownsey (1991), Ostry (1991), Telgarsky and Ueno (1996), Stone *et al.* (1998) and Struyk (1999).

6 'It is a time-honored Japanese gardening technique to prepare a tree for transplanting by slowly and carefully binding the roots over a period of time, bit by bit, to prepare the tree for the shock of the change it is about to experience. This process, called *nemawashi*, takes time and patience, but it rewards you, if it is done properly, with a healthy transplanted tree' (Morita 1986: 158).

7 James Scott (1998: 339) quotes an illustrative passage from Sinclair Lewis' *Arrowsmith*: 'They said … that he was so devoted to Pure Science … that he would rather have people die by the right therapy than be cured by the wrong.'

8 See Ryle (1945–46) for the earlier distinction between knowing how and knowing that; Oakeshott (1991) for a treatment of practical knowledge versus technical knowledge; Schön (1983) for a related treatment of professional versus instrumental knowledge; and Scott (1998) on *metis* versus *episteme/techne*. The tacit/codified distinction looms large in Nonaka and Takeuchi (1995), and they note that Larry Squire (1987) gives a dozen labels for similar distinctions.

9 Even the codified part may suffer from the '*Rashomon* effect' (different people giving very different descriptions of the same phenomenon) described in Schön (1971).

10 That is the brokerage model of the knowledge bank (see Sundquist 1978), which is sometimes juxtaposed to the storehouse or library model. Since explicit knowledge of the best practices (and of the pointers to tacit know-how) can be 'downloaded,' each model has some applicability. It is a question of emphasis.

11 See Hirschman (1991: 168) for a contrast of consensus-building dialogue with the adversarial 'rhetorics of intransigence.'

References

Arrow, K. (1962) 'The implications of learning by doing', *Review of Economic Studies* 29: 155–73.

Bandura, A. (ed.) (1995) *Self-Efficacy in Changing Societies*, Cambridge: Cambridge University Press.

Bell, M. and Pavitt, K. (1995) 'The development of technological capabilities', in I. U. Haque (ed.) *Trade, Technology, and International Competitiveness*, Washington: World Bank, 69–101.

Cohen, T. (1987) *Remaking Japan: The American Occupation as New Deal*, New York: Free Press.

Cole, R. E. (1989) *Strategies for Learning*, Berkeley: University of California Press.

Datta, D. M. (1961) *The Philosophy of Mahatma Gandhi*, Madison: University of Wisconsin Press.

Dewey, J. (1957) *Human Nature and Conduct: An Introduction to Social Psychology*, New York: Modern Library.

Dewey, J. and Tufts, J. (1908) *Ethics*, New York: Henry Holt.

Economic Report of the President (1997) Washington: US Government Printing Office.

Heine, H. (1959) *Religion and Philosophy in Germany*, J. Snodgrass (trans.), Boston: Beacon Press.

Hirschman, A. O. (1970) 'The search for paradigms as a hindrance to understanding', *World Politics* 22 (April).

Hirschman, A. O. (1991) *The Rhetoric of Reaction: Perversity, Futility, Jeopardy*, Cambridge, Mass.: Belknap Press.

Jefferson, T. (1984 (1813)) 'No patent on ideas: letter to Isaac McPherson', 13 August 1813. In *Writings*, New York: Library of America, 1286–94.

Keynes, J. M. (1936) *The General Theory of Employment, Interest, and Money*, New York, Harcourt, Brace & World.

Lane, R. E. (1991) *The Market Experience*, New York: Cambridge University Press.

Langford, J. W. and Brownsey, K. L. (eds) (1991) *Think Tanks and Governance in the Asia-Pacific Region*, Canada: Institute for Research on Public Policy.

Lindblom, C. (1990) *Inquiry and Change*, New Haven, Conn.: Yale University Press.

Morita, A. (1986) *Made in Japan*, New York: E.P. Dutton.

Nonaka, I. and Takeuchi, H. (1995) *The Knowledge-Creating Company*, New York: Oxford University Press.

Oakeshott, M. (1991) *Rationalism in Politics and Other Essays*, Indianapolis: Liberty Fund.

Ortega y Gasset, J. (1961) *Meditations on Quixote*, New York: Norton.

Ostry, S. (ed.) (1991) *Authority and Academic Scribblers: The Role of Research in East Asian Policy Reform*, San Francisco: ICS Press.

Polanyi, M. (1962) *Personal Knowledge: Towards a Post-Critical Philosophy*, Chicago: University of Chicago Press.

Romer, P. M. (1986) 'Increasing returns and long-run growth', *Journal of Political Economy* 94(5): 1002–37.

Ryle, G. (1945–46) 'Knowing how and knowing that', *Proceedings of the Aristotelian Society* XLVI: 1–16.

Samuelson, P. (1954) 'The pure theory of public expenditure', *Review of Economics and Statistics* 36: 387–9.

Schön, D. A. (1971) *Beyond the Stable State*, New York: W.W. Norton.

Schön, D. A. (1983) *The Reflective Practitioner: How Professionals Think in Action*, New York: Basic Books.

Scott, J. C. (1998) *Seeing Like a State: How Certain Schemes to Improve the Human Condition Have Failed*, New Haven, Conn.: Yale University Press.

Seers, D. (1962) 'Why visiting economists fail', *Journal of Political Economy* 70 (4), August.

Shaw, G. B. (1962) *The Wit and Wisdom of Bernard Shaw*, Stephen Winsten (ed.), New York: Collier.

Smith, J. A. (1991) *The Idea Brokers: Think Tanks and the Rise of the New Policy Elite*, New York: Free Press.

Squire, L. R. (1987) *Memory and Brain*, New York: Oxford University Press.

Stiglitz, J. E. (1977) 'Theory of local public goods', in M. S. Feldstein and R. P. Inman (eds) *The Economics of Public Services*, London: Macmillan, 274–333.

Stiglitz, J. E. (1986) *Economics of the Public Sector*, New York: W.W. Norton.

Stiglitz, J. E. (1987) 'Learning to learn, localized learning and technological progress', in Dasgupta and Stoneman (eds) *Economic Policy and Technological Performance*, Cambridge: Cambridge University Press, 125–53.

Stiglitz, J. E. (1995) 'The theory of international public goods and the architecture of international organizations', *United Nations Background Paper* 7, Department for Economic and Social Information and Policy Analysis, July.

Stiglitz, J. E. (1998) 'Towards a new paradigm for development: strategies, policies, and processes, given as Raul Prebisch Lecture at United Nations Conference on Trade and Development (UNCTAD), Geneva, 19 October. Internet: http://www.world-bank.org/knowledge/chiefecon/index.htm

Stone, D., Denham, A. and Garnett, M. (eds) (1998) *Think Tanks Across Nations: A Comparative Approach*, Manchester: Manchester University Press.

Struyk, R. (1999) *Reconstructive Critics: Think Tanks in Post-Soviet Bloc Democracies*, Washington: Urban Institute Press.

Sundquist, J. (1978) 'Research brokerage: the weak link', in L. Lynn (ed.) *Knowledge and Policy: The Uncertain Connection*, Washington: National Academy of Sciences, 126–44.

Telgarsky, J. and Ueno, M. (1996) *Think Tanks in a Democratic Society: An Alternative Voice*, Washington: Urban Institute Press.

Transparency International and IBRD (1998) *New Perspectives on Combating Corruption*, Washington: World Bank Institute.

Wills, G. (1999) *Saint Augustine*, New York: Viking.

Wolfensohn, J. D. (1997) *Annual Meetings Address: The Challenge of Inclusion*, Hong Kong: World Bank. Internet: www.worldbank.org/html/extdr/am97/jdw_sp/jwsp97e.htm

Wolfensohn, J. D. (1998) *Annual Meetings Address: The Other Crisis*, given at the 1998 World Bank/International Monetary Fund annual meetings. Internet: http://www.worldbank.org/html/extdr/am98/jdw-sp/index.htm

Wolfensohn, J. D. (1999a) *A Proposal for a Comprehensive Development Framework*, Washington: World Bank.

Wolfensohn, J. D. (1999b) *Annual Meetings Address: Coalitions for Change*, given in Washington, 28 September 1999.

World Bank (1997) *World Development Report: The State in a Changing World*, New York: Oxford University Press.

World Bank (1998a) *World Development Report: Knowledge for Development*, New York: Oxford University Press.

World Bank (1998b) *Assessing Aid: What Works, What Doesn't, and Why*, Washington: World Bank.

3 The instrumentalisation of development knowledge

Knut G. Nustad and Ole J. Sending

Introduction

The Global Development Network (GDN) is a network in the making of scholars, policy makers and donors that aims to create and share knowledge related to development efforts. Originating from and organised by the World Bank, the GDN forms part of its strategy of becoming a 'knowledge bank'. The GDN thus plays a part in the World Bank's emphasis on, first, the role of knowledge in social and economic development; and, second, the part played by civil society actors in addressing development issues.

The inaugural conference of the GDN in Bonn was organised under the heading 'Bridging Knowledge and Policy'. The main topic raised and discussed was how think tanks, research institutions and others could contribute to making knowledge more relevant to development policy. A key goal, according to the conference programme, was to 'enhance the quality and availability of policy-oriented research and strengthen the institutions which undertake this work'. (www.gdnet.org/bonn).

This is an important initiative that recognises and sets out to redress the general lack of communication between policy makers and researchers. It was therefore with a certain expectation that one of the authors arrived in Bonn hoping that he would be present at the launch of an institution that would provide a forum for discussions that included policy makers and researchers, thereby contributing to the institutionalisation of a sense of critical self-reflection in the development community. Critical analyses and insights about current development practices and problems seem to require a degree of detachment – a certain distance from the imperative of making research directly relevant to the needs of policy makers. The GDN has the potential to become an institution that will assume a certain degree of autonomy from the world of policy making but that could still deliver important insights into it.

However, the Bonn meeting left the impression that establishing the necessary distance and detachment from policy making proved more difficult than anticipated. A possible explanation, and a line of critique that was voiced by several participants at the meeting, was that discussions at the GDN stayed too much within the confines of a neo-liberal approach, where development is conceived in terms of economics. We believe the problem to be of another nature, which has repercussions far beyond the confines of the GDN. An explanation, we will argue, must be sought in the understanding of knowledge and its relation to policy making, which framed the debate at the conference. Knowledge was understood in purely instrumental terms, as an apolitical and objective tool that, if made relevant to policy making, would contribute to the making of better policies. Within such a framework, knowledge cannot serve as an instrument for critical self-reflection because the boundaries within which one can operate and discuss matters are confined to discussions about how to make knowledge more policy-relevant and how to have 'policy impact'.

In our view, what disappears from consideration with such a conception of knowledge is the political implications inherent in defining certain propositions as 'knowledge'. Knowledge has normative and political implications that are often used as a tool to legitimise and rationalise certain positions. The problem extends far beyond the GDN initiative itself and relates to development practices and debates generally. This problem, which we refer to as the instrumentalisation of development knowledge, lies at the heart of many failed development policies. We therefore use the conference as a 'window of opportunity', a platform, to reflect on the role of knowledge in development policy making more generally. What follows is therefore not a critique of the GDN initiative as such but rather an exploration of the limits of the conceptual apparatus within which knowledge for development is discussed and practised.

Our argument runs as follows: knowledge is not objective and value-free but necessarily embeds certain cognitive interests. For knowledge to be relevant to policy makers implies that it has to be produced within a framework, an understanding of what constitutes relevant and meaningful propositions. It is this framework that we, following Habermas (1971), refer to as cognitive interests. The focus on this kind of knowledge excludes other forms of knowledge equally important, if not readily relevant to policy. This is played out in the development field as follows: any agency involved in development policy, if it is to be a supplier of solutions, must define development problems in such a way that they are amenable to the toolkit of solutions available to it. Failing to do so would mean that the agency defined itself away as a possible provider of solutions. In seeking to intervene in society through policies, one particular form of knowledge is relevant: causal knowledge, which identifies variables open to manipulation by the policy tools available to policy makers. It is not surprising that policy makers approach and use knowledge as an instrument and therefore advocate an instrumental view of knowledge. The problem is that this understanding of knowledge also serves to limit and confine the whole development debate within one dominant understanding of the relationship between knowledge and development policy. As we will show through three examples, this has direct practical implications: those aspects of intervening in a society through policies that are not conveyed in the form of variables to be manipulated tend to be left out.

This has two negative effects: first, discussions about knowledge and development perpetuate a conception of knowledge as an instrument, a tool, for the identification of manipulative variables, thus overlooking the importance of creating and sharing knowledge that at first seems irrelevant. Second, attempting to improve development efforts by bridging knowledge and policy in this way portrays development efforts as a depoliticised, technical task. If the point is to develop, share and make powerful knowledge and *new* ideas, the discussions about knowledge and development must include the inherent pathologies of the multilateral aid and development system. One such pathology, in our view, is the instrumentalisation of development knowledge with which this chapter is concerned.

GDN99 in Bonn

The opening conference in Bonn in December 1999 attracted almost 600 participants. At the opening session in the old Bundestag, Joseph Stiglitz, then chief economist at the World Bank, underlined the power of ideas as a key rationale for the GDN. Quoting Keynes' famous dictum that 'practical men, who believe themselves to be quite exempt from any intellectual influences, are usually the slaves of some defunct economist', Stiglitz argued that the GDN should 'scan' for ideas globally, whereas local research institutions and think tanks should 'reinvent' and put these ideas to work locally (Stiglitz 1999). In this way, development knowledge and policy would be formulated in a manner more cognisant of contextual factors. This is how the objective of the GDN99 was presented in the conference programme:

> Sharing both research and practical knowledge related to development as well as to economic and political transition helps bridge differences of perceptions and increases the capacity and effectiveness of researchers and policy institutes to generate policy relevant research and advise decision makers. The spirit of the GDN99 is to provide a communications bridge between the world of the policy practitioner and the world of the researcher to help improve the prospects for development.
>
> (GDN 1999: 2)

During the four days that the conference lasted, the participants engaged in numerous discussions on how to make research and policy analysis more relevant to policy making. Some panels addressed this issue directly by exploring possible means of enhancing the effectiveness of communications with governments, and of how to make knowledge relevant to policy makers. The majority of panels focused on presenting research findings to donors and policy makers, in many cases placing policy makers as discussants in the expectation that they would draw out the policy implications of research. Yet others were concerned with the presentation of 'GDN products', which included web strategies, research awards and assistance in communications strategies to the public and governments.

At least eight panels directly addressed the issue of bridging knowledge and policy. Some of the panels aimed at investigating what role think tanks perform in the policy process and how one could improve on current practice. One panel explicitly addressed the 'knowledge–policy nexus' (*ibid.*: 39). This panel was to discuss questions such as 'How is research used in policy making, and how does it improve the policy process?' and 'Where does knowledge come from and how does it enter into the policy process?' (*ibid.*: 39). Judging from the presentations and the ensuing discussions in this and other panels, the focus appeared to be on how knowledge could be deployed in a way that would have an impact on policy. Frequent statements in presentations and in the subsequent discussions were 'enhancing the efficiency of communicating to policy makers', 'how to make knowledge relevant to policy makers' and 'measuring the impact of influencing through knowledge'. Put simply, the emphasis seemed to be on the issue of 'bridging' rather than on the conceptualisation of how knowledge and policy are related, and on how politics enters into the equation. As noted by a somewhat frustrated policy maker who attended the conference: 'You are talking as if we policy makers are empty vessels to be filled and enlightened by knowledge. That is not the case. We have experience and opinions of our own.'

We will argue that the focus and content of these debates reflect a more general trend in the field of development; a common denominator seems to be that the two things one seeks to bridge – knowledge and policy – are inadequately conceptualised and discussed. This silence on the many aspects of the relationship between knowledge and policy making indicates that these discussions rest on a preconceived understanding of what constitutes knowledge and policy. Knowledge is assumed to be consensual and objective, and an instrument to be used in policy making. Within this instrumental understanding of knowledge, and the 'engineering model' of policy making derived from it, policy makers are assumed to agree on the desired goals but to lack the necessary knowledge of how to obtain them. In the view of Deborah Stone (1997: 8), the policy-making process is therefore seen as a technical task of intervening in society. Correspondingly, policy making is seen as detached from politics; policy making is conceived of as a rational process whereby different alternatives are evaluated, based on their perceived appropriateness given the agreed objectives. This conception of the knowledge–policy nexus corresponds to what Carol Weiss labelled 'traditional wisdom', by which she meant to argue that the idea of knowledge as unproblematically entering into and increasing the rationality of policy making is misguided (1977: 4).

Let us be more specific. Consider the following incident, which occurred at the plenary session at the beginning of the second day of the conference. Around 400 participants had gathered for the session entitled 'Bridging the gap between knowledge and policy'. The panel consisted of one NGO representative, two ministers and one counsellor to a head of state. All panelists spoke of the critical role of knowledge in policy making and illuminated their arguments with examples from their own experiences. After the panelists had made their presentations, a German professor emeritus made an intervention from the floor.

Critical of the lack of conceptualisation of knowledge and how it operates in the policy process, he asked: 'What kind of knowledge are we talking about here?' A certain unease seemed to spread in the audience as it became clear that none of the panelists wanted to address the question. The tension was relieved when the chairman responded with a 'well, thank you for that professorial remark'. The audience laughed and the chairman moved on without any follow-up or response to the professor's question.

What was going on here? Had the professor completely misunderstood the issue of the plenary? Alternatively, had the rest of us who laughed not understood what he was aiming at? The professor posed, in this setting, an irrelevant question. That is why the chairman responded as he did, and that is why the rest of us found his response so amusing. But why was it irrelevant? What does it say about GDN99 and about development knowledge in general?

In all stories, there are those who are cast as heroes and those who are portrayed as villains. The hero in this story is the professor because he invoked an element of self-reflection. It is this invitation to self-reflection, on what bridging knowledge and policy involves, that we would like to respond to here. The 'villain' is not the chairman, or the rest of us who laughed. To identify the villain, we have to make an extended argument about some aspects of knowledge and its relation to policy making. The rest of this chapter is thus an attempt to identify the 'villain'. As will become clear below, the villain lies buried in what we refer to as 'the instrumentalisation of development knowledge'. In order to see what is implied by this term, we have to make our way through a somewhat theoretical argument about the nature of knowledge. This is the topic of the next section. We then proceed by 'bridging' the conception of knowledge to policy making. However, this bridging will be of a different kind than the one advocated at the conference in Bonn.

Knowledge

Before we can discuss the relationship between knowledge and policy making, it is necessary to have a clear understanding of what knowledge is. *The Penguin Dictionary of Philosophy* defines knowledge in terms of the *certainty* that a proposition is true:

> Knowledge is not the same as belief or opinion. To say that a person *knows* that p implies that p, but to say that he *believes* that p does not imply that p. The two statements *A knows that p* and *B knows that not-p* cannot be true together, for the first implies that p and the second implies that not-p.
>
> (Mautner 1997: 296; italics in original)

This definition conforms to our intuitive understanding of knowledge: it is something that we take to be true because we are certain, it is something we *know*. In more general terms, the *certainty* of a proposition that makes it a candidate for constituting knowledge derives from the rules of logical inference, of methods and so forth that define *science*. Knowledge can thus be understood as the sets of propositions that derive their certainty from the rules, standards and procedures that are embedded in and define science.[1]

One question, which is of critical importance for our discussion, seems to have been left unanswered, however: what is it about science that lets us establish with the necessary certainty whether a proposition constitutes knowledge? In answering this question, we will turn to the ideas developed by Jürgen Habermas in his 'Knowledge and Human Interest' (1971). For knowledge to be produced, Habermas argues, there has to be a transcendental *frame of reference* that constitutes the objects to which the scientific inquiry is directed. It is only within such a frame of reference that the rules and the standards of a scientific inquiry attain their *meaning*. This assertion is firmly grounded in epistemological inquiries about the possible conditions of knowledge: any scientific inquiry draws its assumptions and axioms from a prior frame of reference that the methods of this scientific inquiry by themselves can neither prove nor apprehend (see Alcoff 1998). The interesting and more complicated aspect arises when Habermas argues that the frame of reference that makes a scientific inquiry possible, and thus constitutes knowledge, embeds certain cognitive *interests*:

> The approach of the empirical-analytic sciences incorporates a *technical* cognitive interest; that of the historical-hermeneutic sciences incorporates a *practical* one; and the approach of critically oriented sciences incorporates the *emancipatory* cognitive interest.
>
> (Habermas 1971: 308; italics in original)

An intuitive view of the relation between knowledge and interests, theory and practice suggests that scientific knowledge is defined as knowledge free of interests and therefore, at least ideally, value-free and objective. It is only with the introduction of action – that is, how a certain body of knowledge is *used* – that we normally speak of interests in relation to knowledge. Political actors may for example use a certain body of knowledge as a strategic tool with which to pursue certain interests, defined in terms of a specific outcome. When Habermas speaks of interests, however, he speaks of *knowledge-constitutive interests* (*ibid.*: 189); that is, those interests that make possible the generation of knowledge in the first place:

> Orientation toward technical control, toward mutual understanding in the conduct of life, and toward emancipation from seemingly 'natural' constraint *establish the specific viewpoints from which we can apprehend reality as such in any way whatsoever.*
>
> (*ibid.*: 311; italics added)

These cognitive interests in either technical control, practical understanding or emancipation are thus embedded in the respective frames of reference that make possible the production of *empirical-analytic knowledge, historical-hermeneutic knowledge* and *critical knowledge* (*ibid.*: 308). In this way appears a *necessary* linkage between knowledge and interest, because science is constituted by a frame of reference that in turn embeds certain cognitive interests. To avoid any misunderstanding, we want to underline that cognitive interests cannot be linked to a specific group of people or an organisation. These are interests that are constitutive of how knowledge is produced. Consequently, these interests appear, or are embedded in, different kinds of knowledge, regardless of the interests that any group of actors or organisation may have in a particular outcome or political objective.

These knowledge-constitutive cognitive interests may not appear directly relevant to what the GDN project is about. After all, the GDN contains a plethora of institutions and actors with different research interests and political preferences. But in considering more specifically how certain kinds of knowledge are necessarily linked to certain political practices (policies) this aspect will appear at the heart of the GDN initiative.

Before we proceed to discuss empirical-analytic knowledge in the context of the GDN, let us briefly outline the character of historical-hermeneutic and critical knowledge. Central to *historical-hermeneutic* knowledge is the notion of inter-subjectivity; that is, the understanding between individuals and between communities. It is geared towards the production of meaning. It is because of this that it can be said to be predicated upon a cognitive interest in practical and mutual understanding and not on instrumental action. A case in point would be the anthropological project of attempting to interpret cultural expressions within their own local contexts. *Critical* knowledge, on the other hand, seeks to go beyond understanding and describing social phenomena and to determine whether theoretical statements express regularities in the world, or 'ideologically frozen relations of dependence that can in principle be transformed' (*ibid.*: 310). Hence the cognitive interest in emancipation. Central to the framework within which critical knowledge is produced is therefore the notion of self-reflection as it can be said to assess the current state of affairs against certain normative standards (such as equality and liberty).

The Bonn meeting aimed at bridging knowledge and policy making: the idea was to create and share policy-relevant knowledge. 'Policy-relevant knowledge' conforms to Habermas' category of empirical-analytic science; that is, knowledge constituted by a cognitive interest in control, which rests on causal explanations. Specifically for development knowledge, we will see that the object one wants to control is the problem that is addressed (for example, poverty), and that knowledge about this 'object' has to be constructed as causal because causal knowledge informs the practitioner of the likely consequences of his or her policy intervention. To explore this link further, we will leave Habermas and make use of the insights developed by Brian Fay. He approaches this issue directly at the level of political theory and conceptions of social life and not, like Habermas, through a theory of knowledge.

In *Social Theory and Political Practice* (1975), Fay is at pains to identify the necessary relation between social theory and political practice by extending the kind of argument made by Habermas. Fay's argument runs as follows: there is a necessary, internal relation between science – understood in positivist terms as in the case of empirical-analytic science – and the need for *control*. This is because the key feature of empirical-analytic science, or positivist science, is the production of general knowledge in the form of causal explanations. Now causal explanations have a 'structural identity' of the form that makes them similar to predictions. In causally explaining a state of affairs Y through an independent variable X, one establishes the necessary and/or sufficient conditions for Y to occur. This would then imply an ability to predict Y on the basis of the existence of X; or alternatively to manipulate X so that Y will occur if Y is a desired state of affairs. In this sense, a causal explanation is the obverse of a prediction. Since causal explanations have a structural identity that makes them the obverse of prediction and prediction is intimately linked to control, positivist science is intimately related to an interest in technical control and instrumental action. But this is only half the story.

In addition to the intimate relation between causal explanation, prediction and control, there is indeed a constitutive aspect here: reality is defined in such a way as to make it possible for it to be controlled through the methods of science:

> Because science marks out the 'world' as a world of observable phenomena subject to general laws it thereby is *constituting this 'world' from the viewpoint of how one can gain control over it*. It is for this reason that possible technical control provides the framework within which the definition of reality and truth in science occurs ... So the conclusion is not merely that scientific knowledge provides the basis for manipulative control, but also, and more importantly, that what can count as scientific knowledge is that which gives us the means by which one can in principle control phenomena.
>
> (*ibid.*: 40–1; italics in original)

In this way, scientific knowledge, defined as empirical-analytic knowledge (or positivist science in Fay's terminology), is in one important regard intimately connected with a cognitive interest in technical control. The social world is defined in such a way as to make possible the control over it through the development of knowledge in the form of causal explanations. This is no coincidence, as science became institutionalised as an authoritative discourse on society in a specific historical context, that of the increasing rationalisation of modern life in which prediction and control were the key features (*ibid.*: 45; see also Wagner *et al.* 1991). This is a crucial point: what appears as, or constitutes, knowledge is determined by the area or aim to which it is directed. Knowledge constituted by a framework of instrumental action and an interest in technical control differs fundamentally, as we have seen, from historical-hermeneutic and critical knowledge.

Hence, in speaking of 'bridging knowledge and policy' and in explicitly emphasising that the aim of the GDN is to 'share and generate policy-*relevant* knowledge', one should be aware that it is only knowledge of a certain kind, directed towards a certain objective, that one seeks to generate and share. The next section will substantiate this assertion by showing how in general terms knowledge and policy are related. We then continue by identifying its expression in the context of development policy making.

Knowledge and policy

We identified above the constitutive interests of empirical-analytic knowledge as technical control. Within this conception, knowledge is an *instrument* for something else. As we turn the discussion to policy making, the instrumental understanding of knowledge as a means to something else is further clarified, albeit in a slightly different and more direct way. Here, as in the case above, *relevance* is of key importance.

A policy usually contains certain rules, regulations, incentives and disincentives. It represents a pooling of resources (either human, monetary or administrative-regulative) into a programme or project or law aiming at the alteration or prevention of a certain state of affairs. In a broad sense, therefore, policy making is about social control or regulation by governmental intervention in society. This is not to suggest that there is a certain interest or demand for control in a strict sense among policy makers: deregulation is also a key element of policy. However, the point is that actors involved in these processes are subject to one very important constraint: in acting or deciding on a course of action they are constrained by the tools of intervention available to them, either in the form of regulations through law, redistribution of resources of some kind, or deregulation (see Nustad 1996; 1997). What are the implications of this for our discussion of the necessary relation between forms of knowledge and different kinds of cognitive interest?

Above we concluded that what appears as knowledge is structured by its relevance or by the aim to which it is to be directed. In the world of policy making, this relation between knowledge and interests, theory and practice, is transformed into one in which the position of the actor determines what appears as (relevant) knowledge. That is, the policy maker is set to intervene in society through policies. In deciding on what actions to take, the policy maker is confined to choosing from among a specific set of policy tools. Through the manipulation of certain independent variables, these tools are aiming at achieving the occurrence of a desired dependent variable. Policies are means of manipulating social and economic variables; hence, what is relevant knowledge to a policy maker is that which can assist in identifying variables that are open to manipulation. Variables that fall outside the range of possible manipulation through the existing kit of policy tools thus appear irrelevant. It is thus the position, and the corresponding kit of policy tools, that determine what it is possible to manipulate through policy, and hence determine what constitutes relevant knowledge. In conclusion, then, knowledge is constituted by certain cognitive interests, and what appears as (relevant) knowledge for the policy maker is that which can assist in identifying manipulatable variables. The next section develops the relation between knowledge and policy further by introducing politics into the equation.

Knowledge, policy and politics

Policy is the enactment of politics. It is a form of politics that claims legitimacy from being portrayed as the technical implementation of a rational solution to a problem. Scientific knowledge in this sense performs a symbolic task as it legitimises and renders credible – that is, rational and efficient – political action. When a political actor is able to support his actions or opinions with reference to some body of scientific knowledge or facts, it becomes difficult to argue that they are untenable or inappropriate. As the main conveyor of authoritative 'reality', science embeds a substantial form of power in political life. One commentator puts it thus:

> the presentation of public action as a scientifically and technically controlled means of bringing about certain substantive results, conveys the appearance of self-exposure, or readiness to step into the public space of visible actions and become transparent and publicly accountable in a world of 'objective' factual constraints.
>
> (Ezrahi 1990: 147)

The potential 'masking' of political action in technical and scientific language and the legitimising effect of science in politics is always difficult to grasp. It is easier to see with hindsight, when the 'objective' knowledge on which a policy was claimed to have been based has been challenged. Most people would agree that the British government's decision in the 1840s not to intervene in the Irish potato famine but rather to let the people starve was a most brutal political decision. Yet this was at the time portrayed as the rational enactment of sound knowledge: Malthus' theory that famines were nature's way of regulating a surplus population (Shore and Wright 1997).

This example illustrates some of the power inherent in policy making. Policies are the enactment of politics, but politics that are objectified and legitimised with reference to something 'outside' itself: objective scientific knowledge. This does not mean that knowledge only serves this function, or that knowledge is best described as a form of disciplinary power. But it implies that one must recognise the role that knowledge plays through policy in rendering some courses of action more objective, rational and technical than they in fact are. Policy interventions based on and legitimised by knowledge may seem rational, but as they affect people's lives in some way and redistribute resources, rights and obligations they are by definition political. In appealing to knowledge as a benign and rational force, the politics inherent in policy become objectified.

This objectification extends both to politics and to the subjects of policy. Through policy, political power takes on an appearance of technical administration; at the same time, the people who are targeted by the policy are transformed into objects: numbers on unemployment charts, mortality rates, percentages of population under a 'poverty line', and so forth. The political implications of making power appear as policy are many. First, as Shore and Wright have noted, 'the political features of policies are disguised by the objective, neutral, legal-rational idioms in which they are portrayed. In this guise, policies appear as mere instruments for promoting efficiency and effectiveness' (1997: 8). Second, this objectification serves to collectivise responsibility for decisions adopted: it is hard to point to the interest of one particular group as being the motivating factor behind a policy decision. Third, policies legitimise politics by relating them to something larger, outside the domain of political interest: it is difficult to argue against an exercise of power that portrays itself as the rational implementation of 'poverty alleviation'.

The relationship between policy and knowledge, then, has two important political consequences. First, by appealing to a form of knowledge that does not question its own assumptions (what Habermas labels frames of reference), the political implications of policy interventions are objectified. Second, the knowledge used by practitioners is shaped by their need to intervene: what appears as relevant knowledge is therefore knowledge in the form of variables, open to manipulation through policy.

The concrete manifestations of these processes will differ depending on the field of intervention. We will argue that knowledge produced for development interventions and by development practitioners has two chief characteristics. The first follows from the effects of addressing something as a policy field more generally: the political problem of poverty is transformed into a technical problem, and a problem that can be solved locally. As Ferguson puts it:

> by uncompromisingly reducing poverty to a technical problem, and by promising technical solutions to the sufferings of powerless and oppressed people, the hegemonic problematic of 'development' is the principal means through which the question of poverty is de-politicised in the world today.
>
> (1990: 256)

Second, knowledge about the target populations of development projects is structured according to the need of states: knowledge about the people who are targeted by development projects takes the form of objectified variables. They are therefore rendered as knowledge that can fit into the needs of a state to govern them. As Hart has pointed out for West Africa:

> almost everything that the new states do in the name of development means the intention at least of forcing the diversity of remote rural lives into an iron grid of title documents, accounts, censuses, and tax lists – words and numbers.
>
> (1982: 105)

Development policy thus has two effects: it extends bureaucratic structures to those who fall outside the influence of the state (the unemployed, participants in the informal sector, etc.), and it depicts their exclusion as an apolitical problem that can be solved by technical intervention. These effects of development come about as a result of the way that development projects are structured. Developers need to construct the problem in a way that enables them to intervene. This precondition excludes some forms of analysis; if the problem, poverty, is seen as a political problem and the specific instance as a part of a much wider network of power relations, then the potential developer has already defined him or herself away as the provider of a possible solution. This is why development knowledge becomes instrumentalised.

Implications for development policy: three examples

The three examples provided below suggest that what we have identified as the instrumentalisation of development knowledge can have direct implications for development practice. Importantly, what these examples indicate is that the instrumentalisation of development knowledge is of a general character. One can agree or disagree with the claims and the content of the examples below, but they give an apt illustration of some inherent problems in the instrumentalisation of development knowledge.

Governance

The current concern with 'good governance' and 'best practice' provides a good example of the instrumentalisation of development knowledge: what appears as knowledge is shaped by the need to intervene. The appeal of such concepts lies in their apparent instrumentality: if one can identify problems in Third World states as resulting from bad or inefficient practices of governance, the solution would seem to be to reform these practices. Governance is an area that is familiar to development policy makers, and at first sight it might seem like an ideal solution to the problem of 'corruption' in many developing countries. Governance, however conceived, consists of factors that are open to manipulation by development donors, who, at least in the most heavily indebted countries, have a lot to say in budgeting and allocation decisions of national governments.

Bayart's (1993) concept of the 'politics of the belly' is an alternative explanation of the problem that 'good governance', 'best practice' and similar terms are meant to address. It is an academic explanation of the same processes at which the good governance rhetoric is targeted. Bayart begins his explanation of the 'politics of the belly' by comparing it with a notion of good governance:

> [It] is not an overriding factor, similar to a more or less erratic 'political culture', for which it might be possible to substitute the idea of 'good governance'; rather it is a system of historic action whose origins must if possible be understood in the Braudelian *longue durée*.
>
> (1993: ix)

In the rest of the book, he provides an outline of what he sees as a general character-istic of the post-colonial state in Africa. 'Politics of the belly' is an expression that he has borrowed from Cameroon. It refers to a conception of politics as based on an ability to enrich oneself and one's dependants. The Cameroonian proverb 'the goat eats where it is tethered' supplies a metaphor for politics as 'eating'. This is much more than a symptom of corruption or of the decadence of the state. These prac-tices can be institutional, as is evident in Nigeria's draft constitution of 1976. It defined political power as 'the opportunity to acquire riches and prestige, to be in a position to hand out benefits in the forms of jobs, contracts, gifts of money etc. to relations and political allies' (*ibid.*: xvii).

The African state has been analysed, by development practitioners and others, as a modern sector that takes part in the modern world and is opposed to a 'traditional world'. Instead, Bayart argues, the African state must be analysed as an indigenous African institution that has evolved over centuries of participa-tion in the world economy. Put simply, he argues that leading actors in sub-Saharan societies have compensated for the difficulties in exploiting depen-dants and achieve autonomous power by strategies of 'extraversion, mobilizing resources derived from their (possibly unequal) relationship with the external environment' (*ibid.*: 21–2).

This is a process that stretches back to pre-colonial state formations but that was intensified by colonial politics. Dominant groups, according to Bayart, live off income that they derive from their positions as intermediaries *vis-à-vis* the international system. Bayart describes a double process by which African govern-ments, far from being the victims of their vulnerability, exploit the resources of a dependence that is fabricated as much as it is predetermined. Attempts at devel-opment interventions are caught up in the same problem:

> Striking in their scale and the severity of the conditions they impose, the interventions of the World Bank and the IMF are imposed by the harsh laws of economics and are viewed, not without justification, by most African leaders as an attack upon their sovereignty. However, inasmuch as loans granted following long negotiations and ostensibly binding agreements seem to a significant degree to have been used for different purposes from what was intended, even these interventions do not undermine our argument.
>
> (*ibid.*: 27)

This cannot be explained as a cultural resurgence of ancient political forms but must be seen in the context of colonialisation. The Europeans, Bayart argues, mixed up the genres more frequently than the authentically bureaucratic phases of British and French colonialisation might lead one to think. Extortion and confusion over the exercise of public authority were inherent in the company regimes, whose extraordinary greed shocked many travellers. Furthermore, the indigenous intermediaries of the colonial state made fresh use of their privileges as auxiliaries of the administration to enrich themselves. In this sense, 'corruption', as it would be called today, was an organic part of the system of 'indirect rule'.

Bayart, then, supplies an analysis of what he sees as the root causes of 'corruption'. It is an instituted practice formed in the interaction of local elites and the international system. According to this conception of corruption, imposing harsh structural adjustment policies or attempting to improve the practices of governance will only serve to entrench the problem: it fuels the processes that one seeks to avoid.

As this example demonstrates, the problematic outlined above has more than academic relevance: development knowledge excludes the political situation of what it constitutes as the target population because it is not open to manipulation. The frame of reference within which knowledge for development is produced labels as irrelevant the kind of critical knowledge of which Bayart's conception of 'politics of the belly' is an example. Yet if Bayart is right, the processes he draws our attention to will undermine attempts at intervention based on knowledge produced within a cognitive interest of technical control. Whether Bayart is correct in his assumptions is beside the point as far as our main argument is concerned: development knowledge, when it aims to make itself relevant to policy intervention, will tend to exclude knowledge that might have important implications for a process of development. This happens, we have argued, because of the frame of reference within which this knowledge is produced.

Disappearing relations

More fundamentally, the structuring effect of the policy makers' need for knowledge that can serve as a basis for interventions might lead to knowledge production that appears strange to outsiders. James Ferguson, in the 'anti-politics machine' (1990), has described a failed development intervention in Lesotho that illustrates our main point. Looking through the development plan for a project funded by the Canadian International Development Agency (CIDA), he was astonished to see Lesotho, a country completely surrounded by and dependent on South Africa, described as a backward, pre-industrial economy rather than as a supplier of labour for South Africa. He concluded that rather than an example of staggeringly bad scholarship, this 'knowledge' of Lesotho was shaped by the development agent's need to intervene. Had CIDA described Lesotho as intimately connected with South Africa, the development agent would have defined itself away as a possible provider of development solutions. However, the knowledge produced made possible interventions based on an upgrading of agricultural technology. When Ferguson was confronted by a 'developer' (not specified) and asked what his country could do to help 'these people', he suggested that the country in question could contemplate sanctions against apartheid, to which the developer replied, with predictable irritation, 'No, no! I mean *development*!' (*ibid.*: 284). An analysis that placed poverty in Lesotho in the wider context of apartheid domination was resented, not because of reactionary politics on the part of the developer but because he knew that political sanctions against apartheid were outside his sphere of influence. The cognitive interest is thus inherent in the developer's position and not in his or her personal political preferences. This is an apt illustration of the point we are arguing: it was the position of the development practitioners that excluded certain ranges of options: they could not, for example, intervene or change South Africa's domination over Lesotho. Consequently, they constructed the problem in a way that opened up the possibility for their intervention with the tools at their disposal.

In these two examples, there are parallels that can be drawn to the GDN. As an instrument for generating and sharing development knowledge, the GDN appears to operate within a framework that is defined by the imperative to be relevant for policy makers. In short, the GDN is a manifestation of the need of international organisations, foundations and development agencies to intervene. Some forms of knowledge are therefore marginalised in preference to the kind of knowledge that can supplement the 'tools at their disposal'. The technical knowledge that is mobilised is primarily constructed and constituted by professional economists, who have a strong institutional base in international organisations such as the World Bank and the IMF. They interact with their counterparts in research institutes and think tanks that are involved in the GDN; organisations comprising mainly Western-trained professionals and development practitioners. Through their cooperation via the GDN, these organisations have considerable capacity to structure both the supply and the demand for development knowledge. In this way, the GDN is likely to perpetuate the domination of an instrumentalised development knowledge.

Civil society

The concept of civil society has emerged as a development buzzword during the last two decades. As a concept, it draws its strength from its kinship to other positively valued concepts such as 'bottom-up development', 'local ownership' and 'partnership'. Contemporary usage of the term stems from Hegel, who introduced civil society as an intermediate category of social formation between the family and the state. In this sense, civil society represents a democratic element outside state structures. This is the normative rationale for the increased attention to civil society. The more practical rationale lies in that civil society contains the actors that are the real targets of assistance. Civil society represents a more direct channel of aid and development assistance in the sense that it is not tied up with formal, bureaucratic or state structures. The idea, then, is that by circumventing state structures, one can have direct access to those in need. In the development field, however, civil society has been operationalised as non-governmental organisations (NGOs). NGOs are better equipped to deliver certain goods and services because they have local knowledge of and engage in close interaction with those in need of aid. The consequence of this focus has been a substantial increase in the level of funding to non-governmental (development) organisations.

However, there is one serious problem with the way in which the multilateral development system conceives of and approaches civil society through the lenses of NGOs: civil society is defined as NGOs, thus making *formal organisation* the defining element of a diverse civil society. The neglect of the informal aspect of civil society is related to the way in which developers have brought the Western idea of a civil society, which is primarily urban, into a population that is, at least in the case of Africa, primarily rural (see Mamdani 1996). This has had the unfortunate consequence of equating civic-ness with formal organisation, thus ignoring the fact that civil society is infinitely more complex and varied than the density and nature of NGOs would suggest. A related problem, according to some authors, is that NGOs are increasingly becoming homogenised and formalised. This homogenisation can be attributed to their heavy reliance upon external and mostly foreign funding. They begin to 'talk the talk' and adopt the practices encouraged by the donors to secure sustained funding. This has come at the expense of their local civic-ness; the civic values that they were seen to convey and represent are streamlined and replaced by new ones that no longer represent the original democratic element (Fowler 2000: 47; see also Tvedt 1998)

We should not be surprised that civil society is operationalised as NGOs in development policy making. As a term, 'civil society' is too vague to be relevant. However, by operationalising it as NGOs, donors and policy makers are able to target transfers of human and monetary resources and make civil society relevant to the task of intervening in society. In doing so, however, some aspects of a complex reality appear at the expense of others. When we describe, explain and make intelligible social processes, we do so through the use of concepts. Concepts let some aspects appear to us, but not all. In equating civil society with NGOs, policy makers and others overlook critical aspects of what civil society is, aspects that would be of critical importance for formulations and implementations of development projects.

Again, there are insights from this example for the GDN. Think tanks and research institutes are often portrayed as civil society organisations that can assist in development programmes. Yet, in many cases, think tanks in developing countries lack the independence and connections to civil society usually associated with NGOs. They are either quasi-governmental or located within the bureaucratic machinery or constrained by authoritarian and quasi-liberal regimes. Furthermore, these are elite organisations. They usually lack long-term relationships with organisations that are deemed to be of lower social status, groups that are perceived to be radical or disruptive in their demands, or bodies that are in competition with think tanks for media, political and foundation attention. In many respects, think tanks are distant from other civil society organisations and sometimes act as a buffer between other civil society organisations and the state (Stone 2000).

A two-pronged homogenisation is in progress: first, the Western ideal of a research institute is 'exported' by development agencies – most obviously in Eastern and Central Europe – in an attempt to 'grow' or 'force feed' civil society.

These organisations then constitute a familiar structure with which donors can interact instead of traditional and sometimes less organisationally amenable structures. Second, the research institutes themselves are heavily reliant upon foreign funding, which promotes scholarly practices, research agendas and 'knowledge of a certain kind' encouraged by donor organisations as 'policy-relevant'. For civil society institutions to carve out an independent space for themselves, which is their *raison d'être*, is therefore extremely difficult.

These three examples suggest that development policy making and its relation to knowledge is of a particular kind, and the list could have been longer. Our point is simply that it is important to recognise these aspects of the relation between knowledge, policy and politics. In this sense, the knowledge–policy nexus should be widened to a triad of knowledge, policy and politics. The bridging of knowledge and policy must not take place at the expense of the political aspects of development.

Conclusion

Abraham Kaplan wrote thirty years ago that 'when all you have is the hammer, the whole world looks like a nail' (quoted in Deleon 1991). This metaphor captures well what we have been trying to flesh out in this chapter: that policy makers, as they set out to intervene in society through policies, have to define and understand social problems in a way that make them solvable with the tools at their disposal. In seeking to solve social and economic problems with policy tools, policy makers therefore tend to understand the reality in which they intervene as a set of manipulatable variables.

The villain in this story has at last emerged. The question posed by the German professor emeritus was scorned because he questioned the frame of reference within which knowledge for development is produced.[2] As we have seen, this knowledge 'functions' because it does not question its epistemological framework. Our main contention, then, is that 'knowledge' is not a neutral and value-free entity that can be used uncritically to improve policies. Talking about bridging knowledge and policy, or of the 'power of ideas', is a far too simplistic model of the process. Knowledge is produced within a frame of reference that embeds certain cognitive interests. And, in the continuation of this, what appears as 'knowledge' and what becomes irrelevant is determined by the position of the person seeking knowledge. For a policy maker, this involves a bias towards 'variables' that can be 'manipulated'. In this way, politics is turned into policy and knowledge into a prescription for action.

We have intended to make this aspect of the knowledge–policy nexus explicit and have argued that the GDN, if it is to contribute to the production of new ideas, must investigate knowledge constructed outside an empirical-analytic frame of reference. Bayart's concept of the 'politics of the belly' as an alternative explanation to 'good governance' is a case in point. This knowledge, which is not readily policy-relevant, has the potential to illuminate, and give an alternative view of, the processes and problems in which one wants to intervene through development policies. What we need, then, is not just a bridging of knowledge and policy but a clearer understanding of how knowledge for policy is produced, as well as the power residing in the contemporary definition of what constitutes relevant knowledge for development. With this as a background, one can proceed to support the generation of knowledge in the form of new and alternative ideas and conceptualisations, because ideas are powerful. As this chapter has argued, we need knowledges in the plural, including forms of knowledge and ideas that do not turn social processes into nails to be hit by the hammer of policy.

Notes

1   When we refer to science here, we include in it the natural, social and cultural sciences.
2   The concerns of the professor were echoed by a few of the contributors to the electronic discussion group convened by the GDN in November 1999: http://www2.worldbank.org/hm/hmgdn/

References

Alcoff, L. M. (1998) *Epistemology: The Big Questions*, Oxford: Blackwell.

Bayart, J.-F. (1993) *The State in Africa: The Politics of the Belly*, London: Longman.

Deleon, P. (1991) 'Political events and the policy sciences', in P. Wagner *et al.* (eds) *Social Sciences and Modern States: National Experiences and Theoretical Crossroads*, Cambridge: Cambridge University Press.

Ezrahi, Y. (1990) *The Descent of Icarus: Science and the Transformation of Contemporary Democracy*, Cambridge, Mass.: Harvard University Press.

Fay, B. (1975) *Social Theory and Political Practice*, London: George Allen & Unwin.

Ferguson, J. (1990) *The Anti-politics Machine: 'Development,' Depoliticization, and Bureaucratic Power in Lesotho*, Cambridge: Cambridge University Press.

Fowler, A. (2000) 'Civil society, NGDOs and social development: changing the rules of the game', UNRISD occasional paper, Geneva: United Nations Research Institute for Social Development.

GDN (1999) 'Global Development Network 1999: bridging knowledge and policy', conference programme, Bonn, 5–8 December.

Habermas, J. (1971) *Knowledge and Human Interest*, Boston: Beacon Press.

Hart, K. (1982) *The Political Economy of West African Agriculture*, Cambridge: Cambridge University Press.

Mamdani, M. (1996) *Citizen and Subject: Contemporary Africa and the Legacy of Late Colonialism*, Princeton, NJ: Princeton University Press.

Mautner, T. (1997) *The Penguin Dictionary of Philosophy*, London: Penguin.

Nustad, K. G. (1996) 'The politics of "development": power and changing discourses in South Africa', *Cambridge Anthropology* 19(1): 57–72.

Nustad, K. G. (1997) 'The ends of development: comments on an obituary', *Forum for Development Studies* 1: 155–66.

Shore, C. and Wright, S. (1997) 'Policy: a new field of anthropology,' in C. Shore and S. Wright (eds) *Anthropology and Policy: Critical Perspectives on Governance and Power*, London: Routledge.

Stiglitz, J. (1999) 'Scan globally, reinvent locally: knowledge infrastructure and the localisation of knowledge', keynote address, First Global Development Network Conference, Bonn, December.

Stone, D. (1997) *Policy Paradox: The Art of Political Decisionmaking*, London: W.W. Norton.

Stone, D. (2000) Think tank transnationalisation and non-profit analysis, advice and advocacy, *Global Society* 14(2): 153–72.

Tvedt, T. (1998) *Angels of Mercy, or Development Diplomats? NGOs and Foreign Aid*, London: James Currey.

Wagner, P., Wittrock, B. and Whitley, R. (1991) *Discourses on Society: The Shaping of the Social Science Disciplines*, Amsterdam: Kluwer Academic Publishers.

Weiss, C. H. (1977) *Using Social Research in Public Policy making*, Massachusetts: Lexington Books.

Part II

Civil society engagement

4 Think tanks in independent Belarus

Catalysts for social transformation

Oleg Manaev

The civil society connection

Policy institutes and think tanks often claim to be independent civil society organisations that contribute to public debate and the health of democratic society. Furthermore, think tanks perform many functions either independently or in cooperation with community-based organisations. In many instances, think tanks can act as a source of research and analysis that other NGOs may be unable to undertake. In addition, they often provide community services such as education and training. Accordingly, one of the panel sessions at GDN99 in Bonn sought to critically assess the role of think tanks in civil society and as 'third-sector' organisations.

The third sector, where voluntary associations, charities, trade unions, religious bodies and other non-profit modes of activity promote civil engagement, is often regarded as the home domain of think tanks. These organisations are not solely directed towards political parties, government and international organisations. The research they conduct often has broader social purposes. Thus, the contributions by Ratna Sudarshan and by Gabriel Ortiz de Zevallos and Alejandro Salas in the two chapters that follow outline the productive partnerships that think tanks can build with other actors in society to assist in the social provision of goods and services.

In some parts of the world, the rights of citizens to organise, lobby and protest – such as by contributing to the establishment of an alternative think tank – cannot be taken for granted. Such organisations, where they exist, often cannot afford to challenge state prerogatives. Indeed, it can be very difficult for new organisations to acquire credibility and recognition in societies where political subservience is ingrained or where intellectual bodies are viewed with hostility.

In advanced liberal democracies, civil society is usually regarded as a sphere of social relations and activity where there is considerable independence from both the state and the market and where development of civil society occurs autonomously. Where civil society is fragile, it can be the case that think tanks and many NGOs are organised and funded by the state; that is, the growth of civil society can be a state-led process dominated by political elites. Civil society becomes a domain where the state intervenes and manages social and political associations, the media and non-governmental organisations (NGOs). Similarly, international organisations and aid agencies seek to 'grow' civil society, often through the 'export' of ideas, institutions and practices (Carrothers 1999).

Accordingly, the status of think tanks as authentic civil society organisations is sometimes open to question.

In such circumstances, think tanks are associated with political elites rather than with the wider citizenry. Their discourse can be exclusive rather than inclusive. Analyses and publications are 'regime-enhancing' rather than 'regime-critical'. Think tanks can duplicate a closed and secretive environment of policy development. The importance of think tanks to the state lies in their capacity to amplify messages that come from the top down to the rest of society. Instead of widening opportunities for democratic participation or the representation of alternative ideas, the sources of think tank funding, political alliances with national and international elites, and their own elite status as scholarly bodies can sometimes act as an impediment to the inclusion of civil society voices in policy debate. Furthermore, the boundaries between the state, the market and civil society can become blurred to such an extent that it is difficult for interests to develop autonomously within civil society. The 'sponsorship' of civil society development by governments or by foreign actors involves resource decisions and political choices concerning the appropriate objects of funding – usually NGOs (the 'NGO paradigm' is raised in Chapter 8 by Ivan Krastev). A growing criticism among development practitioners is that support for NGOs does not in itself contribute to the development of civil society. Of greater importance is the cultivation of processes and practices that empower local groups and communities to develop and direct civil forms of association.

Notwithstanding these cautionary comments, the research and policy debates of think tanks can be critically important in helping to promote and consolidate institutions in civil society. This occurs when institutes help poor or disenfranchised communities to gain real and meaningful rights as citizens. The provision of alternative information, ideas and analysis is one function that think tanks can perform to empower not only themselves but also other groups in society by giving expression to public opinion. In the following discussion, Oleg Manaev recounts the experiences of Belarusian think tanks in civil society, where institutes are one expression of the rights of individuals to associate voluntarily and to build organisations to proclaim their interests.

Diane Stone (editor)

Introduction

In the USA, a multitude of independent research and analytical centers provide well-grounded policy solutions for various public problems. They are more often called 'the fifth estate' rather than think tanks (Craufurd 1996). Leading politicians and public policy makers, influential businessmen, diplomats and journalists are proud to cooperate with many of 1,200 well-known American think tanks such as the Hoover Institution, the Brookings Institution, the Heritage Foundation and the CATO Institute (Hellebust 1997). Their participation in research and analysis gives an importance to and improves the public recognition of social sciences in social and political debates. Thus, the staff of the East–West Institute based in New York city, where I was a visitor for six months in 1998, boasts such important members as a former minister of Connecticut state, high-ranking officials from the State Department and the Swedish Foreign Ministry, a US ambassador, and a successful American millionaire. On the other hand, many people who hold high positions in think tanks go to work in government authorities and become well-respected and influential politicians, especially during changes in politics or ruling teams. Their participation in decision making gives final resolutions a sense of competence and improves recognition by the authorities. For instance, US Secretary of State Madeleine Albright used to be the head of such a center in Washington before being called to power.

The USA is far from Eastern Europe, and as some readers might note, countries in this region have a different pattern of think tank development. However, our neighbours offer lots of similar examples of the movement of individuals from think tanks into government or politics. Thus, Lesec Balzerovic, founder of the Center for Social and Economic Research in Warsaw, became vice prime minister of Poland. Andrey Illarionov, director of the Institute for Economic Analysis in Moscow, became a senior economics counsel to President Vladimir Putin. Yelena Leontieva, president of the Lithuanian Free Market Institute, became a senior economics counsel to President Valdis Adamkus. And Vyacheslav Pikhovshek, director of the Ukrainian Center for Independent Political Research, recently received the Honorable Order from President Leonid Kouchma for his contribution to democratic reforms.

The Republic of Belarus is one of fifteen republics of the former Soviet Union, and think tank development should be considered in this context. Under Soviet control, research institutes revolved around the Academy of Sciences (Yakubovsky 1998). While many of these institutes continue to operate, from the 1990s new think tanks appeared in Russia. In some cases, intellectuals left state-funded research centers in the wake of funding cuts to carve out an independent existence, sometimes with foreign support. In other circumstances, institutes were formed around the policy agendas of political leaders. Today, independent institutes are well established in this country. In the newly independent states, private institutes are also populating the policy scene. In 1994, the Institute for the Development of Kazakhstan was the first independent institute in Central Asia, but others have emerged in Ukraine, Lithuania, Moldova and elsewhere. In Belarus, new spaces have also opened for independent research institutes, but unlike Russia and some of the other republics, serious constraints and impediments to their activities remain.

A brief history of think tanks in Belarus

There were no think tanks in Belarus before the break-up of the Soviet Union. Various traditional organisations conducted research in the social sciences – universities, the academic institutes of economics, sociology, law, philosophy and history, and departmental institutes (for example, the Institute for Statistics, affiliated to the Ministry of Statistics; the Institute for Labor, affiliated to the Ministry of Labor; the Institute for Criminal Law, affiliated to the Ministry of Internal Affairs). These were completely funded and thus controlled by the state. Sometimes they produced not just new knowledge but also adequate solutions to various public problems (Belarus had one of the most advanced labour and research forces in the USSR). But their influence on public policy could only be through governmental and Communist Party decision-making structures and was therefore limited – and completely unknown to the public.

After the break-up of the Soviet Union and the collapse of the Communist Party in 1991, Belarus became independent and started social transformations focusing on the development of political democracy, a market economy, the rule of law and civil society. These fundamental changes created social, political, economic and legal conditions for the emergence of the 'second sector' (private businesses) and 'third-sector' organisations: that is, various NGOs, independent trade unions and human rights groups. Many social structures, groups and individuals began to identify themselves as social actors responsible for social transformations at organisational, local and national levels. Political parties, business associations, independent trade unions and the mass media began to understand the need for and importance of objective social information, professional analysis and expertise, and effective technologies, and of their impact on public opinion and policy. Even the government had to demonstrate similar interests and needs. Thus, social needs created the necessary conditions for the emergence of think tanks in Belarus.

A small group of young scholars, politicians, businessmen and journalists founded the first think tank, the Independent Institute of Socio-Economic and Political Studies (IISEPS), at the beginning of 1992. Its motto is 'Democracy and the market economy', and its main aim is to promote democratic social transformations through research, advocacy and networking. The most recognised and influential think tanks in Belarus were founded in the period 1992–94, when the newly independent country tried to redefine its national identity, as well as finding an appropriate role in Europe and the world.

The situation changed dramatically after 20 July 1994, when the first Belarusian president, Alexander Lukashenko, took office. The former director of a backward *sovkhoz* (a state-run collective farm) and a strong populist, Lukashenko defeated his rivals and moved forward via an 'electoral revolution' against both the old ruling elite and newly emerging democratic forces. Subsequently, he destroyed a system of political checks and balances (by disbanding parliament, the constitutional court and the central electoral committee), as well as oppressing both the 'second' and 'third sectors'. Lukashenko does not require alternative policy perspectives and ideas; moreover, he perceives proponents of such ideas as challenges to his personal power. The strong authoritarian regime formed by Lukashenko in Belarus inevitably led to strong international denunciation and the isolation of the country.

In these conditions, many Belarusian think tanks have tended to transform themselves from being sources of alternative ideas into 'shelters' for alternative ideas and people. Many prominent politicians had to leave their positions in state structures (government, presidential administration, parliament, constitutional court) and political parties. They were left with little choice but to pursue their interests in public policy making through various NGOs, including think tanks. This led to new challenges for think tanks. On the one hand, they acquired knowledge and experience of 'direct public policy making' (from former ministers, parliamentarians, judges, party leaders). On the other hand, they faced a danger of politicisation and loss of their intellectual independence.

Currently, around two dozen think tanks are functioning in the Republic of Belarus: two-thirds in the capital and one-third in the regions. A medium-sized Belarusian think tank does not exceed five to seven full-time researchers and support staff, along with four or five part-time experts and employees. Most specialise in particular policy activities. Thus, the Sapeha Foundation for Democratic Reforms Support used to organise regional seminars to train the authorities and public leaders in local self-government. The Center 'Belarusian Perspective' organised a 'public university' to educate young citizens in the principles of national sovereignty and democracy. Another body, 'Legal Initiative', and the Center for Constitutionalism and Comparative Legal Studies devised new regulations for elections and promoted ideas about the rule of law. 'Strategy', an analytical unit, conducts research into macroeconomic stabilisation and security issues, while the International Institute for Political Studies focuses on disarmament and non-proliferation of weapons of mass destruction. The Center for Social Resources Development (otherwise known as 'Oracle') in Gomel addresses the problems of farming and the consequences of the Chernobyl accident. 'Logos', a research and educational center in Brest, has focused on problems of private enterprise and gender. The public association 'Humanitarian Initiative' in Mogilev is concerned with human rights issues. Another public association, 'Private Initiatives' in Vitebsk, is involved in training young public leaders. Some think tanks like NOVAK Enterprise and the Center for Social and Ecological Research conduct public opinion polls and have their own network of interviewers. Only a few combine research, advocacy and networking activities. IISEPS, for example, conducts polls and interviews the ruling elite (through its network of 100 interviewers in fifty sites around the country); it undertakes documentary analysis (through its Center for Documentation, which has a database of 40,000 documents and materials); it organises conferences and seminars; it publishes and disseminates books, bulletins, and analytical and policy papers; and the institute constantly appears in the mass media.

Despite their very modest size and resources, the output of think tanks exceeds the output of their rivals. These include such huge state-run organisations as the Economic Research Institute, affiliated to the Ministry of Economy (which has more than 500 researchers and support staff); the Institute for National Security, affiliated to the Security Council; the Institute for Social and Political Research, affiliated to the presidential administration; and the Academic Institutes of Sociology, Economy and Law (each of which has almost 100 researchers and support staff).

All Belarusian think tanks have legal status either as public associations (national or regional) or as private companies (joint-stock company, limited company, private enterprise). Unfortunately, as yet there is no appropriate legislation for non-profit organisations and foundations in the country. Unlike their Russian counterparts, Belarusian think tanks (regardless of their legal status) have to pay taxes as ordinary business enterprises. Usually, taxation takes around half of their revenue. It means that a think tank applying for a grant of $30,000 should in fact apply for $45,000. Many international donors, operating within very strict legal and financial rules, cannot agree to allocations that effectively enlarge the Lukashenko regime's budget. Accordingly, proposals from Belarusian think tanks are often rejected. It is an understandably difficult situation when USAID officials need to convince the US Congress, or program officers of the Open Society Institute need to convince George Soros to increase the expenses of Belarusian think tanks by 50 per cent just because of such brutal legislation.

The annual budgets of Belarusian think tanks range from $5,000 to $50,000 and exceed $100,000 very rarely. In the period 1992–95, many received a significant part of their budgets from private business (relatively few received some funding from the government, and as a rule indirectly through semi-private companies). During political campaigns – presidential, general and local elections, as well as national referenda – some institutes could obtain funding from different political parties or politicians. But since that time, when the embryonic political democracy and market economy were destroyed, and the average monthly salary fell to $40 (and the monthly pension to $20), international donors became the only source of funding. Unlike in Russia and Ukraine, where dozens of international and foreign donor organisations are providing support for think tanks, only a few donors operate in Belarus. They include some US organisations, such as USAID, the Eurasia Foundation, the Open Society Institute, the National Endowment for Democracy, the Center for International Private Enterprise and the MacArthur Foundation. European structures include the Westminster Foundation for Democracy, TACIS, the Council of Europe, OSCE, and several German, Swedish and Polish foundations.

Unlike their neighbours, the Belarusian authorities recognise foreign support not as a means of strengthening their ties outside the country but a way to discredit local think tanks as 'the agents of Western influence'. And there is no need to kill or arrest opponents in a post-communist country (as it was under 'real communism'); the authorities can achieve the same aims more easily. Thus, in the summer of 1997, the Belarusian Soros Foundation, which during the previous five years had supported hundreds of scholarly, cultural and civic projects (and spent almost $13 million) had to discontinue its activities in Belarus. In 1995, President Lukashenko had introduced special tax-free regulations for the foundation because at that time he was trying to obtain international recognition. However, he revoked this decision two years later as he became increasingly concerned and alarmed by the strengthening of civil society. The State Tax Committee retrospectively demanded $3 million as unpaid taxes for the previous five years. George Soros naturally refused, so the foundation's property was requisitioned and its bank account frozen. Similarly, the Foundation for the Children of Chernobyl, which had organised a rehabilitation zone for hundreds of thousands of children from Chernobyl in various Western countries, and the National Center for Strategic Initiatives 'East–West', which created networks between national and foreign civic partners, had to suspend their activities because of pressure from the Security Council. A year ago, IISEPS was accused of joining the political opposition in a conspiracy against 'the legitimately elected authorities' and also faced various difficulties.

As a consequence of the government's policies towards the third sector in general and think tanks specifically, some Belarusian think tanks have serious doubts about continuing their relationships with foreign sponsors. Would their relationship with international donors discredit their image with the public? The results of an IISEPS survey (see Table 4.1) dismiss these doubts completely.

All foreign donors to Belarusian NGOs, even the US and Western European governments, do not appear to perturb the Belarusian public unduly (see Table 4.2). By contrast, they appear to be more hesitant about support for the Belarusian authorities (although a significant section of the public still knows little about most NGOs and has no clear ideas about their funding).

The irony is that a significant proportion of the Belarusian public considers international donors to be more interested in the promotion of democracy, a market economy, the rule of law and civil society than the Belarusian authorities. It is one reason why in transitional countries, where people have little or no confidence in most state and public institutions, think tanks could potentially increase their impact on public opinion and policy by keeping their distance

Table 4.1 Public attitudes to different forms of international support for NGOs (%)[1]

Which of the kinds of international support for Belarusian NGOs listed below do you consider permissible from a moral, political or other point of view?	Permissible	Not permissible	Difficult to answer
Financial support	65.6	8.3	26.1
Educational support (education and training through seminars, conferences in Belarus and abroad)	61.2	7.9	29.9
Technical support (computers, modems, fax machines, photocopiers, etc.)	60.9	12.6	26.5
Humanitarian aid	54.1	16.6	29.3
Information support (delivery of newspapers, magazines, journals, books, bulletins, etc.)	46.9	14.1	39.0
Moral and political support (official statements, discussions with official representatives of Belarus, media campaigns)	44.4	16.2	39.4

[1] According to data in a national public opinion poll conducted by IISEPS in September 1998 (1,486 respondents aged 16+ were interviewed face to face, and sampling error did not exceed 0.03).

Table 4.2 Public attitudes to support from different international donors (%)[1]

Do you think that Belarusian NGOs should get support from:	Yes	No	Difficult to answer
International organisations (UN, UNESCO, etc.)	51.8	9.9	38.3
State-run organisations from NIS	39.9	12.0	48.1
NGOs from NIS	37.5	12.3	50.2
American NGOs (e.g., Soros Foundation)	38.1	14.7	47.1
Western European NGOs	30.5	12.9	56.6
Western European state-run organisations (EU, Council of Europe, British, French, German and other governments)	33.6	16.7	49.7
Eastern European NGOs	28.1	14.3	57.7
Eastern European state-run organisations (Polish, Czech, Lithuanian, etc.)	28.1	14.3	57.6
American state-run organisations (White House, Congress, State Department, etc.)	28.2	21.3	50.5

[1] According to data from the same 1998 public opinion poll conducted by IISEPS.

from both power (that is, government) and money (that is, private business). In this situation, international donors seem the most neutral and trustworthy sources of support for think tanks (as well as for other NGOs). However, a significant number of survey respondents are still dubious about international assistance (even humanitarian aid for the victims of Chernobyl) because of the persistence of Soviet-era stereotypes of a hostile West, as well as aggressive campaigns in the state-run media supporting and cultivating these stereotypes.

The consequences of the hostile attitude of the authorities towards the structures of civil society (including think tanks) supported by international donors have become apparent. Ignoring social and economic realities and sources of information reflecting these circumstances, as well as putting political pressure on groups analysing policy and seeking solutions that are intended to improve conditions, has contributed to poverty in public policy making. This has helped to create a permanent economic and political crisis, social collapse and poverty, international isolation, and even a threat to Belarusian independence.

Impact on public opinion and policy

Even in an oppressive environment, Belarusian think tanks do their best not just to produce new knowledge but also to achieve some impact on public opinion and policy, and to promote ideas of political democracy, a market economy, the rule of law and civil society. Most of the traditional strategies employed by

Western think tanks to influence public opinion and policy (Abelson 1998) are used by Belarusian think tanks. These include:

- Holding open public forums (conferences, seminars, workshops, briefings) at a national and regional level to discuss domestic and foreign policy issues (IISEPS has organised thirty-six conferences and seminars).
- Publication of research results and analysis in national and local mass media (IISEPS alone has published over 1,300 items in dozens of mass publications).
- Publishing books, journals, bulletins and newsletters (such as *IISEPS News, Belarus Monitor, Vector, Problems of Constitutionalism* and *Civic Alternative*).
- Creating distribution lists of leading officials and politicians as well as business and opinion leaders in society and the private sector, who have analytical and policy papers delivered (IISEPS has a distribution list of around 200 for such papers).
- Inviting selected policy makers to participate in conferences, seminars and workshops (actually, all prominent policy makers and public leaders used to make presentations at numerous think tank forums).
- Offering former policy makers positions in think tanks (thus, Dr Alexander Sosnov, former MP and minister of labour, who left the government after Lukashenko disbanded the Supreme Soviet,[1] became deputy director of IISEPS; Dr Alexander Vashkevich, a former judge of the Constitutional Court, also disbanded by Lukashenko, became executive director of the Center for Comparative Legal Studies).
- Creating home pages on the Internet (most influential think tanks have home pages, for example: www.cacedu.unibel.by/iiseps).

The capacity to distribute and publicise their products is all the more significant given the constraints on the press. As noted on the Center for International Private Enterprise website:

> most of the media are not editorially independent and distribution of national newspapers is controlled by the government ... the country's one independent radio station was closed by authorities in 1996, and journalists have been subject to beatings, arrest and intimidation.
>
> (CIPE 1997)

The maximum degree of transparency and openness not only strengthens the impact of think tanks on public policy but also helps to neutralise pressure from the authorities. Let me illustrate this point by a tragi-comic personal experience. During the first years of IISEPS activity, KGB officers used to come to our office and warn us 'not to make contact with foreigners so actively' because we could 'violate the security regulations and sell important state information'. Of course, we ignored these 'warnings'. As a result, some articles discrediting the institute were published in the state-run press. Eventually, as a preventive measure, I decided to include the name of the chairman of the KGB on our distribution list of policy makers (which includes around 200 names) so that he would receive all of our analytical and policy papers. On the next visit from a KGB officer 'to warn' me, I said: 'Officer, if you are really interested in what information we provide to our partners, you should go to your chairman's office and ask him because he gets all the same information. I consider it will be much easier for you.' He was shocked, and it was his last visit to our institute. Moreover, since that time we have received several letters of gratitude from the KGB chairman regarding some of our work.

Unfortunately, the relations of think tanks with the political opposition (including various political parties from liberal to communist, as well as public movements and associations – all those who do not support the existing regime) are far from successful. Any research and recommendations in line with the programs of the opposition – such as a slump in the president's rating, or diminishing trust in basic government institutions – are welcomed and actively used. However, once the results of our work or our recommendations contradict the programs of the opposition parties – such as the president's rating is improving, or the rating of political parties is nosediving, suggesting the need to work with some electorate groups – think tanks are 'cold-shouldered' by the opposition.

Nevertheless, both the authorities and the opposition parties use information, analysis and solutions provided by think tanks. Despite the desire of President Lukashenko and his propagandists to declare 'total public support for his policies', they cannot ignore his real public opinion rating of approximately 40 per cent, revealed by various public opinion polls conducted by think tanks. Moreover, the authorities have to tolerate think tanks and the independent media because they have become virtually the only source of unbiased information and reliable analysis. A picture of real public problems and concerns that is provided by think tanks helps to provide an early warning system of undesirable developments for the authorities. Furthermore, the government cannot rely upon its own research and analytical centers to a great extent because these centers are still accustomed to providing predictable and desirable information and solutions in line with intellectual practices developed under the Soviet system. Psychologically, this mode of analysis reaffirms perceptions of power and symbolises the legitimacy of the regime, but politically it is rather short-sighted and occasionally dangerous for those who are in power. Thus, in the spring of 1994, during the first presidential campaign, most state-run research centers predicted a victory for Prime Minister Vyacheslav Kebich and gave no chance to Alexander Lukashenko. The ruling elite ignored the voices of independent think tanks, which were presenting a contradictory picture, and was unprepared for electoral defeat. It is probable that President Lukashenko has not forgotten that lesson and has tolerated think tanks in the interests of self-preservation.

The state-run research centers also have to follow the results and standards of think tanks, otherwise nobody would believe them: neither the public nor the authorities. For years, many Belarusian research centers used to present the results of public opinion polls and other research procedures without any notes on the date when these procedures were conducted, the size and error of their samples, and so forth. Neither the researchers nor the public could be sure of the reliability of these results and whether conclusions were well grounded. IISEPS initiated debates in the mass media criticising both state-run and independent research centers in the manipulation of data, advocating the use of well-grounded methodological standards in public presentations. It was a difficult task and took some time, but now most media publications based on the results of social research follow these standards.

A failure of the usual strategies of dissent and opposition (such as street fighting) has also forced the opposition parties to take think tank analyses and solutions into account. Since the government broke off negotiations with the opposition under the aegis of OSCE at the end of 1999 and repudiated the agreements already reached,[2] opposition leaders have begun to meet regularly with think tanks to discuss how to meet the challenges of the forthcoming general and presidential elections.

Facing sceptics and distrust from both sides of the political fence, how do think tanks not only survive but effectively inform policy? There are two basic solutions. First, go to the West, where Belarusian think tanks can get professional and public recognition. Thus, independent Belarusian researchers and analysts have been able to participate in major international conferences and seminars from Warsaw to Washington as well as to publish the results of their research and analysis in leading Western journals. And their opinions are taken quite seriously in these venues. This form of international recognition can be important in boosting morale among the Belarusian think tank community.

Second, they can try to gain direct access to the people through media publications, wide distribution of analytical and policy papers, and the organisation of public forums. However, it is difficult to assess their impact on public opinion. A slow but tangible shift in public attitudes towards political democracy, a market economy, the rule of law, national sovereignty and civil society, noted by public opinion polls, can serve as an indirect indicator of that. And there are also some more vivid indicators of their impact on public opinion, as shown in Table 4.3 outlining public attitudes to various public and state institutions.

The trust rating of think tanks is slowly but steadily improving. In 1998, 25.7 per cent of those polled trusted them and 15.9 per cent distrusted them, whereas these figures are 31.6 and 13.4 per cent, respectively, in 2000. The positive ratings for think tanks outstrip not only state-run institutes but also most leading public institutions. However, the meaning of these figures should not be overestimated: it must be understood that the state institutions listed in Table 4.3 have a far wider public impact than think tanks. But most of these institutions have a negative image in society, while most people know relatively little about the activities of think tanks. Nevertheless, people who are aware of think tanks trust them.

Intensive publication in the independent press is not sufficient to raise public awareness of think tank ideas, because this coverage reaches a rather limited audience. Furthermore, the state-run media seldom publish independent think tank material. Despite relatively few public outlets in the country, the Belarusian

Table 4.3 Level of trust in the most important state and public institutions (%)

Institution	Trust	Distrust	Do not care	Trust rating[1] (2000)	Trust rating (1999)	Trust rating (1998)
Church	47.1	18.5	34.4	+0.298	+0.267	+0.329
Independent think tanks	31.6	13.4	55.0	+0.190	+0.122	+0.098
Military	40.5	24.7	34.8	+0.165	+0.085	+0.135
State-run media	38.5	31.6	29.9	+0.072	+0.091	+0.159
President	39.2	32.9	27.9	+0.064	+0.162	+0.258
Advisory and monitoring group from the OSCE in Belarus	20.5	20.5	58.8	0.000	–[2]	–
State-run research centres	22.4	22.1	55.4	−0.003	+0.027	–
Independent trade unions	19.4	24.7	55.9	−0.055	−0.181	−0.126
Associations of entrepreneurs	17.1	23.1	59.8	−0.062	−0.254	−0.292
Independent media	25.7	31.9	42.4	−0.065	−0.159	−0.130
State-run trade unions	20.9	28.2	50.8	−0.077	−0.198	−0.143
Central electoral committee established by president	24.6	33.3	42.2	−0.092	−0.098	–
Government	21.6	38.2	40.1	−0.172	−0.044	+0.038
KGB	20.7	37.3	42.1	−0.173	−0.165	–
Courts	23.6	41.5	34.9	−0.186	−0.186	−0.164
13th Supreme Soviet	11.6	29.4	59.0	−0.189	−0.306	−0.165
National Assembly	11.8	31.5	56.6	−0.207	−0.184	−0.077
Police	20.2	49.0	30.8	−0.302	−0.293	−0.229
Local authorities	16.8	46.5	36.6	−0.310	−0.220	−0.131
Political parties	6.8	36.7	56.4	−0.315	−0.409	−0.320

[1] The trust rating is a correlation between the sum of the positive ('trust = +1), negative ('mistrust = −1) and neutral ('do not care = 0) answers, and all respondents (n = 1,495). The last national public opinion poll was conducted by IISEPS in April 2000, the previous one in June 1999 (n = 1,508) and the one before that in September 1998 (n = 1,486). In all cases, sampling error did not exceed 0.03.
[2] This institution was not included in the questionnaire.

public has another opportunity to become familiar with think tanks' outputs – through Russian TV channels, which are available to the whole population. Accordingly, during the general and presidential election campaigns in 1999–2000, all Russian TV channels presented dozens of programs with well-known analysts from leading Russian think tanks. Growing public recognition of think tanks and confidence in their professional analysis and well-grounded policy recommendations is a good foundation for the ability of think tanks to inform public opinion and achieve some policy impact.

Thus, IISEPS has studied public attitudes towards the most important principles and results of social transformations in Belarus: from totalitarianism to political democracy, a market economy and real independence, as well as towards some actual events of public policy (such as Belarusian–Russian union, negotiations between the authorities and the opposition, and the forthcoming general and presidential elections). To illuminate the impact of think tanks on public opinion, we conducted a comparative analysis of these attitudes of respondents who trust think tanks and those who do not. Significant differences between the attitudes of these groups should demonstrate, to some extent, the level and direction of think tank impact on public opinion.

As Table 4.4 illustrates, people who trust think tanks differ noticeably in their political and economic opinions from those who do not trust them. But what is important is that there are no significant differences in socio-demographic status (sex, age, place of residence, social status, income, etc.); the only exceptional group are residents of the Belarusian capital, who have higher education levels. Those who trust think tanks are characterised by strong positive attitudes towards national sovereignty, the market economy and private enterprise, political democracy and the rule of law, a readiness to engage in dialogue with opponents, and recognition of the role played by international organisations. On some important indicators, those mistrustful of think tanks demonstrate the so-called 'mirror effect'.[3] However, these attitudes cannot be considered a direct result of think tank impact. Many people trust think tanks because the ideas and values articulated by them coincide with their own ideas and values. Even so, these ideas and values are supported, consolidated and broadcast by think tanks through their information and analyses.

One interpretation of the data is that support for the 'radical' ways expressed in the opinions of the first group represents dissatisfaction with propaganda and political control in the country. In other words, existing socio-economic and political arrangements do not meet their interests or even contradict them. In this context, think tanks become not just a source of reliable information, analysis and solutions but also an extremely important means of consolidation for people concerned about a better future. In sum, think tank communications both inside and outside the country are not simply of intellectual value but also represent a civic alternative.

A new level of think tank activity

In order to resist pressures from the authorities, as well as to consolidate their activity and to strengthen their impact on public opinion and policy, fifteen leading think tanks from the capital and most regions of the country founded the national association, Belarusian Think Tanks, (BTT) on 7 June 1997 in Minsk. The think tanks devised, signed and published in the mass media a declaration (see pp. 80–2) that presented their aims and methods of activity to the public.

Table 4.4 Political and economic attitudes of those who trust in and distrust think tanks (independent research centers) (%)

Political and economic attitudes	Trust in think tanks (31.6%)	Distrust think tanks (13.4%)
What economy would you choose?		
• Market economy with insignificant state regulation	56.8	33.5
• Planned economy	15.7	26.1
What type of ownership is more effective?		
• Private	71.7	46.6
• State	21.2	46.0
What kind of enterprise would you prefer to work in?		
• Private	55.0	35.5
• State	32.1	56.9
Have you ever participated in private enterprise?		
• Yes	26.7	21.0
• No, but I'd like to participate	42.4	34.0
• Never, and I'm not going to participate	30.5	44.0
Would you like your children to deal with private enterprise?		
• Yes	52.6	38.9
• No	19.4	34.6
Do you consider the strike by 120,000 Belarusian vendors in February 2000 against tax increases and other state limits on their activity to be well grounded?		
• Yes	65.3	42.4
• No	12.0	24.5
If you were president of the country, what would you start with?		
• Achieving the rule of law	56.8	35.0
• Economic reforms	54.3	42.4
• Achieving membership of the European Union for Belarus	33.1	20.4
• Eliminating the Mafia	29.3	42.1
• Establishing freedom of the press	29.2	9.9
• Unifying Belarus and Russia	22.5	36.9
• Restoring order as it was in the USSR	10.5	26.0
• Eliminating opposition	3.6	10.8

Continued

Political and economic attitudes	Trust in think tanks (31.6%)	Distrust think tanks (13.4%)
Which type of state regulation do you prefer?		
• Division of powers	66.4	40.3
• Concentration of all power in the hands of the president	8.8	21.1
• Do not care/no answer	24.9	38.7
What is your attitude to President Lukashenko's politics?[1]		
• Convinced supporter	6.8	21.2
• Member of vacillating majority	45.2	41.5
• Convinced opponent	48.0	37.3
If a general election were to take place in Belarus tomorrow, what parties would you vote for?		
• Different parties	48.1	27.8
• Do not care/no answer	51.9	72.2
How should conditions and rules for general elections be defined?		
• Through negotiations between authorities and opposition, with agreements being binding on both sides	47.3	23.3
• Through wide public dialogue, but the final decision taken by the authorities	25.4	26.2
• Authorities should define conditions and rules without any dialogue or negotiations	6.0	17.4
• Do not care/no answer	20.4	33.2
Do you have experience and are you willing to express your opinions through:		
• Meetings, demonstrations and pickets?	30.0	15.7
• Strikes?	21.1	9.9
• Armed fighting?	10.2	8.5
Which do you consider the most appropriate relationship with Russia?		
• Neighbourly relations between two independent states	48.7	37.7
• A union of independent states	29.9	30.2
• Unification into one state	19.9	31.5
Which mass media do you trust?		
• Belarusian state-run TV	20.6	34.6
• Russian independent TV (NTV)	49.6	35.9
• Belarusian independent press	23.4	2.5
• Western radio stations	13.0	8.5

Continued:

Political and economic attitudes	Trust in think tanks (31.6%)	Distrust think tanks (13.4%)
Which countries and organisations do you consider a threat to Belarus?		
• NATO	26.5	40.9
• USA	15.6	27.1
• Russia	10.7	3.6
• none	52.4	35.1
The activities of which international organisations operating in Belarus do you consider important?[2]		
• World Bank	67.0	39.5
• International Monetary Fund	68.5	41.2
• Organisation for Security and Cooperation in Europe	64.8	38.3
• European Union	59.4	34.3
• United Nations	67.4	47.5

Note: The table should be read as follows: of those who trust in independent research centers, 56.8% chose a market economy and 15.7% a planned economy; of those who distrust them, only 33.5% chose market economy and 26.1% a planned economy. The poll was conducted by IISEPS in April 2000.

[1] Lukashenko's convinced supporters include those who trust him and consider him an ideal politician, as well as those ready to vote for him in the next presidential elections and in probable elections for the president of a unified Belarus–Russian Federation. His convinced opponents do not trust him, do not consider him an ideal politician and would vote for another candidate in a presidential election.

[2] Organisations are ranked based on difference between two analysed groups.

Declaration of the Belarusian Association of Think Tanks

The weakness of the structures and mechanisms of civil society are among the main reasons for the deepening political and economic crisis in Belarus. Long before the drastic changes in the USSR and other socialist camp countries began at the end of the 1980s, activity to train people who would be able to formulate, propose and implement reforms was underway in the countries of Central and Eastern Europe. Such activity laid the foundation for the ability of political parties and movements to propose and implement programs that are based on the principles of democracy, a free-market economy and respect for human rights. The laborious task of the 'invisible universities' of KOS-KOR[4] and Charter '77 in the 1970s prepared the way for the success of democratic movements in Poland and Czechoslovakia in the 1980s. Sadly, Belarus lacked well-developed social technologies for the transition from totalitarianism to democracy and strengthening the sovereignty of the country: both state and non-state structures, as well as society as a whole, were not ready for independence and the independent choice of its own historic way.

To form and strengthen civil society, all citizens must have access to objective information about the situation in the country, about the attitudes of the state and different groups of population towards the main events and problems of public life. There is a great need for professional analysis and recommendations, new ideas from specialists, based on the results of professional research in sociology, politics, psychology, economics, law and other social sciences. Such information must be accessible to all those who care about their own fate and the fate of the country. In democratic countries, much state and non-state research produces such information and new ideas and analytical centers called 'think tanks'. In Belarus, information produced by the state research and analytic centers is for the most part biased and hardly available to the general public, while ideas produced by these agencies are almost never new. The reason for this is simple: these centers depend completely on the state and serve its interests.

At the same time, during the period of independence various independent public and private research and analytical centers were created in Belarus. These centers provide the possibility for society to assess social problems and perspectives. Though not comparable in their resources to state ones, these independent public and private centers provide society with objective and easily accessible information, and unbiased and well-grounded analysis. But think tanks in Belarus face very difficult conditions today. Very often they meet distrust and even pressure from the state. Different political forces try to use them for their own political benefit. The support of local businesses for think tanks is still very limited. Very often, the information that such centers produce is in greater demand abroad than in Belarus.

We have decided to unite our efforts and to create the Belarusian Think Tanks Association in order to:

- develop the networking of think tanks;
- raise the effectiveness of their cooperation with each other as well as with state and non-state structures;
- guarantee that the public will have the possibility of receiving objective and up-to-date information about major social problems, tendencies and perspectives;
- conduct independent professional analysis of various social projects and programs; and
- strengthen the role of non-governmental research and analytical

centers in preparing reforms in the country and the formation of civil society in Belarus.

The BTT motto is 'Professionalism and civil responsibility'.

The association became well known in the country through various forms of public activity. Since autumn 1997 it has organised quarterly briefings, where the most important results of research and analysis are presented to the public. Dozens of policy makers, scholars, journalists and diplomats have attended these meetings. Daniel Speckhard, US ambassador in Belarus, in his greeting to the first briefing, mentioned the great role of think tanks in public policy in the USA. For Belarus, he stressed that one more important democratic institution was emerging in the country that could provide the impetus for the reform process and for Belarus' entry into the international community. Several seminars were organised to promote BTT ideas and provide training for scholars and policy makers in the regions, such as 'Think tanks and civil society' in Grodno, 'Think tanks and public policy impact' in Brest, 'Think tanks and the rule of law' in Mogilev and 'Think tanks and regional development' in Gomel. A quarterly analytical bulletin as well as three annual editions of *Belarusian Think Tanks: A Comprehensive Directory of Independent Research and Analytical Centres in Belarus*, published by the BTT (Manaev 2000) have been published and distributed among leading state institutions, civil society groups and university libraries. These have become very popular and are much quoted. Since May 2000, the most important results of BTT activity have also become available on its website (http://btt.org.by).

Belarusian Think Tanks is also beginning to have some public policy impact through various civil initiatives. Thus, in 1999, the BTT leadership proposed that it give some assistance to the Ministry of Foreign Affairs in reviving TACIS programs for Belarus.[5] This program had been frozen for political reasons, but through BTT mediation it was revived. The BTT also promoted the OSCE initiative to commence negotiations between the Belarusian authorities and the opposition (the so-called 'Bucharest process') despite strong criticisms of this initiative from radicals in both the government and opposition. Through such activities, think tanks helped to consolidate progressive social actors not only inside but also outside the country by adopting 'civic diplomacy'.

However, the association's attempts to consolidate its impact on public opinion and policy can occasionally be thwarted by the authorities. For example, the association was in the habit of inviting local and national officials to attend its public forums, from time to time asking them to act as keynote speakers. However, their reaction to these invitations could sometimes be quite bizarre. Thus, the leadership of BTT and experts from a dozen think tanks from Minsk, Gomel, Mogilev and Brest, as well as journalists from influential state-run and independent papers, went to Grodno in October 1998 to organise a briefing for local policy makers and scholars. The aim of the briefing was to introduce the association, to discuss the results of recent research and to present a new issue of its analytical publications. Just a few hours before departure time, I received an official reply from the mayor of Grodno, who had been invited to attend our briefing. The document is unmatched in essence, therefore its full text is printed here:

To: Prof. O. Manaev
Chairman of the Belarusian Association of Think Tanks
220030, Minsk
Fax (8-017) 222-8049   October 14, 1998

This is to inform you that your application to organise a briefing in the hotel 'Tourist' was not considered, because it does not correspond to article 6 of the Law of the Republic of Belarus 'On Meetings, Rallies, Marches, Demonstrations and Picketing'. Additionally, we recommend that you organise such events where your public association is located.

A. Pashkevich
Mayor of Grodno City

Almost every word of this document arouses a feeling for which 'bewilderment' is a mild, neutral term. Why does the document say that the 'application was not considered' if there is an official answer to it? How is it that a briefing organised by a think tank association 'does not correspond to article 6 of the Law of the Republic of Belarus "On Meetings, Rallies, Marches, Demonstrations and Picketing"?' The BTT unites well-known researchers and analysts but not street fighters! Where is the location that Mayor Pashkevich recommends organising 'such events'? The BTT is a national public association registered with the Ministry of Justice as required by Belarusian law, and it could organise its forums anywhere in the country. It seems pointless to look for answers to these questions, because this document does not have anything to do with human logic, reflecting the general attitude of the authorities to any structures of civil society.

In this hostile environment, the growing professional recognition of the BTT inside and outside the country becomes a very important factor for its work and efforts to inform public opinion and policy. Thus, at the beginning of our activity, we had to rely on our own very limited financial and technical resources. Then we obtained a small grant from the Westminster Foundation for Democracy, and later a new and significant grant from the MacArthur Foundation. The first edition of *Think Tanks in Central and Eastern Europe: A Comprehensive Directory*, published by Freedom House as part of its regional think tank initiative in 1997, included over 100 research and analytical centers from a dozen countries in the region, but none from Belarus. Its second edition, published in 1999, included eight Belarusian think tanks, five of which are members of the BTT (Wiebler 1999). Due to this financial and moral support, the BTT can increase the number of its briefings and seminars, widen circulation of its analytical bulletins and books and involve prominent new analysts and policy makers in its activities.

Prospects for think tanks in post-communist countries

The Global Development Network (GDN), formed under the aegis of the World Bank and the United Nations, demonstrated at its first conference in Bonn in 1999, the great need, ability and enthusiasm of both intellectuals and policy makers to engage in new forms and levels of cooperation worldwide. Many traditional means of solving public problems at national, international and global levels seem inappropriate in the face of new challenges on the threshold of a new millennium. As the president of the World Bank stressed:

> Despite all efforts of governments, state institutions, and NGOs we will never succeed in a significant reduction of the number of starving children in the world if we do not *build the dynamic coalitions* of governments, civil society and private sector purposeful on building a global economy for the good of mankind. We really need *broad discussion* but not closed meetings, and to make this discussion real we need to know the opinions of everybody.
>
> (Wolfensohn 2000; italics added)

Who could provide the public with trustworthy information, analysis and solutions nowadays? Who among the various social actors seems to be the most neutral intellectual authority for the government, public and private sector? Who could initiate both broad discussions and dynamic coalitions between those actors? Governments? The military? Political parties? Trades unions? Private business?

While I am uncertain about advocating their role in developed and developing countries, it is think tanks (along with the Church and the mass media) that seem the most appropriate groups for this mission in many post-communist countries. Most traditional state institutions (the government, the Soviets, the Communist and other parties, and the 'first sector') and their values have lost their power and people's confidence. On the other hand, private business and civil society (or the 'second' and 'third sectors') and their values have not yet fully emerged and consolidated. Yet the public cannot live in a vacuum of social values and institutions for too long. Without catalysts for a progressive social transformation, the gloomy, rejected past could come back in a new, more terrible guise, preventing the possibility of a better future. As it seems from the experience of think tanks in independent Belarus, they have a considerable ability to provide new values and outline means for their implementation that – and this is most important – become clear and acceptable to the public. It is not surprising that think tanks experienced a new boom after the post-Cold War period. Almost a quarter of think tanks around the world have appeared since the break-up of the Soviet Union, and half of them are in Eastern Europe (McGann and Weaver 2000). It is one reason why I do believe in the mission of think tanks to contribute to progressive social transformation in post-communist countries, as well as at a global level within the GDN.

Notes

1   The Supreme Soviet of the 13th Convocation – the legitimate Belarusian parliament – was elected in 1995 for a five-year term but was disbanded by President Lukashenko following an illegitimate national referendum in November 1996.

2   In order to solve the constitutional crisis in Belarus, the OSCE Parliamentary Assembly initiated negotiations between the government and its political opposition in 1999. A first meeting of the Belarusian opposition and OSCE leaders was held in June 1999 in Bucharest. At first, President Lukashenko accepted this idea and even appointed his aide Michael Sazonov as his official representative for negotiations with the Consultative Council of eight opposition parties. However, six months later, when these negotiations, conducted under the aegis of the Advisory and Monitoring Group of the OSCE in Belarus, had reached some positive results (for example, it made an agreement on access to the state-run media), Lukashenko broke off the negotiations and dismissed his official representative.

3   The 'mirror effect' means that two groups being compared show opposite attitudes on the same indicator. Thus, only 32.1 per cent of those who trust think tanks prefer to work in state enterprises, while 55.0 per cent prefer private enterprise. And *vice versa*: only 35.5 per cent of those who distrust think tanks prefer to work in private enterprises, while 56.9 per cent prefer state enterprises. The 'mirror effect' is seldom noted in social studies and means that the groups compared are not just 'different' but 'antagonistic'.

4   Before the well-known Solidarity trade union appeared in Poland in the 1980s, there were several structures like **KOS-KOR** (that is, committees to protect workers) in the 1970s that acted in various underground forms, including so-called 'invisible universities', where Polish dissidents and intellectuals educated workers.

5   TACIS (Technical Assistance to the Commonwealth of Independent States) is a European Union initiative intended to support democratic and market-oriented social transformations in the former Soviet Union. In 1997, after President Lukashenko had destroyed the system of political checks and balances and oppressed the third sector, most TACIS programs in Belarus were frozen. For example, in 1997 TACIS allocated $6 million for Belarusian civil society development, but the government did not agree with the list of NGOs selected for this program. Similarly, TACIS did not accept the list of NGOs selected by the Belarusian government. This program was frozen for more than two years. At the beginning of 1999, the BTT leadership offered its mediation services to the Ministry of Foreign Affairs to resolve this problem. Later, the BTT took an active part in promoting negotiations between the Belarusian authorities and the opposition initiated by OSCE (see note 2). Thus, a first unofficial meeting of President Lukashenko's representative, Michael Sazonov, and the leader of the opposition, Anatoly Lebedko, took place in IISEPS offices a week before the official meeting in the OSCE office.

References

Abelson, D. E. (1998) 'Think tanks in the United States', in D. Stone *et al.* (eds.) *Think Tanks Across Nations: A Comparative Approach*, Manchester: Manchester University Press.

Carrothers, T. (1999) *Aiding Democracy Abroad: The Learning Curve*, Washington: Carnegie Endowment for International Peace.

Center for International Private Enterprise (1997) 'IISEPS works to build civil society despite stiff obstacles in Belarus', 1997 worldwide update: http://www.cipe.org-/about/report/1997/iiseps.html

Craufurd, G. (1996) 'The fifth estate: research for informed debate in democratic society', in *Think Tanks in a Democratic Society. An Alternative Voice*, Washington: Urban Institute.

Hellebust, L. (ed.) (1997) *Think Tank Directory: A Guide to Nonprofit Public Policy Research Organizations*, Kansas: Government Research Service.

Manaev, Oleg (ed.) (2000) *Belarusian Think Tanks. A Comprehensive Directory*, third edition, Minsk: BTT.

McGann, J. G. and Weaver, R. K. (2000) *Think Tanks and Civil Society: Catalysts for Ideas and Action*, Somerset, NJ: Transaction Press.

Wiebler, P. (ed.) (1999) *Think Tanks in Central and Eastern Europe: A Comprehensive Directory*, second edition, Budapest: Freedom House.

Wolfensohn, J. (2000) 'We live in an epoch of tremendous opportunities', *Belarusian Business Newspaper*, 29 April.

Yakubovsky, V. B. (1998) 'A short history of Russian think tanks', *NIRA Review*, winter.

5 New partnerships in research: activists and think tanks

An illustration from the NCAER in New Delhi

Ratna M. Sudarshan[1]

Think tanks could be defined as policy research institutes that seek to set agendas and to contribute to governance by supplying information and expertise. However, it is difficult to define clear criteria to distinguish a 'think tank' from a 'research institute' since most research institutes would argue that they have (or seek) independence and are engaged in policy analysis. The operational definition of a think tank may therefore have to vary from region to region (Weaver and McGann 2000). A notable feature of Indian think tanks is that the majority of institutions are engaged in both research and training, and relatively few are pure research organisations. All are autonomous of government and have multiple sources of funding, and most are registered under the Societies Registration Act 1860 (NCAER 1974). The research environment in think tanks is clearly different from that of university departments, which traditionally engage themselves in the business of teaching and research without seeking to play an active role in policy making. It is also distinct from research wings of the government in that think tanks lack the executive role of government agencies and to that extent can be autonomous and more critical.[2]

The only well-known institutions to be established in the pre-independence years in India (the first generation of think tanks) seem to have been the Gokhale Institute of Politics and Economics (1930) in Pune, the Indian Statistical Institute (1932) in Calcutta and the Tata Institute of Social Sciences (1936) in Mumbai (NCAER 1974; IDI 1992; NIRA 1996; GDN 1999). Post-independence, most of the second generation of think tanks were set up in one of two phases. The decade 1956–65 saw the establishment of a large number of institutions, and the motivation seems to have been a need to compensate for the absence of a policy research environment in Indian universities. The institutions set up in this period include the Indian Institute of Public Administration (1954), the National Council of Applied Economic Research (NCAER; 1956), the Institute of Economic Growth (1958) and the Centre for the Study of Developing Societies (1963). The Indian Council of Social Science Research (ICSSR) was set up in 1969 both to provide technical and funding support to research organisations and to enable networking among them.[3] It is important to understand that in the Indian context, it would not have been possible, in the immediate post-independence period, to engage in any meaningful dialogue with government and non-government actors outside a development frame. Since the state undertook primary responsibility for initiating and supporting a development strategy after independence, think tanks set up in this period positioned themselves as adjuncts to the government. The task, in the 1950s, 1960s and 1970s, has been to support, by filling in the gaps and niches in the available expertise in government, the larger task of modernising and developing the country.

A second spurt of organisational growth is visible in the 1980s, a decade that saw a shift towards greater liberalisation in Indian macro-economic policy and greater liberalisation in the use of foreign funding. This period was characterised by an increased non-availability of state funds for research but an increase in both donor funding and private domestic funding. These factors, along with the availability of a generation of Indians who had been closely involved with post-independence government policy making and were attracted to the role of advisors and critics in neutral policy institutes, lie behind the creation of the 'second wave' of institutes. Notable among these are the Indian Council for Research on International Economic Relations (ICRIER; 1981), the Indira Gandhi Institute of Development Research (IGIDR; 1986), the Research and Information Systems (1983) and a little earlier, the Centre for Policy Research (1973).

All of these think tanks, with the exception of IGIDR in Mumbai, are located in Delhi. They also share a national orientation, a broad mandate, economic policy and development issues as a *central* not an *additional* focus, and a desire to stay out of advocacy campaigns.

Other research institutes are dispersed throughout the country, reflecting the Indian federal structure and also funding support from both state and central governments. Many of these have been oriented towards state-level development approaches and issues. These are 'think tanks' in the sense described above but have chosen to engage primarily with state policy rather than national policy. Regional policy (and implementation/interpretation of central mandates) thus receives substantive and thoughtful input and critiques from regional think tanks, albeit stronger in some states and less so in others. Many of the strong institutions outside Delhi were started with the explicit intention of countering the centrifugal attractions of the capital. For example, the M.S. Swaminathan Research Foundation in Chennai (1988), the Centre for Development Studies in Tiruvananthapuram (1970), the Madras Institute of Development Studies in Chennai (1971) and the Institute of Development Studies in Jaipur (1981). But the 'price' of being located elsewhere is a natural resistance to seeing national governance issues as the most imperative point of focus, and being responsive to local and regional issues has generally meant playing a smaller institutional role in national think tank activity.

A number of think tanks with a sectoral specialisation and an advocacy stance have been set up at different times. Some of these specialised institutes have played crucial roles in defining policy and advocacy, including the Indian Institute of Population Studies in Mumbai (1956), the National Institute of Rural Development in Hyderabad (1958), and in Delhi, the Indian Institute of

Foreign Trade (1963), the Institute for Defence Studies and Analysis (1965), the Tata Energy Research Institute (1974), the National Institute of Urban Affairs (1976), the Centre for Science and Environment (1980), the Centre for Women's Development Studies (1980) and the Society for Participatory Research in Asia (PRIA; 1982).

The role of government has changed over the years, slowly until the 1980s and more rapidly in the 1990s. There has been a gradual retreat from seeing the government as the main determinant of development outcomes to that of providing an enabling framework for development. Although the opening up of the Indian economy may have been slow in relation to the speed of change in Southeast Asia, there is little doubt that there has been a dramatic change in the country in attitudes, orientation and cultural norms, particularly perceptible in the last decade. The 1980s and 1990s brought significant changes in the policy environment, changes that have had an impact on the concerns and orientation of Indian think tanks. A notable change is the increased visibility of civil society actors.

Civil society and development concerns

Among the significant changes in the country over the last two decades is the growth of autonomous civil society organisations with a development focus. At independence, the only organisations that would probably have qualified for inclusion under this category were those inspired either by religious thinking (such as the Ramakrishna Mission) or by Gandhian ideology. Many of Gandhi's followers carried his beliefs and ideologies with them into distant and remote parts of the country and can be found even today working with the poor or the marginalised in varying efforts, ranging from education to general development concerns. In addition, there have always been some indigenous 'people's organisations' scattered across the country. By and large, these organisations have stayed outside the mainstream of policy making in India.

A new generation of voluntary development organisations began to emerge in the 1970s and 1980s. The leaders of this sector are educated Indians with a relatively elite background, for whom the voluntary sector is a conscious choice and who share a common educational and social background with the elite backbone of the civil service or the emerging private sector. For this group, it has been important to enter into public debate, to seek to set agendas and to engage actively in the advocacy of selected issues. They have been able to form allies with the more indigenous people's organisations as well as with government, and in the new liberalised environment of foreign funding, they have been attractive to foreign donors as recipients. There is little doubt that tremendous energy and creativity has gone into many of their experiments. Without in any way trying to analyse the complexity of this sector, it can be asserted that there are today new actors from civil society with the skills and experience to make a significant contribution to critical debate (Sethi 1998; Sheth and Sethi 1997).

Think tanks and civil society

Civil society can be defined as consisting of intermediary organisations between the citizen and the state. This includes a large and heterogeneous set of organisations, including women's groups, national and local NGOs, the private, non-profit sector, professional groups/associations, including business associations, voluntary citizens' groups, community groups, religious groups, and research organisations and think tanks. One characteristic of think tanks that sets them apart from other groups is that they generally aspire to being neutral and objective in their approach. As Stella Ladi notes elsewhere in this volume, to the extent that they succeed, a valid way of looking at think tanks is to see them as mediators between different interests, with knowledge as the primary tool of such mediation.

It is as true in India as Nesadurai and Stone note is the case elsewhere that 'the ideas that think tanks deal with are inflected with the motives of vested interest'. Neutrality may be virtually impossible to achieve, but an assertion of neutrality and independence is clearly appreciated by sponsors, for whom the credibility of favourable findings is much enhanced. Neutrality does not mean that research (and researchers) should not be engaged with controversial issues. In this context, it is interesting to find that most established partnerships of Indian think tanks are with government or industry. They have also shown some responsiveness to business associations.[4] But the barriers to working with active civil society organisations are generally high. There seem to be two or three underlying reasons for this. One is the emphasis in think tanks on a technocratic and academic orientation, which makes them less accessible, and possibly less interesting too, to the newer and more radical development NGOs, which would like more rapid research outputs and more commitment to action. A second reason is the fear of being too closely associated with advocacy or explicitly political actions because this would 'colour' the think tank as well. Finally, achieving international recognition and being participants in international forums is an increasingly explicit objective and a driving force in research efforts. To that extent, engaging in extensive dialogue with local actors may at times be in conflict with other objectives. Or in the words used by Joseph Stiglitz, wanting an international identity could lead to favouring knowledge that is codified and general; working closely with local development actors may require a greater attention to tacit and local knowledge.

This tendency can be seen, for example, in the particular context of applied economic research in India. With liberalisation and widespread concern with the probable effects of structural adjustment on vulnerable groups, there have been many discussions and many attempts at documentation and research by non-economists and activists. While advocacy think tanks have had easy partnerships with activists, the more academic think tanks have been uneasy about such partnerships. Part of the reason for this may be the persistence of a belief among (some conventional) researchers that 'activists' tend to lobby for or against policies based on an emotional reaction to a situation, and they cannot participate constructively in a process of critical thought. But a reluctance to be drawn into advocacy campaigns may be the more important reason.

Both social science research and social activism are engaged in the attempt to find a way of making sense of a complex social reality. Policy research chooses to do this by using a set of concepts and categories to separate essentials from non-essentials, and thereby to find relevant policy implications. Activism uses a different method to identify the key constraints to change or development, thereby seeking to influence policy makers to remove these constraints. In theory, there is no reason why one set of efforts should not complement the other. The fact that some activist agencies are increasingly well integrated with research and policy discourse and make their presence felt not only in local action but also in consciousness raising and policy advocacy, suggests that there may be opportunities for constructive collaborations (PRIA 1991). PRIA, for example, has been successful not just in national but also in global networking of NGOs and in basing its advocacy on NGO research. From the point of view of think tanks, relevance in research is important, and such collaborations are one way of ensuring this. For activists, good research and objective findings can only strengthen the cause (Dubey and Sethi 1979).

In practice, the relation between think tanks and other civil society organisations is one that is constantly evolving. This paper seeks to examine the constraints and opportunities of partnerships between NGOs and think tanks in the context of the research and policy process as it exists in India. In particular, it addresses the question 'what are the optimal conditions for NGO and think tank collaboration?' and an answer is attempted using the experiences of the NCAER in India. While this experience is undoubtedly specific, it helps in posing several questions that have a wider applicability.

NGO–think tank interactions: an illustration from the NCAER

The NCAER was founded in 1956 (originally as the Council of Economic and Industrial Research, revised after a few months to the National Council of Applied Economic Research) as a registered society under the Act of 1860. The founding members were eminent persons drawn from public life, including the ministers of finance and industry, other members of parliament, senior government officials, and industrialists. The constitution envisaged that there would be multiple sources of funding. An initial grant from the Ministry of Finance was supplemented by a building grant from the Ford Foundation in New Delhi and project grants from central and state governments and industry. The particular niche that the NCAER was set up to fill was to give the government support in the exercise of planning for development. To do this, it was necessary to set up a body of researchers who were capable of generating large-scale primary data on their own and able to provide independent analysis of planning and development problems at the national, state, sectoral and individual industry levels. Over time, the NCAER has come to be recognised as an alternative data source to that of the government.

From its inception, the NCAER has responded to the concerns of both government and industry. The 1964–65 annual report states that in the nine years since its inception, the council completed '128 projects ... of which 69 were sponsored by the Central and State Governments, 49 by Industry, including 19 by Public Sector Undertakings, and 10 on its own initiative' (NCAER 1965: 1). That is, while more than half of the projects were done for government, almost 40 per cent were for industry. Projects undertaken included techno-economic surveys in which the NCAER had special expertise, and which received commendations from within the country as well as from neighbouring countries (*ibid.*: 10). These surveys assessed the physical and financial resources of each state and provided a broad framework for planning with a time horizon of fifteen years or so (NCAER 1974: 94).

Partnerships with government and industry are thus of long standing. The NCAER has also worked with NGOs, but these collaborations were almost exclusively for the purpose of collecting primary data through the NGOs. The significant difference in present-day collaborations between NGOs and think tanks, and those that have taken place previously, is that most NGOs today seek to be equal partners in the relationship. In the past, collaboration has been initiated by organisations like the NCAER mainly to obtain data using the field staff and insights of selected NGOs. This kind of partnership tends to be top-down. The agenda, the methods of data collection and the use of research findings would be dictated by the NCAER because of its research expertise. The role of the NGO was a passive one.[5] Today, more and more NGOs are attempting to document their work and build up research competencies. There are also examples of NGOs attempting collaborative research with research institutions (Bhatt 1999: 3). However, the relationship between activists and academics is a complex one, and partnerships in research are relatively new. Moreover, such interactions usually require financial support from a third agency, so that the agenda also has to meet the priorities and concerns of the funder. Finally, the role of NGOs in policy making is itself an evolving and relatively new one.

Changing policy environment

In the 1950s and 1960s, the approach followed by the government towards development was not questioned within the Council. For example, in describing a project to devise a development strategy for Nagaland, it is stated that:

> The principal objective in agricultural development in the Fourth Plan is to set the pace for converting *jhums* into areas of permanent cultivation. The conversion of the non-monetised rural economy into a market oriented monetised one is taken as essential.
>
> (NCAER 1965: 8)

This reflects official policy at the time.

Changes in the policy environment in the 1980s and 1990s have had an effect on the research environment for think tanks like the NCAER. Interaction between think tanks and government explicitly lay behind policy formulation between the 1950s and the 1970s. The Planning Commission, in particular, has had a tradition of widespread and open consultations, which have included research institutions. In the past decade and a half, other actors, such as the voluntary sector/NGOs, have begun to have a presence in different kinds of forum for policy dialogue. For example, consultations with NGOs were first held by the Planning Commission prior to the finalisation of the Eighth Plan (largely in recognition of the fact that NGOs had begun to acquire an institutional identity).[6] Even if largely a symbolic gesture, this kind of formal consultation is now widely used by most ministries. Another example is the much greater responsiveness to users that is being displayed in the statistical agencies of government. Once again, the significance is in the process. The Central Statistical Organisation, for example, has appointed NGO representatives on several advisory committees, so at the level of ideas at least, channels of communication have been established.

These and other changes in the working of the government reflect to some extent the requirements of international donors, particularly the World Bank and the United Nations. Internationally, there is greater recognition of the need to involve civil society in development interventions, and this has been accompanied by a larger flow of funds to NGOs. The increasing sophistication of representatives of civil society, and their more visible presence in global networks, has led to greater interest on their part in using research for advocacy. Local interventions do not require extensive research. But research-based interventions are far more effective in lobbying for policy change, and for a consciousness-raising exercise. More and more, NGOs engaged in local action are beginning to recognise that an enabling policy framework can increase the impact of locally designed interventions and, conversely, can fail to be successful if policy initiatives favour a different set of actions. Addressing policy makers thus becomes a necessary part of local action.

What these changes mean for think tanks is that there are more users for research output and, potentially at least, more sources of funding (NGOs now have both research needs and access to funds). Over the years, the relative contribution of different sponsors has been changing systematically. For the NCAER, the ratio of government to non-government funding in the 1960s and 1970s was roughly 60:40. In the period 1980–81 to 1989–90, this ratio had changed to 39:61. Of the 61 per cent coming from non-government sources, 37 per cent came from domestic industry and 25 per cent from international donors. In the period 1990–91 to 1993–94, the contribution of government fell to a little under 30 per cent and that of industry to 17 per cent, while international agencies provided 53 per cent (NCAER 1994: 1). Taking the period 1990–91 to 1998–99, the ratio now stands at 32:68. Of the 32 per cent from government, 6 per cent came from the public sector. Of the non-government funding, 8 per cent came from the domestic private sector and the remaining 60 per cent from international organisations. Much of the donor support in the 1990s has been for research into the impact of liberalisation and for data on related economic issues. The result of this change in sources of funding is that today, the assured funds that the NCAER receives from the government and returns on an endowment fund together cover less than 10 per cent of its annual expenses (NCAER 1999: 9).

Institutional response

Such a financial situation could contribute to greater user responsiveness and force stronger attempts to improve the quality of research. Evidence of the need for organisational renewal can be found in the annual reports of the early 1980s. This period marked the transition from a reasonably stable financial situation, largely dominated by government funding, to one that is more volatile. It was anticipated that improving research quality and hiring new people would raise the costs of research, and that 'the extent to which we can succeed will therefore depend on the extent to which we can convince our sponsors' (NCAER 1984: 14).

Other changes followed. From being largely a provider of information, NCAER research began to become more explicitly policy-oriented:

> Since the beginning of the major turnabout in economic policies in recent years, the projects have tended to become more oriented towards developing specific policies for government or industry.
>
> (NCAER 1994: 1)

New processes of research were noted:

> In keeping with the changing economic environment, NCAER is building networks with research institutions and scholars in India and overseas, and engaging in exchanging views on considerations of alternative policies and their impact.
>
> (*ibid.*: 3)

How far research methods and processes have actually changed in an organisation like the NCAER is a moot point. On the one hand, a quick survey of NCAER staff suggests that although the changes in the policy environment mentioned above are real enough, much less change has been perceptible inside the organisation. By and large, the same methods of data collection and analysis are in use (although with some added sophistication attributable to better information technology and econometric abilities). The end product of a research process is still seen as a report (or publication). Dissemination in the popular media is usually done more in response to a demand from journalists than from a sense of reaching out or attempting to generate public debate (although there may be some exceptions).

Organisational change is inevitably slow. The 'ideal types' suggested by Kent Weaver and James McGann (2000) for think tanks are useful in understanding the transition currently underway at the NCAER. From being largely a 'contract research organisation', it is moving in the direction of an 'academic think tank'. In response to this changing environment, the NCAER has developed an active recruitment policy with a conscious attempt to recruit PhD holders from prestigious universities, and the staff profile has changed significantly over the last five years. Greater use of information technology is seen as one of the tools for improving research quality and keeping abreast of international as well as national developments. But it differs in many ways from the IGIDR, for example, which is a 'pure' academic think tank with a status equivalent to that of a university (Parikh 2000). Since the transition to an academic think tank is necessarily incomplete, it is most accurate to describe the NCAER as a hybrid of these two types. Research output continues to include survey findings and descriptive reports, but there is an increasing role for econometric analysis. Being a hybrid has generated some internal tensions, but in so far as think tanks have to play a part in the market for policy advice as much as that of knowledge, it has probably on balance been a source of strength.

Collaborating with others: the NCAER–SEWA project

The NCAER–SEWA project is the first think tank–activist collaboration that the NCAER has participated in, and furthermore, a partnership in which the sponsor is the activist organisation (although the collaboration was made possible by the (silent) support of a donor agency, the Ford Foundation).[7] The two parties have been 'equals' in the research process, albeit contributing to different aspects of the work. In this project, the Self-Employed Women's Association (SEWA) formulated the basic research question (What is the contribution of the informal sector to the economy?). However, the specifics and methodology used relied more on the technical expertise of the researchers involved.

The members of SEWA, which was registered as a trade union in 1972, are poor, self-employed women workers. Over the years, it has expanded into different areas of activity, so that today it can be said that:

> SEWA is both an organization and a movement. The SEWA movement is enhanced by its being a 'sangam' or confluence of three movements: the labour movement, the cooperative movement, and the women's movement. But it is also a movement of self-employed workers – their own, home grown movement with women as the leaders.
>
> (SEWA 1999: 5)

It has a strong field base, but is also well integrated into both national and international networks and policy dialogues concerning the informal sector, workers and women. International networks in which SEWA has played a critical role in founding include HomeNet, Women in Informal Employment Globalizing and

Organizing (WIEGO), and the International Alliance of Street Vendors (*ibid.*).[8] In the new environment of liberalisation and free trade, it is interesting to note that SEWA has not taken a standpoint opposed to the new thinking. Instead, it argues for greater recognition of and support for workers in the informal sector on the grounds that their contribution is significant to the functioning of the economy:

> With globalization, liberalization and other economic changes, there are both new opportunities and decline in some traditional areas of employment. More than ever, our members are ready to face the winds of change. They know they must organize to build their own strength and to meet the challenges. There are still millions of women who remain in poverty ... They must be brought into the mainstream, so as to avail of the new opportunities that are developing with regard to employment.
>
> (*ibid.*: 5)

This approach is fundamental to the success of the NCAER–SEWA collaboration. At no point have researchers involved in the project been under any pressure to formulate an alternative economic policy; rather, the stress has been on generating numbers, finding out what is the size, contribution and dynamics of informal employment from available macro-data and field surveys. Such detachment on the part of the NGO concerned is also testimony to its own ability and confidence in using the findings, as also in working out strategies for its own work that can draw on environmental resources rather than attempting to oppose them.

Developing partnerships: the role of networks

From the experience of one project and one interaction one can at best conclude that there is further potential for think tank–NGO collaboration. Before examining the opportunities for and constraints of such interactions, it is helpful to look at the ways in which think tanks are currently embedded in economic and political structures. One way of doing so is to use a network frame of analysis and the categories outlined in Chapter 10 on Southeast Asian think tanks.

Networks at the NCAER

Networks represent a new form of governance, providing points of connection, contact and decision making that run parallel to formal governance structures. Among the different research and policy networks of which NCAER has been a part, a recent UNDP-sponsored project network may be mentioned.[9] The first phase of this project involved the collection of data on health, education and employment/poverty from around 33,000 households, yielding a national data set with valuable multi-dimensional information on aspects of human development. In the second phase, a number of researchers from different institutions have been given access to this data, and a set of studies is being undertaken to extract as many insights as possible using the data. With an advisory committee in which several policy makers are represented, these insights are shared easily and quickly, and any queries or additional requirements can also be supplied to them. This experiment is interesting because it is probably the first time that such a data set is being made available to researchers outside the Council, and the network aspect encourages a stronger partnership between a range of researchers and policy makers on matters of contemporary policy debate. Such a network contributes to the strengthening of a 'policy community' that intersects with the NCAER but extends beyond to include a wider range of actors.

A different kind of network, created as a donor initiative, is the IDRC-sponsored MIMAP (Micro Impact of Macro and Adjustment Policies) network.[10] MIMAP projects have been started in several countries, with the general purpose of strengthening economic research that examines the links between macro-economic policy and micro-economic impacts. The strength of the research–policy nexus varies from country to country. However, this is an important part of the network's objectives, which include 'developing and examining micro–macro linkages in a rigorous manner; enabling indigenous capacity for policy analysis and research for policy; and promoting sound policy dialogue' (Medhora 1995: 28). Such a network has the potential to recognise the relevance of 'tacit' knowledge on the one hand and 'codified' knowledge on the other. Knowledge transfers can be provided in an organised and systematic way, as in training in new techniques, for example. The MIMAP network is largely a network of southern researchers and can perhaps be described as a 'discourse coalition'; that is, it seeks to define a policy problem in a certain way and to find a set of ideas, concepts and categories through which the problem can be understood.

The only experience that the NCAER has had so far in participating in or coordinating a network that includes an activist organisation as a research partner is the NCAER–SEWA project network. The immediate network is relatively small, consisting of two other research institutions, the Gujarat Institute of Development Research and the Institute of Social Studies Trust, in addition to NCAER and SEWA (for a full discussion, see Sudarshan 1997). Thus, while each of the studies was institutionally embedded and drew upon institutional resources, the project has gained substantially from being simultaneously part of a network structure. An advisory committee was appointed, and meetings of project researchers were held frequently to share interim findings. Although the life of a project network is clearly limited and restricted to the duration of the project, the emergence of a network structure as a means of coordinating and developing ideas follows a pattern that is becoming increasingly common. Apart from the immediate project network, the project resulted in wider interaction through related international networks, including the informal and international WIEGO network in particular as well as the Delhi Group (a network of statistical agencies set up in 1997 to examine data issues relating to the informal sector). Exposure and contributions to international ideas, approaches and thinking have been made possible by networking, with institutional consent but not necessarily involvement. The motivation behind using networks undoubtedly varies from case to case, but in this instance two factors have been particularly important. On the one hand, the network has been a way of drawing upon existing institutional resources and simultaneously participating in related events and thinking in other countries and from other disciplines. This can be easier within a network structure. Second, some activities that may not fit within an institutional mandate but would strengthen the policy impact of the project could be accommodated in a network framework. For example, advocacy does not fall within the institutional mandate of most research organisations, including the NCAER, but working together in a network means that it is possible to collaborate in research while leaving some activities (in this case advocacy) to a partner (in this case SEWA).

Taking the South Asia region as a whole, there are important issues of collective interest and attempts have been made in the past to network, set agendas and seek to influence policy. But such second-track diplomacy has been much less successful here than in Southeast Asia and seems to flounder on the 'big brother' perception of India by other countries in the region or by the emergence of political turmoil and conflict. The SAARC Poverty Forum is an example of such a network. The NCAER has not participated in such networks partly because of its commitment to technocratic analysis and partly because it has been more deeply engaged in Indian development debates rather than regional governance issues.

Evaluating and using networks

Networks play a functional and practical role apart from the more strategic roles discussed above. In general, networks will be more sustainable where both institutions and individuals perceive some benefit from being part of the grouping. Networks are often described as networks of institutions. But as voluntary associations, they are viable and sustainable only when some individuals, or an individual, is committed to the purposes and activities of the network. The relation of the individual to the institution and the institution to the network are both of relevance. The common understanding that 'one can either work or network' draws attention to potential problems that excessive networking can create. However, well-managed networks should add to productivity and not detract from it. Networks enable some understanding of the role of tacit knowledge without the need for permanent relocation. Individuals may well relocate to different places or to different types of work, and networks would facilitate more informed choices than may otherwise be possible. Many institutions (such as the NCAER) have begun to encourage contractual employment, thereby weakening the individual–institution link. In such situations, networks may provide the additional support that individuals need to stay in organisations that offer more tenuous employment contracts now than they did in the past. Networks are essentially non-hierarchical and hence likely to stimulate creative energies.

Where an institution is based largely on one disciplinary orientation (as the NCAER is on economics), networks can facilitate access to other disciplines and contribute to a more holistic understanding of a given problem.

Through the flexibility they offer, networks represent an opportunity, but some problems can also be anticipated. While project networks are fairly well established, there has been little analysis of how networks interact with institutional norms and systems. There can be many reasons to favour a network frame for research: first, a quick sharing of ideas (especially relevant with 'discourse coalitions') and training in new techniques, management systems and so forth; second, providing peer review and reactions more quickly and from a wider range of people than would normally be possible; and third, encouraging and enabling a wider dissemination of research findings, including policy advocacy.

These outcomes largely benefit the individuals who participate in networks. For the institution, networks have the potential to be energising through access to new ideas and different forums, and by cutting across institutional hierarchies. There could be conflicts if institutions resist these, for whatever reason, but it is clear today that while networks need to be responsible and responsive to valid institutional concerns, it is increasingly unsatisfactory to undertake projects that are wholly contained within institutional boundaries. Despite the fact that networks are usually voluntary and informal associations, successful networking does imply some relocation of 'power' both in identifying research priorities and in attracting funding. Despite their non-permanent nature, many networks have acquired the credibility to attract direct funding, and even to influence the direction of institutional grants.

Are networks simply a new form of organisation, or do they also result in a new kind of output? Is there some visible product differentiation? At the point of departure, it is institutional resources, including research methods and priorities, that people bring with them. Where networks consist of like-minded people with similar backgrounds it is not clear that networking will change the nature of the product greatly, except by broadening the perspective of the researcher. However, networks are often more ambitious, bringing together different disciplines or attempting academic–activist combinations, and such networks have greater potential for changing the nature of the product. It is possible that the new knowledge generated is more relevant, gives visibility to the invisible and attempts to be more holistic. It is equally possible that it will fall outside the boundaries of conventional disciplines. The question then is whether this poses a problem for the researcher. To the extent that organisations stand behind such networks, these problems are less likely to surface. But on occasion, experienced researchers have opted out of mainstream organisations. This option is less feasible for those who perceive their fall-back options to be weaker, and who may in consequence reduce their participation in the network.

A wide range of likely outcomes is thus possible as a result of networks impacting upon organisations. In a general sense, there is a quality of apprenticeship and learning that is better fostered within the more durable and stable structure of an organisation. But it is clear that in a world that is increasingly networked, organisations cannot stand outside. The net result may be that those organisations that will survive are those that are able to accommodate to the new imperatives in research that networks tend to foster – quicker, more oriented to policy or action concerns. But if they are to add value to such networking, they need to have the space and the time for more conventional roles as well. It may be possible to do both only with a high level of transparency and integrity within organisations, and an acceptance of the less hierarchical manner of interaction that characterises the network community.

The most comfortable networks are those where the various participants share an intellectual and social background, but the challenge to the network structure comes from the ability to create viable interactions between people of varying backgrounds and orientations. For example, attempts to bring together activists and researchers generally require some 'ground rules'.[11]

Sustained interaction between researchers located in think tanks and activists may require some reorientation in the think tanks. To understand why, a slight deviation into an understanding of research processes is needed. Research processes can be of different kinds, and the contractual research undertaken by the NCAER, and think tanks in general, tends to be 'reactive' research. That is, the research responds to a question raised by the sponsor. Independent research done by NGOs usually falls into the 'action research' category, where the emphasis is on documenting experience in order to understand the constraints and the opportunities. Both of these types of research tend to ignore the complexities inherent in any situation. Academic research would not do this, but it risks losing policy relevance. In contrast, research that draws upon grass-roots experience to conceptualise development issues and pose relevant questions, but allows for complexity, has the potential to stimulate the application of academic abilities to policy-relevant matters while taking explicit note of the concerns of local actors. This could be described as 'pro-active' research.

In the past, the NCAER has seen its most appropriate role as being somewhat passive, providing the information base for policy decisions (or reactive research). In the new environment of policy making – in which a more pro-active role is less controversial and indeed probably necessary – the institution needs to strengthen its skills in such activities as (1) organising policy dialogues with relevant partners; (2) popular dissemination and the use of the media; and (3) sharing information through networks, in addition to the known skill of academic publication and presentation. It would then be possible to engage effectively in pro-active research.

The divisions between different groups of actors may not be as rigid as this discussion suggests, but on the whole, while the government–think tank interaction is relatively well developed, the addition of activists to the picture requires some care and consideration at present, and until such time as more experience is gained in this area. In particular, there needs to be a clear understanding of each other's domains. For example, academics sometimes resent the role of activists in defining a research agenda, perhaps more so because there are fewer examples of the reverse influence, of academics on the activist agenda. Such partnerships can work where there is a shared sense of the importance of the issue being researched. Similarly, the usual methods of policy or applied research are considerably dependent on the data that may be available, and they may permit fewer clear-cut answers than the activist would like. Finally, dissemination in the popular media is an activity with which academics are often uncomfortable, because civic education is not their primary purpose. However, the activist's purpose is not served unless this can be done.

There are thus considerable differences in the perceptions and world view of conventional academics and conventional activists. Notwithstanding the tensions, there could be mutual gains from developing such interactions.

Conclusion: optimal conditions for NGO–think tank collaboration

The question posed earlier in this paper concerned the 'optimal conditions' for NGO–think tank collaboration. Two conditions emerge from the above discussion. The first is that there needs to be an acceptance of a conceptual framework that places both research and its policy implications within the same canvas. That is, a purely academic stance is not conducive to such partnerships. The second is the need for realistic expectations on the part of the NGO. Quick research that will generate a directly useful product is not always possible.

Colonial rule, with its accompanying territorial annexation and the need to create an elite with a shared world view and language, meant a strong rejection of local and tacit knowledge in India. It is perhaps only fitting that a revival of concern for the role of such knowledge in development transformation should emerge as a global issue. Researchers in local think tanks may well have a better understanding of these, as Stiglitz suggests. But their world view has been derived from within the boundaries of codified and general knowledge, and to revive the missing dimensions is a challenging, though not impossible, task.

Notes

1 Opinions expressed in this paper are personal and do not necessarily represent the official view of the NCAER. I would like to thank my colleagues for sharing their perceptions of the Council and its work with me; Director-General Dr Rakesh Mohan for encouragement and helpful discussions, and Harsh Sethi and Diane Stone for their input.

2 Although this section tries to develop a rough typology of Indian think tanks/research institutions, some caveats need to be made. Institutions named have been selected to illustrate different types, and this is not an exhaustive list. More importantly, there are probably few pure 'think tanks' (policy advocacy institutes) in India. The actual situation is complex: there are policy advocates in universities, research institutes that confer degrees, and so on. One reason behind the jumbling of functions may be that mobility across institutions, such as from universities to think tanks and back again, has proved to be difficult in India. The result is that different organisational types have diversified into a multiplicity of functions. But it may still be appropriate to treat the term 'think tank' as equivalent to 'research institute' in the

Indian context because these organisations are certainly attracted to the attributes of think tanks: autonomy and policy relevance.

3 Setting up the ICSSR was recognition by the government of the large number and importance of the research institutions started in the 1950s and 1960s (the ICSSR itself is neither a research organisation nor a statutory body).

4 Liberalisation appears to have led to more open policy advocacy by business associations. For example, the Confederation of Indian Industry has jointly sponsored several events with organisations like the NCAER and ICRIER in the last five years. Sponsored research for business associations has an older history. As an example, the NCAER annual report for 1983–84 lists the following sponsors: the Vanaspati Manufacturers Association, the Organization of Pharmaceutical Producers of India, and the Northern India Flour Mills Association.

5 Based on an informal survey of about fifteen senior researchers at the NCAER conducted by the author in September and October 1999, including a few written responses.

6 The approach to the plan was formulated in 1990, but implementation was delayed by a couple of years. The Eighth Plan was implemented over the period 1992–97.

7 The NCAER–SEWA project on the contribution of the informal sector (Ford Foundation 0970–0379) started in early 1997.

8 HomeNet International is a foundation registered in the Netherlands, No. 41098260. It has home pages at the following addresses: http://www.homenetww.org.uk. See also WIEGO at http//wiego.org and StreetNet at http://www.streetnet.org.za.

9 UNDP project number IND/91/100.

10 The MIMAP–India project (IDRC 93–8307 and 04592/98–0234) started in 1993.

11 It should be noted that there are several examples of successful networking among individuals around an issue of mutual interest where some may be 'activists' and others 'academics'. Such networks of individuals need to be distinguished from networks that are embedded in institutions, which is the focus of the discussion here. The latter too require commitment from individuals but also need to be responsive to institutional concerns.

References

Bhatt, E. (1999) 'Bridging the gap between knowledge and policy: one that liberates is knowledge', Global Development Network Conference, Bonn, 6 December 1999.

Dubey, P. S. and Sethi, H. (eds) (1979) 'Action-research: proceedings of a seminar', New Delhi: ICSSR mimeo.

Global Development Network (GDN) (1999) *Profiles of Organizations*, Washington: GDN Secretariat.

International Development Information Network (IDIN) (1992) *Directory of Research and Training Institutions and Organizations on Economic and Social Development and Planning in Asia and the Pacific*, Kuala Lumpur: Asian and Pacific Development Centre and Association of Development Research and Training Institutes of Asia and the Pacific.

Medhora, R. (1995) 'The Micro Impacts of Macroeconomic and Adjustment Policies (MIMAP): experience to date and future directions', Ottawa: International Development Research Centre mimeo.

National Institute for Research Advancement (NIRA) (1996) *NIRA's World Directory of Think Tanks*, second edition, Japan: National Institute for Research Advancement.

NCAER (1965) *Review of Work and Activities 1964–65*, New Delhi: National Council of Applied Economic Research.

NCAER (1973) *Review of Work and Activities 1972–73*, New Delhi: National Council of Applied Economic Research.

NCAER (1974) *Research and Training Priorities in Economic Development and Planning: A Survey in India*, New Delhi: National Council of Applied Economic Research.

NCAER (1984) *Annual Report 1983–84*, New Delhi: National Council of Applied Economic Research.

NCAER (1993) *About NCAER*, New Delhi: National Council of Applied Economic Research.

NCAER (1994) *Annual Report 1993–94*, New Delhi: National Council of Applied Economic Research.

NCAER (1999) *Annual Report 1998–99*, New Delhi: National Council of Applied Economic Research.

Parikh, J. (2000) 'Indira Gandhi Institute of Development Research: a leading think tank in Asia', in J. G. McGann and R. K. Weaver (eds) *Think Tanks and Civil Societies: Catalysts for Ideas and Action*, Somerset, NJ: Transaction Press.

PRIA (1991) *Holding Together: Collaborations and Partnerships in the Real World*, New Delhi: Society for Participatory Research in Asia.

Sethi, H. (1998) 'Micro struggles, NGOs and the state', in M. Mohanty and P. N. Mukherji, with O. Tornquist (eds) *People's Rights: Social Movements and the State in the Third World*, New Delhi: Sage Publications, pp. 405–20.

SEWA (1999) *SEWA in 1998*, Ahmedabad: Self Employed Women's Association.

Sheth, D. L. and Sethi, H. (1997) 'Representations and reality: the NGO sector', in V. A. Pai Panandikar (ed.) *A Survey of Research in Public Administration 1980–1990*, Delhi: Konark Publishers, pp. 259–88.

Sudarshan, R. (1997) 'The contribution of the informal sector to the economy: the NCAER–SEWA project', *Margin* 30(1): 1–4.

Weaver, R. K. and McGann, J. G. (2000) 'Think tanks and civil societies' in J. G. McGann and R. K. Weaver (eds) *Think Tanks and Civil Societies: Catalysts for Ideas and Action*, Somerset, NJ: Transaction Press.

6 Building productive partnerships for the promotion of reform

The APOYO Institute in Peru

Gabriel Ortiz de Zevallos and Alejandro Salas

Introduction

The emergence of think tanks[1] in Peru is recent when compared with their Western counterparts. The context in which each has been created, their financing and staffing choices, research agenda priorities and product development options are diverse, but some fundamentals are common. Because of low salaries, strong bureaucracies and a lack of independence, a significant proportion of professionals interested in the general area of public policy have not been attracted to the public sector or to universities.[2] Instead, this professional group has created think tanks and/or consulting firms, looking for different sources of funding to finance the studies by which they want to contribute to the policy process.

International funding has played a key role in shaping the structure and agenda of think tanks in Peru, probably more than would have been desirable, without denying its usefulness. Some think tanks have adopted a more typical organisation, similar to those of Western countries, while others have not. All have struggled with the difficult task of obtaining funds from foreign sources and influencing local decision makers, some with better results than others.

The first wave of think tanks emerged in the 1960s and early 1970s in the context of military and populist regimes, with the predominant vision of those times in favor of a large and interventionist state as the engine for solving social problems. A second wave of research institutes and consulting firms emerged in the 1980s, a period of high macroeconomic instability for the country and of dramatic change of the state–market paradigm in the whole world. These first two waves were characterised by the availability of significant funding from European and American sources. Since 1990, however, funding has been more restricted and more practically oriented. A few more think tanks were created during the 1990s, but it is still hard to judge whether these efforts will be sustainable in this more competitive environment.

From the standpoint of a developing country, this chapter looks in detail at the constraints and difficulties in the Peruvian policy environment encountered by think tanks. All in the think tank community face the severe information failures of the policy process in Peru, which most probably are common to other developing countries (Myers 1997). It seems useful to delineate these problems in general terms. For the past thirty years, political parties have been dysfunctional, responding more to charismatic leaders than to voters, and their credibility deteriorated terribly at the end of the 1980s. With a few notable exceptions, political parties did not develop strong technical structures within their organisations. Since 1989, all elections have been won by 'independents', several times in 'lucky strikes'. This reflects how unstructured and unpredictable has been the definition of who, from the perspective of a think tank, will be the policy makers to influence. With a few exceptions, the public sector has faced a severe shortfall of well-trained bureaucrats, with the few qualified public officials in each agency usually being overwhelmed with different tasks. Because these officials have no time to read research papers and analyses, research by itself has been of very little use in defining public policy. Finally, the public debate over policy options has often strongly distorted or oversimplified the options at stake. This has to do primarily with two factors: (1) the electoral rules determine a general structure of incentives that promotes confrontation and opportunistic behavior among political leaders (Sardón 1999); and (2) the lack of technical staff in Congress and in the media prevents debate focusing on the real policy issues.

These difficulties shape the organisational choices faced by think tanks and limit the strategic options for their activities. This chapter will further suggest that the promotion of partnerships is an effective strategy for overcoming some of the difficulties found in this context. In other words, building partnerships is suggested as a core issue for making research products influential in the policy process. However, building partnerships in this type of environment is not an easy task. From a think tank perspective, when are partnerships effective? What are the central elements to successful partnerships? Who are the best partners for think tanks? How can think tanks leverage their comparative advantage with other groups? Are the lessons drawn from the APOYO Institute's experiences useful for other think tanks? These are the major questions this chapter will address.

The first section will review the general dimensions of the think tank industry in Peru and the APOYO Institute's agenda. The second section illustrates the APOYO Institute's recent experience on partnership strategies, including successes and failures. The third section identifies the limiting and enabling factors found in the policy environment that shape the strategic options of think tanks in Peru. The final section summarises the chapter's findings and conclusions.

Think tanks in Peru[3]

James McGann and Kent Weaver (2000) argue that at least in the USA and Western Europe, think tanks can be understood as variations on one or more of four basic 'ideal types':

- *universities without students* – academic institutes that focus on staff with strong academic credentials and non-partisan research;

- *contract researchers* – institutes mainly in the form of for-profit consulting firms;
- *'advocacy tanks'* – institutes attracting staff with political credentials and oriented to currently topical issues; and
- *political party think tanks* – institutes that focus on party members and party loyalty.

In the Peruvian case, most think tanks do not fit neatly into these categories but share many of the characteristics of the first three, which, together with the particularities of the policy environment and the availability of resources, constitute hybrid organisations.

The first think tanks in Peru can be traced back to the 1960s and early 1970s. Their creation was a response – and sometimes a contribution – to the social reforms instituted by the military government. These organisations were created in an environment of abundant sources of funding from European and American foundations and worked mainly on projects aimed at favoring the poor and the development of social sciences.

The most prestigious think tanks of this era are the Instituto de Estudios Peruanos (IEP) and the Centro de Estudios y Promoción del Desarrollo (DESCO). In the first case, a group of scholars interested in social reform based their activities on academic research and their dissemination through publications. With a similar background, DESCO focused on the improvement of living standards and the participation of marginal sectors in Peruvian civil society. In both institutions, the basic dissemination strategy for research results is through publications (books, magazines and newsletters), use of the national media to reach public opinion, networking in seminars and conferences with national and international agencies, and national and international networks.

By the late 1970s and early 1980s, a second wave of think tanks had emerged in the context of a deep economic crisis, characterised by an overgrown public sector, a large public deficit and a growing sense that more market-oriented policy research on development issues was needed. Several types of institution were created in this environment. The professionals who led their formation, mostly economists with advanced degrees from US universities, resorted to the funding opportunities available to them, based on their previous experience, and their internal organisation adopted more business-like procedures.

In general, these organisations, in contrast to the ones created earlier, were more focused on applied than on academic issues, although this is a questionable average of a diverse set of products developed by all these organisations. These think tanks had different strategies and organisational structures but shared a more favorable vision of market forces in the development process. Grupo de Análisis para el Desarrollo (GRADE) was created in 1980 with the typical structure of a research center, with a relatively large number of researchers with advanced degrees from foreign institutions, and with strong ties to Canadian and American foundations. A very different type of organisational structure is that of Macroconsult, a consulting firm created in 1985 that is basically dedicated to providing services to the private sector but whose professionals have contributed to the policy debate with products that are typical of a think tank. Another organisational format is the APOYO Institute. It is a non-profit institution that was created in 1989 by the APOYO Group – a firm founded in 1977 that is dedicated to economic consulting, market research, polling and economics journalism. The world-renowned Instituto Libertad y Democracia (ILD) had an organisational structure that was more typical of a think tank at its nascence, but it has now moved more towards consulting. It specialises in the area of land titling of informal property.

The 1990s brought along a more restricted availability of international funds and the most recent trend in think tank developments. The Instituto Peruano de Economía (IPE), another non-profit think tank, resulted from an alliance of the government, leading firms and the World Bank in 1994. Although the IPE organisational structure was completely private, it was conceived as a direct counterpart to the national Ministry of Economy and Finance (MEF) to complement its limited research capacities at the time. The IPE has confined its research strictly to economic analysis, and it disseminates its findings only to the MEF and its associates, with the exception of a newsletter of small circulation for paid subscribers. However, the resignation of the minister of economics in 1998 resulted in the migration of most of his senior staff to the IPE, and the institutional character changed in ways that are still not fully predictable.

This section does not intend to give a full description of the think tank industry in Peru. It aims to identify some important trends that facilitate for a foreign reader a general comprehension of the development of think tanks in Peru, as well as of some of the different types of organisation that contribute to the policy debate in the country. The section does not include private university research centers with a tradition in the area of economic policy. The most notable are the Universidad del Pacífico (CIUP) and the Pontificia Universidad Católica del Perú (CISEPA). Both centers are comprised of a group of the professors of the university, who develop their own research projects and consultancies. In general, universities do not fund research with their own resources.

All these think tanks, with others, have contributed substantially to the policy process in different areas and periods of time, from their own perspectives and models of development, with their own successes and failures. With the instability of the Peruvian public sector, think tanks fill a vacuum by providing a more stable and rewarding environment for professionals interested in public policy issues. However, society in general is not quite conscious of this role.

The APOYO Institute

The APOYO firm was created in 1977, during a period of military government, to provide information on and analysis of the economic situation and perspectives of the country, and of desirable policies and reforms that the government should undertake to combat the economic crisis of that time. In 1977, after almost a decade of strong interventionist policies in every sector of the Peruvian economy, the country was in a deep crisis. Shortly before, a prominent businessman who had been critical of governmental policies had been named minister of economics by the government, only to resign forty days after his nomination when it became clear that the government had no intention of undertaking the necessary reforms. One of the principal advisors on the minister's staff then decided to create APOYO as a firm dedicated to publishing the first monthly economic report in Spanish to inform the business community about the problems of the economy and possible solutions. Demand was high in the business sector for this form of economic reporting, ensuring the long-term sustainability of the project. Later, other non-profitable projects were undertaken to improve the awareness of these issues in universities and through other magazines, to touch on issues of the political and cultural aspects of development.

In 1982, as competition in the market for economic information became stronger, APOYO developed a service of economic information and analysis for the most important firms in the country. In 1984, it created its own polling division, initially with the intention of monitoring political and economic information for the service created in 1982. Market opportunities determined that this division gradually conducted more and more market research studies. In 1986, it created a non-profit effort to develop an alternative measure of inflation to that of the government following the enactment of a general price control policy and extremely expansionist monetary and fiscal policies, which led the country into hyperinflation.[4] This alternative price index was designed to prevent the government being tempted to manipulate official inflation figures and became very prominent through the press. This project was financed with resources obtained from profitable projects such as market research studies and the advice service. In 1989, after a process of strategic planning, APOYO separated its profit and non-profit activities, creating the APOYO Institute for the latter.

The APOYO Group gives institutional support to the APOYO Institute, providing staff, information and organisational resources. Although the APOYO Institute aims to be self-sustaining financially, the APOYO Group has given financial support to specific projects or under specific circumstances. This allows for more flexibility and sustainability in an unstable environment. The synergies and positive externalities of this type of partnership are extremely significant. However, there may also be negative externalities, which need to be addressed very clearly. For example, business clients of the firm need to understand that research from the institute is completely independent. In 1996, a client of the consulting firm asked the institute to prepare a study on a tax exemption that had been eliminated, and when it was clarified that this study would be fully independent, they backed away from the idea of funding it. In a 1990 project, one member of the Task Force on Health Reform (see below) who worked for a pharmaceutical firm asked for some considerations against the mandatory prescription of generic pharmaceutical products to be included in the final report. In this case, these comments were followed by the opinions of those in favor of mandatory use of generic products. The Institute's mission statement and this case-by-case management of specific situations is enough to resolve such misinterpretations, which arise from time to time. In this respect, the institute in some way benefits from the fact that conflicts are more frequent between the clients of the consulting firm (APOYO Consultoría S.A.) and the business magazines firm (APOYO Comunicaciones S.A.). Several times each year, some clients need to understand that although they may be clients of the first this does not mean they will receive any special treatment from the second.

The initial work of the APOYO Institute was strongly influenced by the extreme economic crisis that the country was facing. This is illustrated in Figure 6.1. The institute started promoting first-generation reforms to confront the economic crisis at that time.

The first projects of the APOYO Institute had a strong emphasis on disseminating information and analyses to promote stabilisation, liberalisation, deregulation and privatisation measures. There was no time for the in-depth, more academic type of research as policy makers needed to make decisions in these areas with the best information and analysis available. At this stage, most of its work consisted of publishing short bulletins and reports,[5] as well as organising monthly meetings with Congress members. Research projects started in two areas: how the policy debate and policy implementation processes work in Peru, and judicial reform.

From 1990 to 1994, Peru has undergone one of the most ambitious economic reform programs in the region. The interest of the APOYO Institute shifted from macroeconomic stabilisation reforms to institutional or 'second-generation' reforms (Naím 1995). The research agenda focused on state reform, decentralisation, judiciary and congressional reform, violence and police reform, and the social policy issues of education, health and poverty. Table 6.1 provides a description and comparison of first- and second-generation reforms.

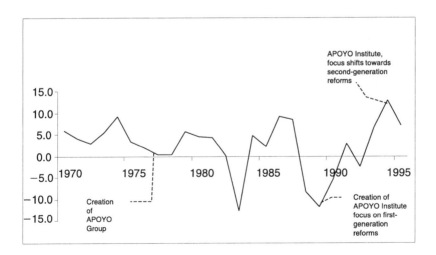

Figure 6.1 Peru: growth in GDP, 1970–1995

Table 6.1 Challenges in the reforms

	Phase I (first-generation reforms)	Phase II (second-generation reforms)
Priorities	• Reduce inflation • Re-establish growth	• Improve social conditions • Increase international competitiveness and maintain macro-stability
Reform strategy	• Change the macroeconomic rules • Reduce the size of government • Dismantle protectionist and statist institutions	• Create and rehabilitate institutions • Increase the competitiveness of the private sector • Reform production, finance and supply of public services (education) • Create the 'economic institutions of capitalism'
Typical instruments (reform objectives)	• Drastic budget cuts and tax reform • Liberalisation of prices, trade and foreign investment • Deregulation of the private sector • Creation of social 'emergency funds' • 'Easy' privatisations (hotels, airlines, some manufacturing companies)	• Labor reform • Reform the civil sector and restructuring of the government • Revise the administration of justice • Improve capacity for regulation (of privatised public services and other monopolies, foreign trade, financial sector, environment, etc.) • Improve capacity for tax collection • Convert and restructure individual sectors (industry, agriculture, banking, etc.) • 'Complex' privatisations (infrastructure, water, mining) • Prepare incentives for exports • Restructure relations between central and regional governments

	Phase I (first-generation reforms)	Phase II (second-generation reforms)
Main players	• Office of the president • Economic cabinet • Central banks • Multilateral financial institutions • Private financial groups and foreign portfolio investors	• Presidency and cabinet • Congress • Public bureaucracy • Judiciary • Trade associations • Mass media • Local and regional governments • Private sector • (Think tanks)[1] • Political parties
Public impact of the reforms	• Immediate • High public visibility	• Medium and long term • Low public visibility
Technical and administrative complexity	• Moderate to low	• Very high
Nature of the political costs	• 'Temporary corrections' well distributed throughout the population	• Ongoing elimination of special benefits for specific groups
Main government challenges	• Macroeconomic administration by isolated, elite technocrats	• Institutional development highly dependent on mid-level administration of the public sector.

Source: condensed from Naim 1995.

[1] Added by the authors.

The APOYO Institute invited Nobel Prize winner Professor Douglass North and organised a series of activities to disseminate the importance of institutions for economic development. At this time, one of Professor North's doctoral students started working for the APOYO Institute, and recently another has joined the staff as chief economist. The Institute has recently added a multi-disciplinary team of associated researchers and consultants to its core staff of economists, including lawyers, sociologists, psychologists, political scientists, medical doctors and educational experts. At this stage, the initial emphasis on dissemination and brief reports was complemented by more typical academic research, although with a preference for an applied perspective.

Promoting institutional reforms is very tricky, as Naím (1995) has clearly pointed out. The odds are against institutional reforms. Political costs come up front in exchange for unclear future benefits. There are no clear paradigms to follow. The success of the reforms depends critically on an ill-trained middle-level bureaucracy. There is a need for a common vision and coordinated efforts from many institutions at the same time. Any improvement is difficult to make and easy to lose. These reforms are difficult, even for developed countries that have to address issues such as educational or state reform. However, in the case of countries where policy processes have severe information failures, the complexity of these reforms is compounded significantly. Partnerships, often informal, flexible and based on relationships of trust with individuals in the business community, the bureaucracy, the media and politicians from diverse groups, seem to be indispensable if progress is to be made in the area of institutional reform. Accordingly, we will now turn to describing specific successes and failures of past and present partnership experiences.

Partnerships for the promotion of reforms: the APOYO Institute experience

A partnership can be understood as a voluntary association between two or more individuals, groups and/or organisations to reach desired objectives based on collaboration that are more difficult to obtain if pursued individually. The partnership can be formalised with a contract, or informally through verbal agreements or implicit shared values and interests. From this basic definition, an effective partnership can be defined as one that allows all participants to reach most or all of their original set of objectives in accordance with the expected timing and amount of resources invested.

Collaboration is a key concept in the above definition. From the communication philosophy literature, Michael Schrage (1995) defines the act of collaboration as an act of shared creation and/or discovery. Collaboration is a purposive relationship that aims at solving a problem, or creating or discovering something within a set of limitations. These limitations usually include:

- *expertise* – one person (or an institution) alone does not know enough to deal with complex topics;

- *time* – collaboration is a real-time effort;
- *budget restrictions*; and
- *competition* – individuals or groups may threaten to undermine a partnership.

People and institutions collaborate when they have limited resources to deal effectively with the challenges that they face individually. Collaboration becomes a necessary technique for mastering complex multi-dimensional themes.

The general principles above apply to think tanks. Many different types of agent could be potential partners for achieving their purposes. Each part involved will imply pros and cons, and think tanks need to develop strategies to define the rules of these partnerships to make them more effective.

It is critical to have the best possible understanding of the interests and resources that the potential partners have at their disposal. One should not over-estimate the level of interest or the amount of resources – time, staff, knowledge, funds – of potential partners on the basis of the importance *per se* of the reform that is being advocated. Judicial reform is critical, without doubt. However, if partnerships are going to be developed to promote judicial reform with any politically relevant actor – politicians, bureaucrats, businessmen, the media – a think tank needs to know how much interest these potential partners have and the resources available on their side for this purpose.

Since its creation, the APOYO Institute has supported partnerships as a strategy for strengthening its policy advice capacity and broadening the dissemination of its research results. Some were very effective, but others were not. Following are three examples of these efforts. At the end of the chapter, we will try to conceptualise those strategies for partnerships that are more effective.

The attempt to modify the economic regime of the 1979 constitution

In 1993, after the elections for a Constitutional Congress that followed the self-coup of 1992, a new constitution had to be drafted. The APOYO Institute had been working on the promotion of economic reform through a series of monthly bulletins between 1990 and 1992 and had realised several times that some articles in the 'Economic Regime' section of the 1979 constitution limited different areas of economic reform.

The effort to 'liberalise' this part of the constitution was complicated because, traditionally, discussion about constitutional issues was restricted to lawyers, who had a very strong consensus in favor of these articles. Lawyers in Peru have no economic training, especially the most experienced ones, who were those incorporated as the experts on constitutional reform. The message of the adverse economic consequences of these constitutional articles was difficult to convey to the public, and most deferred to the authority of the lawyers.

The APOYO Institute developed a partnership with CONFIEP,[6] an umbrella business association, to discuss and disseminate a proposal for a complete change of this section of the constitution. One of these dissemination activities was to publish and distribute among Congress a complete report and six bulletins from an economic perspective on how to reform the constitution. These reports were well received by most members of Congress, and a more informal type of partnership with several, from both the government party and the opposition, was developed. One of the main leaders of the opposition and the president of Congress became especially involved in these reforms, and the APOYO Institute provided both with all the information and analysis they requested.

A partnership was also developed with Propuesta, a small NGO directed by a highly respected former prime minister that at that time had USAID support to organise debates in several provinces to discuss constitutional reform as a whole. In the end, two proposals for constitutional reform were presented, one by the government and one by the opposition. Both reflected many of the recommendations considered in the APOYO Institute's reports.[7]

In retrospect, partnerships were a key element in the success of this case of informing constitutional debates. Other institutions that presented very interesting proposals on their own had much less impact because they were unable to generate a wider constituency of support for their policy proposals. In the case of APOYO, informal, trust-based partnerships with individuals were essential to overcoming the very strong inertia against reform.

The business association partnership to improve police station performance

In 1999, the APOYO Institute developed a partnership with a local business association that supports the police. The APOYO Institute was approached by this association because of the public profile that APOYO has in the general area of designing indicators and surveys. The Institute was commissioned to design a methodology, through a household survey in each police district, that would allow the police station that had improved its image the most over a one-year period to be identified. The officials of that police station were then entitled to a monetary prize donated by the business association.

An important additional factor was that the 10,500-household survey was also designed to collect information on the characteristics of crime in Lima (the victimisation survey), which would allow the police to improve their strategies to combat crime. The first survey was conducted at the beginning of 1999. Initially, the partnership seemed to be flourishing: police officers asked for recommendations on how to improve their statistics, and alternatives to improve police performance from an institutional perspective were discussed. After the results of the survey were processed, the business association asked the APOYO Institute to give an interview to the most important newspaper in the country to present the methodology and its implications. The following day, a front-page article distorted the data and presented Lima as more violent than it actually is. The journalist took a sensationalist approach. Although the Institute immediately clarified the issue with the newspaper, and the newspaper published the clarification, the partnership lost all its drive. The victimisation part of the survey was dropped from the project, and the prize to the police station is now nothing more than part of a few isolated, highly noticeable yet ineffectual measures to improve police performance. This potential partnership between business, the police and a think tank could have made important improvements in the way police stations operate in Peru. It was lost because a relationship of trust had not been built with newspaper editors or the specific journalist.

The Civil Society Task Forces Initiative

In response to the challenges that the policy debate faced in the pre-electoral period and beyond (Peruvian general elections were held on 9 April 2000), in 1998 the APOYO Institute initiated the 'Agenda for the First Decade' project, otherwise known as the 'Task Forces Initiative'. Eight task forces were established to examine and develop policy agendas around essential themes and issues. Each task force focused on a specific policy topic: state reform and decentralisation, local government, political and legislative reform, judicial reform, citizen safety, education, health, and the fight against poverty. The object of the project was to develop a greater degree of consensus about the need for institutional reforms and to suggest viable options to address complex reform issues by a multi-disciplinary civil society team.

Each task force was convened by one of the researchers from the APOYO Institute. At least one or two politicians from different groups across the political spectrum, one or two top-level public officials, a leading journalist, a businessman/woman and researchers from other think tanks and NGOs were included to make a total of eight–nine people. Each task force met monthly over a four-month period to discuss and produce a 20–25-page document that identified the main issues and problems faced and suggested viable policy alternatives for their solution. The final document generated by the researchers from the APOYO Institute was approved by all members of the task force. The compilation of the eight task force reports was disseminated widely among politicians, presidential candidates and their teams, public officials, civil society, journalists, development cooperation agencies, and universities.

Partnerships were a key element during the elaboration of the policy papers and were even more central for the dissemination phase. Producing a policy paper entails 'informal' partnerships with all members of the task forces. They did not receive any payment for their participation. Partnerships were also built with local NGOs in two provincial cities. This gave the opportunity of sharing and discussing the documents outside Lima, enriching their content from a local perspective.

Among the dissemination activities there was a partnership with the Instituto Peruano de Administración de Empresas (IPAE), which organises the Annual Conference for Executives (CADE) – the most important meeting of entrepreneurs, journalists and politicians in Peru. This year, the main interest was on the elections, and almost 1,000 people attended. Some presidential candidates were invited and presented their government agendas. The APOYO Institute distributed the documents at this forum.

Dissemination is still in progress through direct distribution of the documents, and web page and e-mail information services. As these activities are in progress, it is hard to anticipate how effective the project will be in the long term for promoting and influencing policy reforms in these areas. However, the feedback on the process has been very positive from the different partners who had an active role and from the requests for information and the documents that have been received from academic institutions, research centers, public agencies and others interested in the project.

Successful partnership strategies in the policy process

A fundamental element needed to define effective partnership strategies for think tanks is an understanding of the main characteristics of the environment in which they operate and the agents that interact in relation to the policy process. In Peru, since 1990, the government of President Fujimori has had many authoritarian characteristics. This may give the impression that the policy process is completely closed to think tanks, which is false. The policy debate has been closed around those issues that were instrumental to his attempt for a third and unconstitutional re-election, as well as in issues sensitive to the armed forces. However, it is a government that has undertaken many reforms in different sectors, and a wide variety of public institutions have been open to advice from think tanks. In the economic arena, the government has mostly been market-oriented,[8] so it is this type of think tank that has been more influential in this area. However, in areas like the agricultural sector and gender issues, profes-sionals from think tanks with a left-wing orientation have also been influential. This is not to say that bureaucracies and politicians have not made up their own minds about what to take and what not to take from the research and consultan-cies developed by these professionals, and in some cases they have significantly distorted what was recommended. But this is always part of the policy process, and it is predictable that this will happen in any country (Wallace 1998). The degree to which this knowledge influences the policy process will depend on the limitations that the country faces in its policy development.

In this scenario, the Peruvian experience has shown that building mutual rela-tions of trust is easier with individuals than with institutions. In institutions, political control is more likely to exist, and information is more easily distorted. The police stations case described in the previous section illustrates how infor-mation was misinterpreted by a journalist, causing the cancellation of a fundamental part of the overall project and very probably the loss of the trust and complete cooperation of police institutions. On the other hand, the Civil Society Task Forces Initiative was more careful in its design and diffusion campaign. It emphasised the participation of task force members as individuals and not as representing their institutions to avoid possible lack of trust, especially of Congress members, government officials and journalists, who are commonly suspected of being susceptible to political influence.

Insufficient technical capacity and limited communication

Peruvian think tanks operate in an environment in which, with few exceptions, public institutions have limited technical and economic resources.[9] Most are also unstable, since they rely on a political support structure that may be subjected to sudden change. As a result, most public agencies do not offer substantial autonomy to public officials or attractive salaries and working environments. It dissuades many professionals from working in the state sector. The most qualified professionals in the public sector are usually overwhelmed with tasks and have very little chance to keep track of research that may be useful for their policy decisions.

In contrast to other countries, where it is common for professionals interested in policy issues to assume posts in public agencies and think tanks at different points in their careers, in Peru this is rare. These circumstances result in limited interaction between think tanks and policy makers. Research tends to be less practical, while policy is not sufficiently based on research efforts. State support for public policy research is mostly limited to short-term consultancies for specific projects, usually diagnostic or evaluative studies needed for the preparation or implementation of multilateral or bilateral loans or grants.

This isolation of research from policy making and vice versa is a common problem in many countries. But there are different degrees of isolation, and these differences can be very important with regard to how informed the policy process is. For the developed world, Ela Bhatt (1999) refers to two constraints that prevent policy makers seeking the support of researchers and using independent policy analysis. On the one hand, policy makers demand a strategic picture to help them to take immediate decisions, while researchers offer a comprehensive picture of the policy issue, which requires more time and analytical capacity for its understanding and practical use. On the other hand, researchers who constantly advise the government sometimes start to think as if they are policy makers and recommend policy prescription. As a consequence they 'compete' with public officials.

In the case of Peru, and this is probably applicable to many other developing countries, the gap is much wider: most researchers and policy makers do not even interact. Several policy makers are unaware of almost any research unless they have specifically contracted it. Researchers, for the most part, have very little capacity to put themselves in the shoes of policy makers. Short-term consultancies for private researchers and think tanks, as well as some improvement in the availability of trained professionals in the public sector, is slowly creating these linkages, which are essential to a more informed policy process and to encouraging research that is more usefully oriented and specifically applied. It is with this diagnosis in mind that the Task Forces Project was planned to bring together multi-sector participants to start a dialogue in a non-politicised arena, to bridge the gap not only between researchers and policy makers but also with politicians, leading journalists and businessmen.

Funding

Think tanks everywhere are constrained by the search for funding. Research on public policies has the characteristics of a public good, which discourages private sector funding (Antonio 1999). In the case of Peru, as in many other countries, local funding for research is extremely limited.

Think tanks in Peru have a strong and longstanding reliance on funds from foreign foundations and development agencies. One possible consequence of this dependence on international funds is the distortion of a national policy agenda. Although public policy research funded externally may be quite useful, the priorities may be different, having a greater impact on some think tanks than others. Lastly, since international funding tends to be related to changing political realities in the donor countries, this exposes the analysis of policy in Peru to continued disruption. For example, the APOYO Institute had to stop a project to improve legislative procedures funded by USAID, which had gained recognition from all political parties represented in the Peruvian Congress, following several questionable political decisions by the congressional majority. These sudden changes interrupt projects and processes that probably would have produced the greatest benefits in the medium term.

Some think tanks have attempted to develop local funding sources, but very few have had some degree of success. Although several private firms do donate money or services or products as a normal practice, this is basically oriented towards more concrete purposes (Instituto APOYO and SASE 1996). Private firms tend to donate funds directly to tangible projects or to those that will improve their institutional image. It is relatively common for the private sector to give donations for social works or cultural events, but it is rare for these same institutions to fund public policy research, especially if this is not directly in the interests of the donor.

Different examples of how funding determines the think tank agenda can be found in the APOYO Institute's experiences. The police stations case is an example of a short-term consultancy that opened up an opportunity for policy change. However, the project was dependent on the interest and support of the business association. Similarly, a comparative project on violence financed by the office of the chief economist for Latin America and the Caribbean region for the World Bank permitted the Institute to study the determinants of violence in greater detail. Several diagnoses and evaluations considered as conditions for loans by the World Bank, the Inter-American Development Bank and bilateral cooperation agencies have allowed the Institute to conduct research and consultancies on issues of health, education, social funds, decentralisation, state reform and others. In sum, think tanks are often beholden to the policy concerns and funding priorities of international organisations in their determination of research agendas.

The labour market for researchers and the quality of public debate

The size and characteristics of the professional sector in Peru also play a significant role in think tank activities, both internal and external. The 'brain drain' occasioned by the violence of the 1980s and early 1990s has only recently begun to be reversed by the return of some professionals. For 'first-generation' reforms this is not such a complicated problem, because these are easier to design and implement, and foreign knowledge is relatively useful. However, for 'second-generation' reforms to take place, local knowledge has to be developed on these issues, because institutional change implies ownership and path dependence, so it is not replicable.

Furthermore, professionals who remained in Peru and entry-level professionals are beginning to leave think tanks for the few government agencies that offer competitive salaries and working conditions and private sector posts with higher salaries. This combination of factors has left a smaller pool of professionals available for think tanks. The availability of sustainable funding to maintain staff doing local research on public policy issues is fundamental for institutional change.

A related constraint that Peruvian think tanks face is that they operate in an environment in which the debate of public policies is vulnerable to superficial analysis and subordination to political interests. Several of the key players who are influential in public policy debate often lack the expertise required to provide adequate input into the process. Neither the Peruvian Congress nor the press, for example, has sufficient technical resources to be able to identify clearly the real nature of policy dilemmas or the implications of policy options. It is not uncommon for Congress and the media to distort more than clarify the real issues at stake. Relatively complex problems can easily be reduced to a 'war of slogans'. The failed police case illustrates this aspect.

The lack of a well-articulated public policy process is due in part to the traditionally weak investigative and analytical capabilities of Congress and the public sector. Currently, every Peruvian Congress member has a monthly allowance of approximately $2,000 to hire advisors, and every permanent congressional committee has two advisors hired at this same salary level. In 1990, salaries for advisors barely reached $300–400 per month. Although policy analysis has improved in a few public institutions, modernisation of the state remains a pending issue on the national agenda. As a result, research that is not directly related to policy options has very little chance of impacting upon policies, because the few policy makers who are sufficiently trained to make use of it are overwhelmed by more urgent priorities. Likewise, research that is not effectively communicated to policy makers and/or influential political players also has little possibility of being noticed.

Peruvian politicians, public officials and think tank researchers develop strategies as a result of this situation. Because politicians and public officials do not have the time or resources to read policy reports, they base their positions on a superficial understanding of report recommendations. In this respect, Antonio (1999) argues that if targeted decision makers are not adequately equipped with the tools to understand and respond to the ideas proposed, think tanks will have insignificant influence. Capacity for policy analysis must also be internal to the state.

In this kind of environment, the 'brand name' of the think tank often has a greater impact than that of the research product itself in determining how or whether its policy recommendations will be absorbed into the policy-making process. Politicians will seldom devote time or be open to recommendations from think tanks that they do not perceive to be either neutral or close to their political positions. This becomes particularly relevant in developing countries, where ideological disputes and debates are still deep-rooted. The general climate of policy thinking is drawn into the confrontational debate between key actors. The credibility gained through years of work and research products that provide correct information, reliable analysis and a dispassionate perspective can be severely damaged if the 'brand name' becomes trapped in political debate.

While political labels may affect the institution's credibility, mainly on national issues, a small number of players in the public policy field have created an opening for all think tanks, especially for specific, short-term projects. In other words, when a think tank establishes a new 'niche', it is likely to enter the public policy process – regardless of the perception of its political position – since no other think tanks are specialising in that field, and none will appear in the short term. Gender issues, for example, has been an area where the most prominent feminist NGOs and researchers have been able to be very active.

In addition, politicians and policy makers develop greater trust in think tanks that maintain some distance from the press. In some cases, this secrecy may prevent the public learning fully about relevant policy issues. In countries where the media have greater analytical capacity, they play a key role in disseminating the work of think tanks, which in turn help to shape a better policy debate. In countries where only top journalists have the knowledge and training to understand and adequately portray the implications of policy research – this is the case in Peru – using the press may be risky because it may substantially distort both the results and the implications of research. A measured and neutral public image of the think tank probably increases the possibility of influencing policy decisions.

A related issue is that influencing the policy process is more probable if researchers and think tanks are not interested in claiming 'property rights' for policy ideas for themselves. Think tanks that are not interested in obtaining recognition for their ideas but instead concentrate their efforts on informing policy are usually better partners for policy makers and politicians. This creates a conflict when funding comes from external foundations and cooperation agencies, because usually they require that think tanks prove their impact on policy making by getting recognition of their ideas.

Conclusion

There is no single model of effective partnerships. With respect to influencing policy decisions, think tanks in countries where the market for information on policy issues fails significantly need partnerships if they want to influence policy decisions. Typical research will not on its own be fruitful, because potential users are not well equipped to process the information. Bridging the gap between research and policy at the local level is essential. However, three major forces that shape the organisational structure and products of think tanks and potential for influence are the labour market for professionals interested in policy issues; the availability of funding for research and consultancy on policy issues; and the capacity of both politicians and the bureaucracy to listen to and absorb the different forms of analysis.

In the case of the APOYO Institute, with respect to politicians, it looks for projects that allow it to provide information and analysis to all the political spectrum. Staff do not participate in politics. In the case of the relationship with the media, it does not look for a high profile, relying on its own bulletins to disseminate research. It does not claim property rights for whatever policy recommendations are considered. It takes care to develop partnerships and relationships of trust with key journalists. The Civil Society Task Forces Initiative is a project that attempts to integrate partnership development into the core of promoting institutional reform. We believe that adding actors through participation in the dialogue process and/or by consultation will promote a feeling of 'ownership' (Stiglitz 1998) that will eventually generate an increase in the number of stakeholders to support and communicate the ideas and research developed. In general terms, informal partnerships have worked better than formal ones, and the relationship of trust with individuals – politicians of all parties, policy makers, leading journalists, businessmen – is a critical element. Choosing adequately is fundamental in order to construct a brand name that opens up the possibility of influencing the policy debate across the political spectrum.

Notes

1   The definition of think tanks outlined by Stella Ladi in Chapter 11 will be adopted in this chapter; that is, organisations distinct from government and pure academic research centers that have the objective of providing advice on a diverse range of policy issues through the use of knowledge and networking.

2   The Central Bank has been the most notable exception in the public sector, but even the Central Bank lost its independence during the hyperinflation period of 1985–90. A few private universities have also been relatively attractive for this type of professional.

3   This section is based on a previous article by Gabriel Ortiz de Zevallos (2000).

4   Annual inflation was 62.9 per cent in 1986, rising to 1,722.3 per cent in 1988, 2,775.3 per cent in 1989 and 7,649.6 per cent in 1990 but dropping to 139.2 per cent in 1991 and 56.7 per cent in 1992 (see Figueroa 1995).

5   The 'APOYO al Congreso' (Support for Congress) project included drafting, publication and free distribution of copies of a monthly newsletter including an economic analysis of the most important bills discussed in Congress. The newsletter was distributed among Congress members, high-ranking executive branch officials, professional and labor organisations, universities, think tanks, the media, and others. Topics included tax reform, liberalisation of foreign trade, deregulation in the labour market, budget issues, antitrust legislation, environmental legislation and privatisation. This project aimed at enhancing law making in areas of crucial importance for the economic and business environment.

6   CONFIEP (Confederacion Nacional de Instituciones Empresariales Privadas) is the association that encompasses the various sectoral business associations (mining, banking, fishing, industry, exporting, etc.).
7   Servicio de Asesoría Económica 'APOYO al Congreso' Nos 8 and 9, November 1992; No. 10, December 1992; Nos 11, 12 and 13, January 1993. Published by Instituto APOYO with financial support from the Center for International Private Enterprise (CIPE).
8   This applies mostly to the 1990–96 period. Very little economic reform was undertaken in the remainder of the decade.
9   Although the Peruvian economy has undergone an ambitious program of economic reform, there has been limited success in the reform of state institutions. A few modern public institutions coexist – the Tax Collection Agency, Customs, some regulatory agencies and the Central Bank – but the majority of the public sector is hampered by strong technical limitations and a lack of professional skills.

References

Antonio, E. T. (1999) 'Towards enhancing the effectiveness of think tanks in generating and marketing policy perspectives: some notes of experience', paper presented at the Global Development Network Conference, Bonn, 5–8 December.

Banco Central de Reserva (1998) 'Memoria anual 1998', Lima: BCR.

Bhatt, E. R. (1999) 'One that liberates is knowledge', paper presented at the Global Development Network Conference, Bonn, 5–8 December.

Figueroa, A. (1995) 'La cuestión distributiva en el Perú', in J. Cotler (ed.) *Peru 1964–1994: Economía, Sociedad y Política*, Lima: Instituto de Estudios Peruanos.

Instituto APOYO and SASE (Servicios para el Desarrollo) (1996) *New Trends in Contributions to Social Development*, Lima: Instituto APOYO and SASE.

McGann, J. G. and Weaver, R. K. (eds) (2000) *Think Tanks and Civil Societies: Catalysts for Ideas and Action*, Somerset, NJ: Transaction Press.

Myers, C. (1997) 'Policy research institutes in developing countries', in M. S. Grindle (ed.) *Getting Good Government, Capacity Building in the Public Sectors of Developing Countries*, Harvard Institute for International Development, Boston: Harvard University Press.

Naím, M. (1995) 'Latin America's journey to the market: from macroeconomic shocks to institutional therapy', International Center for Economic Growth Discussion Papers No. 62, San Francisco: ICS Press.

Ortiz de Zevallos, G. (2000) 'Public policy think tanks in Peru', in J. G. McGann and R. K. Weaver (eds) *Think Tanks and Civil Societies: Catalysts for Ideas and Action*, Somerset NJ: Transaction Press.

Sardón, J. L. (1999) *La Constitución Incompleta*, Peru: Instituto APOYO.

Schrage, M. (1995) *No More Teams! Mastering the Dynamics of Creative Collaboration*, USA: Currency Doubleday.

Stiglitz, J. (1998) 'Distribution, efficiency and voice: designing the second generation of reforms', paper presented at the conference on asset distribution, poverty and economic growth sponsored by the Ministry of Land Reform of Brazil and the World Bank, Brazil, 14 July. [http://www.worldbank.org/html/extdr/extme/jssp071498.htm]

Wallace, W. (1998) 'Ideas and influence', in D. Stone, A. Denham and M. Garnett (eds) *Think Tanks Across Nations. A Comparative Approach*, Manchester: Manchester University Press.

Part III

Reform and reconstruction

7 The challenges of intervention for Cambodian think tanks

Kao Kim Hourn[1]

The participation of intellectuals and experts in the reconstruction of conflict-ridden societies is assumed to be essential but is rarely investigated. This brief preface to the chapter addresses the general themes covered in two panels at the Global Development Network Conference in Bonn on the role of think tanks in transition and conflict. The main body of the chapter is written by Kao Kim Hourn, who discusses the part played by these organisations in Cambodia, and in particular, the role played by the Cambodian Institute for Cooperation and Peace in the reconstruction of Cambodia.

Think tanks in conditions of conflict and rapid change

Two of the more innovative panel sessions at GDN99 in Bonn were those that sought to address the role of think tanks and researchers in societies undergoing significant upheaval. One panel addressed 'Policy research for economic reform and political change' while the other focused on 'Critical interventions in civil conflict'. Most studies of research institutes and think tanks have focused on political systems that are relatively stable and where relative economic prosperity has provided the public space, the philanthropic support and intellectual foundations in universities, the media and the professions for research institutes to emerge and participate in policy debates. Yet it is in more uncertain circumstances of social disruption, ethnic conflict or economic disintegration that these organisations can sometimes effect critical interventions.

The panel on economic reform and political change began with the proposition that think tanks can be agents for regime change and transformation. On the other hand, they can be closely connected to the state, providing the ideas, arguments and justifications that help to bolster and legitimise incumbent governments. These issues are covered in the following chapters by Ivan Krastev and Simon James. They detail how the break-up of the Soviet Union and the emergence of new nation-states produced new political spaces for think tank entrepreneurs. Furthermore, the transition economies created enormous demand for policy guidance in building new social, political and economic architecture. This demand came not only from the new governments in Eastern and Central Europe but also from many international organisations and Western foundations keen to export ideas about the operation of market economies.

The panel on 'Critical interventions' was more concerned with the activities of think tanks in situations characterised by ongoing conflict or a recent history of political strife. Here, think tanks can play an important role in conflict resolution, peace dialogues and rebuilding political and economic institutions in war-torn societies and collapsed states. Nevertheless, ethnic hostilities, cross-border tensions and communal strife present difficult environments for policy institutes to operate in and where intellectuals (no less than others) may face intimidation, harassment or violence in the course of their work. The politically sensitive nature of some policy research (or what might be regarded as critical, disruptive or oppositional) means that institute directors must be extremely responsive, flexible and innovative in their relations with the holders of power.

The situation and the responses of think tanks and the intellectual community in general will differ from country to country. Nevertheless, as the discussion below on Cambodia indicates, when a polity has been left in ruins, think tanks can fill 'knowledge gaps' in new governments as well as providing the intellectual resources and training events to build knowledge capacity in government over the long term. Similarly, many institutes are sometimes regarded as independent organisations that can create neutral territory in the form of closed meetings or private dialogues where all parties to a conflict can meet (secretly if necessary) to discuss possibilities for peace, reconciliation or reconstruction. This is sometimes described as informal diplomacy.

Informal diplomacy entails activities or discussions involving academics and intellectuals, journalists, business elites and others as well as government officials and political leaders 'acting in their private capacity'. The notion that bureaucrats and politicians are acting in their private capacity is to be treated as a 'polite fiction'. Official and non-governmental participation in seminars, conferences and organisations is 'mixed' or 'blended', suggesting that the demarcation between official and unofficial involvement is unclear (Kraft 2000; Stone 2000). For example, in the People's Republic of China, government think tanks have been established within the orbit of the Chinese Academy of Social Sciences or the leading universities, a few of which monitor relations with Taiwan. On occasion, there have been discreet exchanges with counterparts in institutes based in the Republic of China (Shai 2000). Due to the unique international status of the ROC, institutes based in Taiwan have long been engaged in this quiet, non-confrontational mode of political communication (Mengin 1997).

The Israel/Palestine Center for Research and Information (IPCRI) is one institute at the centre of conflict. It was formed in the shadow of the *intifada*, which emerged in the refugee camps, the most dispossessed parts of Palestinian society (see al Qaq and Baskin 1999). This institute is built around the political position that the Israeli–Palestinian peace process needs to be a joint dialogue with political leadership from both sides. Towards this end, ICPRI has two directors and two chairs: one Israeli and the other Palestinian. While balanced political participation took a considerable time to engineer, ICPRI argues that it is now valued and recognised as a relatively neutral forum where issues can be debated together by establishment Israelis and Palestinians. These forums allow participants 'to learn about each other's position and to begin to develop new ideas for creating peace between them' (*ibid.*: 4). Towards this end, ICPRI has become a player, behind the scenes, in 'track-two diplomacy'. In the Israeli–Palestinian case, the deliberations were more often than not held in secret and in circumstances where the Israeli Foreign Ministry denied any association with ICPRI. However, ICPRI was prepared to participate in this 'fiction' in order to achieve its institutional objective of influencing the policy process.

Nascent groups of policy entrepreneurs frequently benefit from the trend in many nations towards democratisation and democratic consolidation or the reinstatement of democratic practices after a period of civil unrest. For example, think tanks in Guatemala are playing an important role after the civil conflict ended in 1996 with the peace agreements, especially in helping to rebuild the institutions and constitutional architecture that were destroyed and in overcoming the lack of sufficiently developed technocracy within the Guatemalan executive (Urizar 1999: 25). Indeed, these organisations are frequently viewed not only as forces for democratisation by Western governments and foundations but also as organisations that are based in civil society and that provide the foundation for grass-roots pressure for democratisation. The founders of the first think tank in Kosovo – Riinvest, established in 1995 – argue that the building of democratic institutions needs to start with the development of the capabilities of a wide spectrum of think tanks (Muhamet and Gashi 1999). Think tanks are portrayed as intermediary organisations that facilitate the participation of Kosovars in the interim administration by convening business associations, the NGO sector and new decision makers as well as functioning as institutional vehicles for cooperation between international organisations and local groups. In particular, they state that think tanks are 'very important in increasing the capacities for human capital for participation in building up a new free society in Kosova' (*ibid.*: 2). In comparable circumstances, think tanks in Cambodia are helping to rebuild a country.

Diane Stone (editor)

The Cambodian story

The role of think tanks in Cambodia must be examined in the context of the country's recent history. In doing so, a picture can then be formed as to the unique challenges faced by such institutions and the critical position they hold in contributing to the rebuilding of a country emerging from political, economic and social disorder.

The historical context

Cambodia entered a very tragic period of its modern history in the late 1960s that continued for almost three decades. The country had been economically self-sufficient and politically neutral. Yet, for all its efforts, Cambodia could not avoid becoming entangled in the web of regional geopolitical conflicts at the height of the Cold War, which ultimately erupted into a 'hot war' on its very doorstep. As a result, conflict and instability reigned for the final third of the century.

The political stability of the country was shattered in 1970 by a bloodless *coup d'état* that installed General Lon Nol, who established the Khmer Republic with himself as president. Internal conflict increased as political repression became common and different political factions struggled to gain power. The massive bombing of the Cambodian countryside that was initiated by the United States in 1969 escalated to a peak in 1973. Rural refugees from the bombing flooded into the cities, decimating rice production and resulting in the collapse of the rural economy. Any hope of a resolution to this political and economic turmoil progressively dimmed and was completely extinguished by the fall of Phnom Penh to the communist Khmer Rouge in April 1975. For almost four years, the country was enveloped in the nightmare of the violent revolution of the Pol Pot regime. All existing political institutions were dismantled and the civil service dissolved. The economy was restructured into a centrally planned and dictatorial authoritarian regime. Banks were closed (the National Bank was literally destroyed), and money was abolished completely. Cities were emptied as the entire remaining population was forced to become part of an agrarian, murderous revolution based on the example provided by Mao Zedong in China. The social and cultural fabric of society was ripped apart as children were separated from their parents, husbands separated from their wives and religious practices forbidden. Personal possessions were forfeited as life became communal. People were forced to work in groups that had daily production targets, and everyone ate together in a communal kitchen.

A new mentality emerged among the Cambodian people during this period. The slightest comment indicating disenchantment with the revolution or disgruntlement over working conditions and food rations could be overheard and repeated. Many people disappeared as a result of this. During the Pol Pot regime, mistrust and suspicion became entrenched into the psyche of the Cambodian people, from workers in the fields to cadres in the governing regime. It can be argued that this frame of mind remains to a large extent to this day. The spirit of mistrust could be called a Cambodian dilemma. It creates a difficult environment for the functioning of policy research institutes engaged in the analysis and criticism of different policy options.

To compound this atmosphere of mistrust and suspicion, Cambodia was isolated and ostracised by the international community from 1975 onwards. With the fall of the Khmer Rouge regime in early 1979 to the invading Vietnamese army, a revised notion of state evolved from this period that still remains embedded to a large extent in the mindset of government officials twenty years later. Even with the collapse of the Khmer Rouge regime, the country remained a victim of Cold War rivalries and did not emerge from its international isolation until 1991. The signing of the 1991 Paris Peace Accords and the eventual deployment of the United Nations Transition Authority in Cambodia (UNTAC) in March 1992 laid the groundwork for a new era in Cambodia's political, economic and social history. This was a turning point away from the country's preceding dark decades. The culmination of this initial phase of Cambodia's transition into a modern democratic society was the successful undertaking in 1993 of the first national elections in almost thirty years.

This groundwork set the stage for think tanks and other civil society organisations such as the Cambodian Institute for Cooperation and Peace (CICP), the

Cambodia Development Resource Institute (CDRI), the Khmer Institute of Democracy (KID), the Cambodian Institute of Human Rights (CIHR) and the Center for Social Development (CSD) to emerge and begin contributing to rebuilding and rehabilitating the nation. However, as alluded to above, the atmosphere that ensued as a result of the country's historical baggage presented unique challenges to the founders of Cambodian think tanks and civil society organisations. Even before the country spiraled into turmoil, the post-independence regime that ruled for fifteen years (1955–1970) was wary of opposition to the point of not accepting dissenting opinions: of the political right at first, and then the political left. Therefore, any think tank that was to operate in the country would have to do so in a challenging environment in which decision makers were unaccustomed to receiving advice from sources outside immediate government circles, never mind receiving criticism with regard to the government's operations.

Both internal and external factors contributed to the opening of social and political space in Cambodia in the early 1990s. There were at least seven internal factors:

1   The people's general mistrust of the government and politics. The Cambodian people had suffered under various governments since 1970. They had little faith in the government. They considered politics to be 'dirty' and manipulative.

2   The people had witnessed war, conflict and violent revolution in the recent past. They were in fact tired of war and conflict, especially the constant power struggle, which made no sense to them. They wanted peace, stability, security and the development of the country.

3   The people generally viewed the international isolation of Cambodia as a critical challenge that deprived the country of the importance of international relations and the benefits of development. That was the rationale behind Cambodia's fast approach to adopting an integrationist policy.

4   The polarisation and the fracturing of Cambodian society to some extent meant that there was a need for a new pole or a new center of neutrality in which the people could trust. The emergence of think tanks and civil society in Cambodia could in part serve the needs and interests of the people and society. Experiences in the 1990s demonstrated that think tanks and civil society were strongly needed and would play a constructive role in the rehabilitation and development of Cambodia.[2] However, the polarisation and fracturing of Cambodian society made the role of think tanks and civil society organisations more difficult, at least during the initial period. Any think tank that has recently been set up needs to define and defend its role because it is inevitably labeled one way or the other – meaning that it is not considered politically neutral and thus questions of its legitimacy are quickly raised (Kanter 1997: 1–3).

5   The lack of human resources capacity in the country, which is essential for nation building, necessitated think tanks and civil society to provide skills

training and capacity building for officials in a wide range of areas, from the English language to diplomacy to economics. Cambodia lost many of its intellectuals during the three long decades of war and conflict.

6   To some extent, the opening up of Cambodia to the outside world impacted on the way of thinking of some Cambodian leaders who realised that the country could no longer afford to remain isolated. This meant that Cambodians needed to change their mindsets and their views of the way they perceived the region and the world.

7   The role of Samdech Preah Bat Norodom Sihanouk, king of Cambodia, was decisive in the promotion of a liberal democracy and an open society in Cambodia. The king also played an important role in promoting national reconciliation and enhancing trust building among the leaders of Cambodia.

In essence, these were the dynamics of the internal factors that contributed to the opening up of political, economic and social space in Cambodia.

However, there were also external imperatives that had a positive impact on Cambodia. First, the end of the Cold War opened up the possibility of ending the Cambodian conflict. The international settlement of the Cambodian conflict that began with the peace process in 1987 and ended with the success of the United Nations peacekeeping operations in 1993 made it possible for Cambodia to move from war to peace – an important transition for a war-torn, conflict-prone society. The UN peacekeeping operations and the 1993 elections laid down a strategic framework for building peace in the country. Second, the Association of Southeast Asian Nations (ASEAN) played its part in the so-called 'comprehensive settlement of the Cambodia conflict' through an active engagement with Cambodia throughout the 1980s and the early 1990s. ASEAN's involvement in Cambodia was a recognition that Cambodia was an integral part of Southeast Asia, and this constituted a positive externality that to some extent helped to stabilise the internal politics of the country. ASEAN diplomats kept dialogue with Cambodia open. Third, the donor community, including international non-governmental organisations (NGOs), contributed to development and change in Cambodia's political, economic and social reconstruction. As a country shattered by war and conflict, Cambodia fortunately benefited from a positive response from the donor community.

When Cambodian tank tanks and civil society organisations were established in the early 1990s, they had to take into consideration the country's political, economic and social context. For example, when CICP was founded in 1994, it had to work in this challenging and uncertain environment. Nevertheless, CICP came to define its mission statement in terms of five objectives:

1   to promote the broader concept of human rights and advance democracy in civil society in Cambodia;

2   to promote peace and cooperation among Cambodians, as well as between Cambodians and others both regionally and internationally;

3   to enhance the capacity of both officials in government and the public at large to make informed decisions about public policy;

4   to promote research in the context of Cambodian development issues, including publication of such research;

5   to promote an open policy debate on strategic issues affecting Cambodia's national interests.

However, CICP was aided in its task of creating a vehicle to enhance opportunities for dialogue, consultation, cooperation and networking. This assistance emanated from the work initially done by the UNTAC mission in Cambodia in 1992 and 1993. The UNTAC mission, first of all, was able to get the four factions vying for power to sit down together for the first time to discuss Cambodia's future and create a formula for sharing power. This was previously unknown in the political dramas that had unfolded in Cambodia. Second, the opening up of Cambodia to the outside world was a result to some extent of the constructive role of King Norodom Sihanouk and other Cambodian leaders. Third, the peace-building process that evolved in Cambodia allowed for a wide range of NGOs to form and operate within an albeit shaky and uncertain political environment. Nonetheless, NGOs promoting human rights, health, gender issues, education and food security, among other issues, proliferated in the cities and throughout the countryside (for a full discussion, see Kao 1999a).

At the time of the founding of many civil society institutions and think tanks such as CICP, government institutions were in their infancy in many respects. The bureaucratic machinery was trying to function while lacking any great expertise and having virtually no resources. In this respect, think tanks had the opportunity to fill some information gaps in the government bureaucracy. Although some improvements have been made in these areas, the lack of expertise and resources remains true to this day. These deficiencies were compounded by the fact that the Cambodian government that resulted after the 1993 election was confronted with a plethora of pressing problems and issues where policy formulation and recommendation were lacking or non-existent. The issues facing the government were complex and needed the consideration of numerous factors requiring various strategies and options. Foreign development aid assisted to some extent in some areas, but it was not adequate to address all the priority issues confronting the country. Here is where think tanks such as CICP, CDRI and others could fulfill their mandates in terms of organising meetings, conducting research and providing policy recommendations to the government. Cambodian think tanks have engaged in various issues, ranging from social and economic issues to the political and security agenda of the country (Muravchik 1996).

The founders and the policy-oriented researchers of think tanks undoubtedly have an important contribution to make to nation building – especially with national reconciliation, trust and confidence building at the leadership level – and to generating policy debates. For instance, CICP saw its function as delineating important policy issues by providing an analysis of alternatives and 'best scenario' prescriptions or policy recommendations to the government. The founders understood that dialogue with various government ministries was needed to facilitate the exchange of ideas and the offering of 'second opinions' or alternative views on emerging key issues. The idea was to push the limits of the possible in generating new ideas. In this capacity, Cambodian think tanks could act as an integral conduit that would allow people who are experts in their own fields to express their perspectives and insights to various governing authorities. Likewise, specific authorities could make their own views known. This exchange of ideas and views then allows for the greatest number of ideas to be presented and debated, sometimes only among the policy makers but at other times between policy makers and the larger public (Kao 1999b).

Furthermore, the research findings resulting from the work done by think tanks such as CICP, CDRI and others can be complemented by the discourse emanating from the dialogue between researchers and the authorities. The combination of data from different sources can then be disseminated to the general public. Think tanks' publications, workshops, presentations and conferences then serve to educate the general public as well as inform the local media of the discourse transpiring with regard to issues of public policy. Disseminating this information on a regional and international level is the logical next step in the process. In the course of disseminating information about Cambodia at these other levels, a network of like-minded institutes can be formed, and strategies and progress can be compared. In this respect, the formation of networks at the regional and international levels is very beneficial to institutes originating from countries like Cambodia in terms of refining methodologies, research capacity building and determining funding sources in order to implement the work that needs to be done.

Political realities and the parameters of influence

This policy discourse, theoretically, is what could be expected under ideal conditions. However, as already outlined, conditions in Cambodia for the operation of think tanks have been wanting. Deficiencies with respect to resources, research skills and human resource capacity, and the high cost of conducting operations in a constantly advancing high-tech world (that is, telephone and Internet costs), combine to hinder Cambodian think tanks in achieving all their objectives. At the same time, the lack of understanding of the role of think tanks by people in general and policy makers in particular presents a major constraint for institutions like CICP. Funding is another important area in which most think tanks in Cambodia face difficulties. Most, if not all, Cambodian think tanks do not receive funding from the government. They also do not receive any support from the private sector, because the private sector in this country is still relatively weak.

While Cambodia is a country that has opened up significantly in the past ten years, the pervading atmosphere of mistrust and suspicion requires that politically sensitive issues be handled with extreme tact and diplomacy. In a climate where opposing political parties are very wary of each other's motives, it is important to reaffirm in a consistent way the non-partisan, neutral stance of think tanks on the issues in question. To this end, for example, CICP strives to maintain a representative balance on its board of directors with respect to the country's major political parties.[3] The board thus includes former government officials, members of the national assembly and academics. While the role of the board is to help to set policies, guidelines and directions, at the end of the day it is senior members of staff who are in charge of the day-to-day operations and activities of the think tank. Senior CICP staff members play important roles in steering the work and activities of the institute and balancing political relations.

To some extent, government and political leaders have been open to studies and have contributed or participated in meetings in the absence of adequate analysis and advice from within bureaucracy or the political parties. On the one hand, the Cambodian bureaucracy lacks not only the capacity but also the expertise and experience in policy formulation and policy analysis. On the other hand, the Cambodian bureaucracy is a young state machine in comparison with many other bureaucracies in the region. Individual senior bureaucrats who were better educated and trained were either overused or were pushed aside. On the latter point, in Cambodia as in other places it is not what one knows but whether one has sufficient connections with the right people. Accordingly, it was difficult to expect too much from a bureaucracy characterised by strong patron–client relations. Most political parties in Cambodia also lack party strategists and policy analysts to help them to develop and strengthen policies and parties. Key individuals in political parties were sometimes either overstretched with tasks or tended to hold multiple positions at one time. In essence, what the government bureaucracy and political parties seem to share is the lack of capacity, human resources, time and the ability to think long term.

The ability of Cambodian think tanks to have more influence is dependent on a number of factors. These include staff capacity, budgets, access to government decision makers, expertise, experience, networking and the right approach. Sometimes, the ability to influence or the power to persuade is dependent on issues and the willingness of government leaders to accept policy inputs from think tanks. In this context, the question of influence is always relative and subject to change due to changes in political leadership and environment. Having said this, one could argue that CICP and CDRI are two of the leading think tanks in Cambodia in their own areas of specialisation and expertise. For example, CICP is well known for its critical work on regional integration, especially ASEAN. CDRI, on the other hand, is well regarded for its work on economic development. A few policy-oriented institutions are involved only in human rights and democracy. A few other think tanks are involved primarily in economic issues such as macroeconomics and economic development. This specialisation in Cambodia has entailed little duplication or rivalry within the think tank community.

It is important that think tanks have amicable relations with the government, and to date, both CICP and CDRI have established such working relationships. However, having a good relationship with the government does not mean that think tanks should always have to agree. On the contrary, most Cambodian think tanks want to be independent of the government; they want the luxury of having the freedom to think. However, it is more difficult for a think tank to have close relations with a political party, because it may be perceived that it does not serve the public interest. If a Cambodian think tank were to be linked to a political party, the chance is that it would lose not only its credibility but also its impartiality in the eyes of the public or the government. Impartiality is the key to the building of trust and confidence between Cambodian think tanks and the government and with the public.

In fact, think tanks have been more inclined to look at issues beyond party politics; they tend to focus on national issues or regional and international issues affecting Cambodia. The challenge is to ensure that when the views of think tanks differ from those of the government they are not necessarily represented as the perspective of the opposition party or a radical group in society. The political risk is that sometimes a few government leaders are more inclined to label think tanks based on their views on certain issues. In this respect, they put the think tanks and opposition party in the same basket. However, in recent years the government has been very much more open and willing to accept dissenting or oppositional views on issues of national interest. The ability of the government to accept different views reflects a growing tolerance of Cambodian leaders facing not only the reality but also the diversity of perspectives on critical problems facing the country. As a result, the working environment for Cambodian think tanks has been significantly improved.

The achievements

Think tanks such as CICP and CDRI were a new phenomenon when they appeared in Cambodia. In the case of CICP, over the six years it has been functioning, it has been able to establish itself as an impartial source of information and a policy advisor to government ministries and institutions, especially with respect to policy debate and policy formulation. During this period, the Institute has sponsored and organised over 100 lectures, workshops, and national and international conferences on topical issues such as leadership, Cambodia's regional economic relations, foreign policy and national defence policy, and issues relating to the Greater Mekong sub-region, ASEAN and the broader Asia-Pacific region. Cambodia's reintegration into the region with the country's admission into ASEAN in April 1999 has made policy-oriented think tanks such as CICP more valuable than ever to the present coalition government, regional organisations such as ASEAN, and civil society organisations in Cambodia.

Moreover, Cambodian think tanks and civil society institutions have been conducting numerous training programs to contribute to the human resources development and capacity building of Cambodians. The country suffers from a serious shortage of human resources due to the loss of intellectuals in war and genocidal revolution. In the 1990s, Cambodia has relied extensively on international consultants to help to execute some of its development programs. Most of the international consultants were paid under the technical assistance programs of various bilateral and multilateral donors. Cambodian civil society has also utilised international consultants to strengthen its programs and activities. However, overdependence on international consultants could result in some critical challenges. First, most international consultants are expensive and could mop up all technical assistance. Second, there is a need to build local capacity and to ensure that there is a transfer of knowledge and skills from the international consultants to local experts. Third, there is a need to use available local experts first. In the area of training initiatives and programs, CICP has undertaken to train Cambodian government officials, the staff of the national assembly, personnel from civil society, students, and individuals from the private sector in order to upgrade their knowledge and expertise on a variety of topics. These areas include leadership, negotiation skills, economic development, the Asian Free Trade Area (AFTA) and other aspects of ASEAN regional integration, multilateralism and international affairs.[4] Training is a vital component of most Cambodian think tanks because the need for human resources development is great.

At the same time, Cambodian think tanks have been conducting research projects that contribute to policy inputs in the government, the national assembly and civil society. Since its inception, CICP has conducted research on national, regional and international affairs related to Cambodia's foreign policy, economic development, democracy, peace and conflict resolution, and election issues, as well as in terms of the development of civil society and Cambodia's participation in ASEAN and AFTA. Research findings have been made available to government officials and the general public through numerous publications. In August 1999, CICP inaugurated its home page in order to have information about the work of the institute accessible to the world at large. While these have been the achievements of recent years, the challenge ahead is to continue to expand activities and improve the quality of work.

The strategic importance of networking

In terms of underlining the importance of creating links and maintaining networks with similarly minded regional institutions, think tanks in Cambodia have joined sub-regional and regional networks. For instance, CICP joined the network of regional think tanks known as the ASEAN Institutes of Strategic and International Studies (ASEAN–ISIS[5]) in April 1997. Comprised of institutes from each ASEAN member country with the exception of Brunei and Myanmar, ASEAN–ISIS serves as a vital forum for the exchange of ideas on issues affecting ASEAN, the Asia-Pacific region and the broader international community (see Kraft 2000; Noda 2000: 167–93). This regional network of premier think tanks has proved its merit with respect to providing timely policy recommendations at gatherings of top-level ASEAN officials (Katsumata 1999; Ronas 1999: 207–17).

ASEAN–ISIS memoranda have been influential in making the case for ASEAN involvement in Cambodian reconstruction through technical assistance such as language and professional training for Cambodian bureaucrats (Hernandez 1997). Moreover, for CICP, its inclusion in this regional network of think tanks means a strategic window on the outside world, where it can engage in policy debate and joint research, access other sources of funding support, collect documents and materials for its library, and pool resources and experts in different fields. CICP's involvement in the various activities and meetings of ASEAN–ISIS – a leading 'track-two' institution in the Asia-Pacific – has not only helped put CICP on a bigger map but also exposed CICP staff, researchers and board members to regional and international experiences in the important work of track-two diplomacy. It is important to note that CICP's membership in ASEAN–ISIS preceded Cambodia's full admission into ASEAN by two years. In this respect, CICP could be described as an important intermediary institution that helped to generate support more widely in Cambodia and the region for the entry of Cambodia into ASEAN. At the same time, it could be argued that ASEAN–ISIS was not only a means for Cambodia to open itself to the wider world but also a strategic venue for other ASEAN actors to engage Cambodia. This is a two-way process for Cambodia and ASEAN.

Moreover, in 1997 CICP joined another network, the Development Analysis Network (DAN). Made up of institutes from Cambodia, Laos, Vietnam and Thailand, DAN was established to promote collaborative research and networking in the countries of mainland Southeast Asia, especially among those transitional economies. At present, DAN consists of seven members and is active in joint research.[6] While it is too early to look at the benefits of its involvement in the DAN, what is important is the fact that CICP has attempted to push forward its research agenda and research capacity building within this network. DAN is primarily a research network in a sub-regional context in which Cambodian research institutions such as CICP and CDRI have tried to look at some key economic issues. So far, DAN has been able to engage in two research projects. The first was a collaborative research effort looking at the impact of the Asian financial crisis on Southeast Asian transitional economies, especially the four new members of ASEAN – Cambodia, Laos, Vietnam and Myanmar. The second project, which only started recently, is a labour market study. This project is vital given the sensitivities and problems facing Cambodia and other new members of ASEAN regarding the labour situation. For Cambodia, the important approach to DAN is to look at Cambodia in relation to a sub-regional framework, especially in economic and social issues.

In addition to these two networks, CICP has continued to work closely with other institutions outside the framework of ASEAN–ISIS and DAN through its bilateral relations and on a project-by-project basis. Nevertheless, it is clear that networking can help to strengthen the relations of like-minded think tanks, improve the quality of collaborative work and enhance constructive dialogue and consultation. There are numerous opportunities for dialogue in the Asia-Pacific region (Morrison and Evans 1995) in which CICP and other Cambodian institutes can seek participation. European think tanks such as the International Institute of Strategic Studies and Chatham House in Britain, the Foundation for Science and Policy in Ebenhausen, the Friedrich–Ebert–Stiftung, the Konrad Adenauer Stiftung and the German Society for Foreign Affairs in Germany, and the Institut Français des Relations Internationale (IFRI) among many others have established research links to institutes in the region (Maull 1995). In many respects, these links preceded European Union interest in these organisations, which has been instituted through the Asia–Europe Meeting (ASEM) to which Cambodia is seeking entry. A number of schemes, such as the Asia–Europe Foundation's 'people-to-people exchanges,' provide ample opportunities for further engagement with the international community and regional partners (Yeo 1999).

The future role of think tanks in Cambodia

Cambodia's socioeconomic and political society has made progress in many respects between the 1993 election and the present. This has been accomplished in spite of many obstacles, challenges and setbacks. The brief outbreak of fighting in Phnom Penh in July 1997 undermined the confidence of the donor community, resulting in the suspension or in some cases outright termination of development assistance to the country. In addition, the problem of continued conflict with the Khmer Rouge guerrillas was not resolved until 1998. Fortunately, such setbacks have been offset to some extent by other factors. The current coalition government, which was formed as a result of the successful 1998 election, is a more viable and thus more stable government than the coalition formed after the 1993 election. Additionally, since 1993, the Royal Government of Cambodia has committed itself to pursuing a market-oriented economy and creating one of the friendliest investment climates of any country in the region. Overall, Cambodia has made improvements in all vital social indicators, as noted in the 1998 United Nations Human Development Report.

This is not to say that there is not more to be done or that there are no daunting tasks ahead for nation building. Many more obstacles need to be overcome, and many issues remain outstanding, especially concerning national development. In this regard, CICP and similar think tanks continue to have an important role in helping to rebuild and restructure the country by providing valuable and relevant information to specific government ministries and the general public. Numerous outstanding issues will require close monitoring and analysis over the coming months and years. Perhaps the most notable of these issues, and one garnering worldwide attention, concerns the manner in which the forthcoming trial of former Khmer Rouge leaders will be conducted. Much scrutiny will be given to this event in terms of whether justice will be served according to international standards. Another current issue that has brought pressure upon the government from donor countries concerns the demobilisation of the country's 150,000-strong armed forces and the future role of the military in Cambodia. Another key issue concerns the impact of the Asian crisis and the economic development of this country given the current stage of the economy and the integration of Cambodia into ASEAN and AFTA.

It is anticipated that towards the end of 2000 or early 2001, the first commune and district elections in Cambodia's history will be organised. Debate has ensued over the manner in which these elections will be conducted in order to ensure that they are free and fair. Other issues that will be in need of policy analysis and debate concern the role of the newly inaugurated Senate, the new legislation planned to establish an NGO law, the national poverty reduction strategy and Cambodia's foreign policy and diplomatic efforts to bring the country into organisations such as the World Trade Organization (WTO), Asia-Pacific Economic Cooperation (APEC) and ASEM. At the same time, there is a need to follow up closely on the current process of East Asian integration, ASEAN Plus Three (ASEAN-10 plus China, Japan and South Korea).

Ongoing issues specific to Cambodia remain with respect to the government's attempts to curb corruption and efforts to increase its revenue base by improving tax collection. Similarly, there is the question of whether the present coalition government will be able to maintain the stable and open environment in which it now functions. For the immediate future, there are also issues that will have an impact on Cambodia as well as beyond its borders, with repercussions regionally and internationally. These issues include the effects of globalisation and non-traditional security or transnational issues such as the environment, trafficking in drugs and humans, illegal migration, and small arms proliferation. The evolving security threat is not of a traditional nature in terms of being exclusively military but is transnational in character. Current phenomena such as population growth, non-sustainable development patterns, unregulated population movements and transnational crime are particularly pertinent in the Southeast Asian region. The combination of unmitigated population growth and non-sustainable development has caused rapid environmental degradation, with the ensuing effect of creating resource shortages that could result in increased possibilities of food scarcity. Ever-increasing migrations of people within the countries of Southeast Asia have put an added strain on governments in terms of providing more jobs and services, as well as possibly heightening cultural and ethnic tensions.

Cambodia's re-entry into the international community is likely to mean that globalisation trends will have a more abrupt impact on the country's political, economic and social institutions. However, Cambodia has a young population (50 per cent below the age of 18) that will be more accepting of rapid change and embrace it accordingly. Another aspect of Cambodia's demographics to be considered in this context is that the country will experience an estimated 50 per cent growth in population in the next ten years, putting pressures on all sectors of Cambodian society. The complexity of these human security issues in a rapidly changing, technology-dominated age can then be aggravated further by the inexperience and inability of countries to deal with them. The possibility of failure in terms of devising solutions and applying appropriate measures to address these issues adequately is then intensified.

In the light of the challenging issues outlined above, it is clear that the Cambodian think tank community will have to become more involved. The question remains as to whether Cambodian think tanks have sufficient capacity to address the multitude of complex issues confronting the country effectively. There is no doubt that these issues are putting more pressure not only on the think tanks but also on civil society organisations as a whole. To be sure, Cambodian think tanks have limited staff, skills, resources and funding to carry out necessary research projects. In order for them to be more effective and more dynamic, they would have to strengthen their research capacity and expand their resource bases.

Think tanks will have to cover more ground and more issues. While there is no direct competition among the think tanks because of their areas of specialisation or policy niches, in the past few years there has been a move towards collaborative research. For example, CICP and CDRI have been working together in the DAN framework to carry out research projects jointly. CICP and CDRI are undertaking another joint research project on labor markets. The trend is that more think tanks may have to team up to work on collaborative research projects, pooling together the available experts and resources in the country.

Government leaders do make informal suggestions or direct requests for policy studies concerning certain policy issues when they need more policy inputs. Similarly, from time to time government officials comment positively on the role and work of think tanks in Cambodia and provide feed-back on studies or institute strategies. For example, CICP has received a number of comments concerning its work in the past seven years. Some have said that CICP should invite more government officials to its meetings. Still others have suggested that CICP should work more closely with government institutions. In fact, CICP has welcomed all the suggestions and feedback from government ministries, public institutions and other organisations so that the quality of its activities and research agenda could be improved to meet the changing needs of society. In this context, like other think tanks, CICP strives to remain relevant and take on the challenges.

Thus it is evident that the role of think tanks in Cambodia is vital in terms of making government leaders and law makers, as well as the private sector and the general public, cognisant of all aspects of issues affecting them, especially the impact of globalisation and regionalism. Policy analysis and vigorous debate will continue to be the cornerstone by which policy-oriented institutions such as CICP carry out their mandate. Striving to build human resource capacity through training and workshops will also continue to be an avenue by which Cambodian think tanks and civil society institutions will contribute and thrive. Disseminating information through distribution of the think tanks' publications and use of the 'information highway' as well as hosting lectures and conferences will ensure that the information gleaned by the research institutes and their policy recommendations are made known to as wide an audience as possible. In undertaking these challenging tasks, Cambodian think tanks and civil society organisations help to create a constructive and non-confrontational process for rehabilitating and rebuilding one of the world's newest democracies.

Notes

1   Kao Kim Hourn wishes to acknowledge the contribution made by Michael Barton and Din Merican. The views expressed here regarding CICP and Cambodia are solely his and do not necessarily reflect the position of the institutions with which he is affiliated.
2   Up to January 2000, the Cambodian government estimated that the number of local civil society organisations (more commonly known as NGOs) exceeded 400. The Council for the Development of Cambodia (CDC), a government institution, estimated that a total budget of $82.85 million would be spent by civil society organisations in 1998 (see Royal Government of Cambodia 1998: 1).
3   From the outset, think tanks founded by politicians usually suffered political labeling and suspicion by people in general and by other political leaders specifically. Without a transparent, non-partisan approach, think tanks in Cambodia may be subject to question by political parties and others, and their long-term survival may not be guaranteed.
4   See background information on CICP at http://www.cicp.org.kh.
5   This organisation consists of the Cambodian Institute for Cooperation and Peace; the Center for Strategic and International Studies, Indonesia; the Institute of Foreign Affairs, Laos; the Institute of Strategic and International Studies, Malaysia; the Institute for Strategic and Development Studies, the Philippines; the Singapore Institute of International Affairs; the Institute of Security and International Studies, Thailand; and the Institute for International Relations, Vietnam.
6   This organisation consists of the Cambodia Development Resource Institute, the Cambodian Institute for Cooperation and Peace, the Central Institute for Economic Management of Vietnam, the Institute of Economics of Vietnam, the National Economic Research Institute of Laos, the National Statistical Center of Laos and the Thailand Development Research Institute.

References

Al Qaq, Z. and Baskin, G. (1999) 'Creating a think tank partnership between conflictual partners: attempts to influence adversarial governments in developing policies of peace making', paper presented at the Global Development Network Conference, Bonn, 5–8 December.

Hernandez, C. G. (1997) 'Governments and NGOs in the search for peace: the ASEAN–ISIS and CSCAP experience', paper prepared for the Alternative Systems Conference, 'Focus on the Global South', Bangkok, 27–30 March. [http://www.focusweb.org/focus/pd/sec/hernandez.html]

Kanter, J. (1997) 'The future role of media in peacebuilding in Cambodia', CICP Lecture Series Report No. 13, Phnom Penh: Cambodian Institute for Cooperation and Peace.

Kao, K. H. (1999a) *Grassroots Democracy in Cambodia: Opportunities, Challenges and Prospects*, Phnom Penh: Cambodian Institute for Cooperation and Peace.

Kao, K. H. (1999b) 'Emerging civil society in Cambodia: opportunities and challenges', Conference Working Paper Series No. 2, Phnom Penh: Cambodian Institute for Cooperation and Peace.

Katsumata, Hiroshi (1999) 'The track two network and security cooperation in the Asia-Pacific: an analysis of the ASEAN–ISIS, Asia-Pacific Roundtable, CSCAP', an unpublished manuscript.

Kraft, H. J. S. (2000) 'ASEAN–ISIS and the dilemma of track two diplomacy in Southeast Asia,' *Security Dialogue*, forthcoming.

Maull, H. W. (1995) 'European think tanks discover Asia', *NIRA Review*, spring. Accessed at http://www.nira.go.jp/publ/review/95spring/maull.html

Mengin, F. (1997) 'Taiwan's non-official diplomacy', *Diplomacy and Statecraft* 8(1): 227–48.

Morrison, C. and Evans, P. (1995) 'Enhancing cooperation among policy research institutions in Asia-Pacific', JCIE Papers No. 18, Japan: Japan Center for International Exchange.

Muhamet, M. and Gashi, L. (1999) 'A think tank in Kosovo', paper presented at the Global Development Network Conference, Bonn, 5–8 December.

Muravchik, J. (1996) 'The role of think tanks, NGOs, and advocacy groups in influencing public policy,' CICP Lecture Series Paper No. 7, Phnom Penh: Cambodian Institute for Cooperation and Peace.

Noda, Makito (2000) 'The role of nonstate actors in building an ASEAN community', in Sekiguchi Sueo and Noda Makito (eds) *Road to ASEAN-10*, Tokyo and New York: Japan Center for International Exchange.

Ronas, M. C. (1999) 'ASEAN–ISIS as a forum on regional policy issues: a Philippine perspective', in K. H. Kao and J. A. Kaplan (eds) *Dynamo or Dynamite: Cambodia's Future in ASEAN*, London: ASEAN/Academic Press.

Royal Government of Cambodia (1998) *Non-governmental Organizations in Cambodia*, Phnom Penh: Council for the Development of Cambodia.

Shai M.-C. (2000) 'Elite politics and China's policy towards Taiwan', PhD dissertation, Department of Politics and International Studies, University of Warwick.

Stone, D. (2000) 'Private authority, scholarly legitimacy and political credibility: think tanks and informal diplomacy', in R. Higgott, G. Underhill and A. Bieler (eds) *Nonstate Actors and Authority in the Global System*, London: Routledge.

Urizar, C. (1999) 'Institutional reforms: the modernization of the executive branch in Guatemala', paper presented at the Global Development Network Conference, Bonn, 5–8 December.

Yeo, L. H. (1999) 'ASEM: Beyond Economics', *Panorama* 4: 5–38.

8   Post-communist think tanks

Making and faking influence

Ivan Krastev

Introduction

The think tank explosion is a remarkable feature of the reform decade in Central and Eastern Europe. The birth rate of independent policy research institutes in the post-communist countries is higher than in most other places in the world. Their media visibility is impressive. Their charm is irresistible. The number of studies on their ideas and influence is growing (Quigley 1997; Struyk 1999). There is a general feeling that post-communist think tanks are a powerful illustration of the critical link between democracy and development. A journey through the web pages of Central and Eastern European public policy institutes gives the impression that papers and conference reports produced by independent researchers are valuable fragments of the inside story of the transformation of the communist system. In the virtual reality of the web, think tanks appear serious, influential and knowledgeable. But are post-communist think tanks influential in the non-virtual world? Who are they, and what are the sources and limits of their influence?

In its second edition of *Think Tanks in Central and Eastern Europe: A Comprehensive Directory*, Freedom House (1999) lists 101 independent public policy research institutes that are non-profit, independent or autonomous with respect to governments and political parties and visible in the policy process.[1] Not all of the organisations included in the directory are 'real' policy institutes. Some would feel more at home in a directory of NGOs or advocacy groups,[2] others are part of the Academy of Sciences in their countries,[3] while one inclusion, Hungarian GKI, is a consultant company.

In post-communist societies, a think tank is something everybody hears about but nobody actually knows much about. In the academic literature, most experts agree that notion is a slippery term. Diane Stone (1996) has called 'think tank' an 'umbrella term that means different things to different people'. It is precisely the vagueness of the definition that makes think tanks a 'fashion' in the post-communist policy environment. In Eastern European dictionaries there is no word for 'think tank'. The introduction of the phrase 'think tank' into the vocabulary of policy makers is the one indisputable achievement of independent post-communist public policy institutes.

Studying think tanks

Theoretical interest in the think tank phenomenon historically has come through two separate roads. Researchers of institutes such as Kent Weaver (1989) with Jim McGann (2000), as well as James Smith (1991), were interested in explaining why and how think tanks emerged and why think tanks (or at least some of them) are important. They focus on distinguishing independent public policy institutes from academic research centers, government research units and lobbying groups. They have explained what makes a think tank successful and why independent policy institutes have flourished in America for many years, have survived in Europe and could never be born in Japan. Researchers into this organisational phenomenon were interested in how think tanks are managed, who funds them, who quotes them and whom they try to influence. The rise of conservative think tanks in the USA convinced many that revealing the mystique behind think tanks is necessary for an understanding of why many Western societies made an ideological right turn in the 1980s.

Contrary to those who research institutes, researchers into the policy process view think tanks not as part of a question but as part of an answer (Hall 1990). Through a study of policy institutes they have tried to answer the question: how do ideas influence policy? Introducing theoretical notions such as 'policy community', 'advocacy coalitions' (Sabatier 1991), 'discourse coalitions' (Hajer 1993) and 'epistemic communities' (Haas and Haas 1995), researchers of the policy process try to figure out the infrastructure that makes ideas powerful. These researchers stress the social functions of think tanks in the utilisation of knowledge and not their organisational specificity. Researchers of institutes (and not researchers of the policy process) prevail in the study of Central and Eastern European think tanks, and it is easy to explain why. In post-communist countries, new ideas did not come from think tanks. After being exported to Central and Eastern Europe by the International Monetary Fund (IMF), the World Bank and Western foundations, think tanks became the local repositories for these ideas.

All the recently published studies on Central and Eastern European think tanks (Quigley 1997; Struyk 1999; McGann and Weaver 2000) are implicitly or explicitly comparative in nature, basing their analysis on a more or less fixed point of departure. That is, they all try to interpret post-communist policy research institutes through the experiences, performance and philosophies of American think tanks. Such an approach is legitimate in many respects: for a long time, think tanks were perceived as typically, if not exclusively, American institutions (Weaver 1989). It is the American environment of policy making marked by fragmentation and the separation of executive and legislative power, the American mistrust of federal bureaucracy, the weak American party system, the American philanthropic tradition, and, finally, the American tax regime that has made policy research institutes such as the Brookings Institution, the American Enterprise Institute and the Center for Security and International Studies into autonomous and influential players. Anglo-Saxon culture, founded upon the power of rational argument, is the proper context for an understanding of the power of twentieth-century independent policy research institutes in both the USA and Britain.

It is not coincidental that in Eastern Europe, Latin America and Asia no one tries to translate the term 'think tank' but rather adopts the concept in its English wording, with all the cultural connotations that this implies. It is also not by chance that influential think tanks are still exceptional in Germany and France. The American stamp on the think tank phenomenon and the fact that it is mainly North Americans who write and publish on the role of independent policy research institutes has resulted in the prevalence of an 'NGO paradigm' in the analysis of post-communist think tanks.

At the heart of the NGO paradigm is the notion that independent policy research institutes are mainly educational institutions that contribute to the opening up of policy making. The conviction that open public debate contributes to the quality of policy decisions constitutes think tanks as powerful instruments for the democratisation and rationalisation of the policy-making process. It is this democracy-building function that has encouraged the export of American think tanks over the past ten to fifteen years. What the United States is eager to export in the post-Cold War world is not only particular economic policies (deregulation and competition) and values (multiculturalism and respect for human rights) but also a specific process of policy making. The structure of policy making has been recognised as the primary guarantee of the sustainability of reforms.

That many Central and Eastern European think tanks have been sponsored by American sources (both private and government) has contributed to the dominance of the NGO paradigm. The popularity of the NGO approach in analysing post-communist policy institutes is also rooted in the fact that it is a donor-serving approach. Most studies focus on the management of the institutes, their funding, public relations strategies, media–government relations and sustainability. Post-communist policy institutes have been the object of well-designed studies, but they have been studied much more as management units than as policy units. They are funded as NGOs and are treated as a special kind of NGO.

The present study takes the 'policy road'. We are not interested in the performance of particular institutes, or in those that are really influential and those that fake influence; we are not even interested in measuring the influence of independent public policy institutes in Central and Eastern Europe. Our study is fascinated by the question: why are think tanks influential in transition policy making, and what future awaits them?

The policy landscape

The great majority of independent Central and Eastern European policy institutes have been founded since 1989. In communist times, there were policy-oriented research entities, but they were not free to define their research agendas. The state dominated the pre-1989 policy landscape (Krastev 1999).

The newly created independent policy research institutes were designed as an instrument for promoting democratic and market reforms. They were a negation of and alternative to the old policy research units. The state think tanks were big; the new institutes are small. The old institutes were hierarchical; the new ones are horizontally structured. The state think tanks were conformist; the independent think tanks declared themselves dissident. The state think tanks were Marxist in their ideology; the new think tanks are predominantly liberal.

Words like 'free market', 'liberal', 'democratic', 'civic' and 'reform' are present in the names of thirty-one of the institutes to be found in the Freedom House directory. Judged by the titles of their papers, post-communist think tanks look like laboratories for democracy and market reforms. Judged by their personnel, think tanks are academic refugee camps populated by young and middle-aged researchers, some with political experience. Judged by their reports, think tanks are an influential policy advisor to both governments and the public.

But is it enough to be pro-reform in a time of reform in order to be influential? A closer look at the research and advice capacity of the institutions surveyed gives a more complicated picture. It is true that more than 1,000 researchers are employed in the Eastern European policy institutes on a full-time basis. It is also true that out of the 101 think tanks only sixty-eight have annual budgets in excess of $50,000, and less than fifty employ more than five in-house researchers (Freedom House 1999). The post-communist think tanks do not focus on long-term academic research, and their studies are neglected in academic circles. Few publish in respected journals. Few publish academic books. Only twenty-nine of the institutes devote more than half of their time to policy research. The Western model of think tanks as 'universities without students' cannot be applied to the newly created policy institutes (Weaver 1989). Institutes committed seriously to research are either big entities like the Institute for World Economics in Budapest, which is part of the Hungarian Academy of Sciences, or very small research groups that work on one or two projects. Foreign policy and security think tanks and some of the institutes working in the field of economic policy are the only clearly specialised post-communist research entities. Most of the others cover various research and policy areas. The fashion for catch-all parties in transition politics is complemented by the fashion for catch-all, grant-driven think tanks.

The sources of funding are the other distinctive feature of the post-communist 'fifth estate' institutions (Goodwin 1995). The majority of funding comes from Western sources, and the financial sustainability of these institutes after the withdrawal of external donors will be highly problematic. Western funding also reflects on the research agenda of the independent institutes. The key words of donors are easily traced in the conference titles and research projects of the post-communist think tanks.

Interviews with policy makers from the region do not support claims about think tanks' impact on decision making (Struyk 1999). In some countries, policy makers are friendly to the policy institutes (Bulgaria, Hungry, Albania). In other places, policy makers are less friendly, but in both cases the research coming out of think tanks is not regarded as an important contribution to policy making. Politicians are ready to recognise the influence of the think tanks' directors but not the influence of the think tanks' research. As in many other parts of the world, it is think tanks that claim their own importance, and it is the media that are most ready to believe them.

An approach to the question of influence

Comparing the strength of the think tank community in different post-communist countries with the success of the reform process in each shows that there is no direct correlation between the spread of think tanks and the success of reforms. Think tank communities in unsuccessful Albania and semi-successful Bulgaria are much stronger than in successful Estonia or the Czech Republic. The type of the constitutional regime and the type of the party system do not explain why some Eastern European countries enjoy better-developed think tank communities than others. The parliamentary regime in Bulgaria and the semi-presidential regime in Poland appear to be equally hospitable for institutionalising independent policy advice. Intellectual and political traditions are the other non-explainer. Why some post-communist societies are more friendly towards think tanks than others, and why Western donors invest more in think tanks in some places and less in others, are open questions.

In the present study, we construct the post-communist think tank as an 'ideal type' and discuss the role and influence of this 'ideal post-communist think tank' from three analytical perspectives:

- direct think tank influence on the work of governments and parliaments;
- think tank influence on the general policy debate (Simon James in Chapter 9 of this volume defines this influence as 'atmospheric'); and
- the future of the post-communist policy institutes in the new global context.

Think tanks are self-reflective bodies, and their story can best be narrated as a process of constant redefining and readjustment to the policy environment. The study of think tanks should not be divorced from the art of inventing and reinventing think tanks. At the heart of the present study is the understanding that a certain period in the development of post-communist think tanks is over and it is time to think about the future.

The policy advice market: think tanks and governments

In the American think tank literature, the Heritage Foundation has always been cited as a model for success in direct influence on the governmental agenda and government decisions. Heritage, alongside the Hoover Institute and American Enterprise Institute, was viewed by many as the kitchen cabinet for the early Reagan presidency (Stefancic and Delgado 1996). In the early stages of the reforms, several post-communist think tanks had their fifteen minutes of fame of 'being Heritage'. The Lithuanian Free Market Institute played a critical role in introducing a currency board in the country. The Center for Social and Economic Research worked closely with Balceroviz's team in achieving macro-economic stabilisation in Poland. In Sofia, the Center for Democracy, the Institute for Market Economics and the Center for Economic Policy drafted important pieces of legislation that were subsequently adopted by the Bulgarian parliament.

However, it was not the strength of the independent research but the weakness of the other players in the realm of post-communist policy making that made think tanks influential players. The lack of confidence between the reform governments and the administration that they inherited, the weak policy capacities of the political parties, the unwillingness of the universities and academies of science to commit themselves to policy research, and the underdeveloped business community are the main factors explaining the 'Heritage moment' of the post-communist think tanks.

Think tanks versus government research units

Research and advice produced within the administration traditionally shape governmental decision making. Zbigniew Brezinski and Henry Kissinger, who have lived on both sides of the think tank–government line, are the first to accept the marginality of independent policy advice in the day-to-day work of administrations (Abelson 1998). However, it was the decline of the research and advice capacity of governmental agencies that promoted think tanks as an important source of policy advice in Central and Eastern Europe. There were four reasons for the decline of the advice capacity of the administration:

- Funding for policy research was reduced in the early years of transition;
- Many research units were shut down, and personnel changes were implemented;
- The policy agenda of the governments changed radically, and expertise in 'planning economic activities' became irrelevant; and
- Former communist research units did not enjoy the confidence of the new democratic governments.

In the context of the declining research and influence capacity of in-house research, post-communist think tanks capitalised on their major competitive advantages: that is, informal relations with the reform governments, access to foreign funding and media visibility. The ideological closeness between post-communist governments and the most prominent research institutes was the critical factor in think tank influence on the governmental process.

It was informal access to the new governments or presidents that provided institutes like CASE in Poland and the Institute for Public Policy in Bratislava with the opportunity to influence government decisions and shape the government's agenda. These 'moments of influence' indicate a common pattern. Post-communist policy institutes are more influential during the first year of the government, and their influence declines steadily with the passage of time. The ideas of think tanks are more welcome in the areas of foreign policy and monetary policy than on local government or privatisation. Vested economic interests and an environment of corruption dramatically reduced the influence of think tanks in those areas where the redistribution of wealth was taking place. However, the increasing influence of the leaders of think tanks often results in them joining government administrations. The fact that ministers, even prime ministers, are serving on the boards of the policy institutes does not necessarily lead to greater openness with respect to independent policy advice.

Foreign advisors were the other source of legitimacy and influence for the newly emerging Central and Eastern European think tanks. In the euphoria of the first years of transition, many prominent Western economists took on the burden (and honorariums) of advising Eastern Europe on reforms. All needed local partners or at least translators, and it was these support groups around foreign advisors that constituted the first generation of policy institutes. The emergence of independent policy institutes in Central and Eastern Europe can be interpreted as the replacement of foreign advisors with local 'free advice brigades' (Stone 1996: 10).

Think tanks versus political parties

In the European context, political parties perform many of the functions that think tanks perform in the American policy context. German and Dutch political foundations or institutes attached to the parties are doing classical think tank business (policy research, educational activities, pressure for ideas and policies). The influence of German political foundations on the formation of party systems in Central and Eastern Europe was founded on an argument that political parties will be major rivals to think tanks in the effort to capture the imagination of both governments and publics. In the medium term, this argument is correct. But in the early years of transition, political parties focused on building a national infrastructure and played the role of a client rather than a competitor to the think tanks.

Central and Eastern European think tanks were successful on several occasions in influencing policy making inside the parties. The best example of a successful intervention in party life is the introduction of primary presidential elections in Bulgaria. A decision was taken on the basis of a policy paper produced by the Centre for Liberal Strategies in Sofia. The paper was widely debated by the party leadership and was finally adopted. In general, it was the weakness of the parties in supporting policy research that helped the independent institutes to gain significance and visibility. In the initial stage of their formation, political parties did not invest in research capacities. The anti-intellectual make-up of most post-communist parties helped think tanks to keep their monopoly over policy research.

Think tanks versus university and business

Universities and their research institutes remained non-players in the policy advice market in the first reform decade. Under the old regimes, there was a wall between the academic world and the world of policy making. In order to secure independence and moral comfort, the best scholars chose internal emigration, consciously avoiding research areas that had policy relevance. Aristocratic disregard for empirical work was another characteristic feature of many pre-1989 policy science departments.

In the early years of the transition, policy-interested researchers either entered politics or joined the think tanks. It was the marginality of the academic community in the process of policy making that stimulated the flourishing of the think tanks. Universities were not a competitor but a resource for the independent policy institutes.

In Western societies, business is a major producer of policy-relevant knowledge, and a number of research institutes and lobby companies now populate the market for policy advice. Advice coming from business is not viewed as interest-free, but it contributes by gathering new data and linking research to the policy process. In the early years of transition, private business did not have either the capacity or the interest to enter the realm of research. This allowed think tanks to function in a policy environment that was favorable for the presence of 'free advice brigades'.

Capitalising on their informal contacts with the new holders of power, their intimacy with Western institutions and growing financial support from outside, the first generation of post-communist think tanks achieved influence on the day-to-day work of governments rarely enjoyed by even the most prominent American and European think tanks. In the period 1990–98, some think tanks played the role of collective advisors to reform leaders. It was the charisma of the think tank guru more than the quality of research that distinguished the influential from the less influential think tanks. It was the success and visibility of this first generation of independent post-communist policy institutes that enthused Western donors with the will to fund think tanks.

But 'first-generation influence' had its limitations. The market for policy advice changed with the second wave of reformers who gained office. Both political parties and government agencies closed the door on outside advice, shifting their preference to in-house advice. In 1997, the Bulgarian government declared that only legislation drafted by the government enjoyed governmental support. Without making such declarations, many other governments have limited the opportunities for outside influence on decision making.

Ten years after the beginning of transition, think tanks operate in a policy environment that is more competitive than the one in which most of them started. The quality of in-house government research has improved. Governments feel more comfortable listening to in-house researchers than to their ideological allies in the think tanks. The reform process moved from strategy making to implementation, for which think tanks often lacked the relevant information. The fifteen minutes of 'being Heritage' seemed to be ending.

The new moment in the post-communist environment is the emergence of the second generation of state tanks. Most of these institutes are registered as independent entities, but they are closely affiliated to governments, and their research agendas are shaped by governments. The Moscow Center for Strategic Development, established in 1999 by the then prime minister, today President Vladimir Putin, is the best-known post-communist state tank. The Center, headed by German Graff, was entrusted by Putin with developing a strategic vision for Russia in the next twenty years to be adopted by the government. George Soros, a prominent American philanthropist and the best-known supporter of post-communist think tanks, took the initiative in founding and funding public policy institutes attached to the reform governments in the region. His idea was to assist reform governments in the field of European integration (although it is too early to assess their impact on government decisions). Such institutes were established in Bulgaria, Romania, Slovakia, Ukraine and some other countries.

This general overview of the present policy environment in most Central and Eastern European countries suggests that think tanks have consolidated over the last decade, but their opportunity to influence governments on a day-to-day base has decreased. It is influence on the general public and not 'decree making' that keeps think tanks in the policy game.

Think tanks and the policy debate

In her book on the role played by think tanks in shaping public discourse, Diane Stone (1996) makes a distinction between the two ways in which think tanks can exert influence on the policy-making process. In the narrow sense, 'influence' can be defined as the direct impact of policy research institutes on legislation or particular government decisions. 'Influence' in the broader sense can be interpreted as 'the power to change the prevailing consensus or to preserve the existing climate of opinion' (*ibid.*: 110) Most think tanks came into existence as part of an effort to change the prevailing policy paradigm. Conservative think tanks in the United States were a fundamental part of the new policy consensus that came to prevail under President Ronald Reagan. It was the very idea of changing the earlier consensus that shaped the structure and strategies of the 'new partisan' institutes like the American Enterprise Institute, Heritage and others. 'Third way' think tanks such as DEMOS and the Constitution Unit were instrumental in Tony Blair's 'velvet revolution' in Britain.

In the case of Central and Eastern Europe, think tanks did not prepare the policy reversal that took place in 1989–91, but they were critical in explaining it. The object was not to change the *status quo* but to preserve the policy paradigm that had been established in 1990–91. The policy paradigm established for economic management in 1990–91 was anti-Keynesian in its orientation and had its origin in the Washington consensus centering on privatisation, limited state intervention in the functioning of the market, support for private initiatives and anti-inflationary measures (Williamson 1990).

The policy role of the think tanks in Central and Eastern Europe cannot be understood outside the dominance of the Washington consensus. It was the new liberal orthodoxy that captured the imagination of the best-known institutes in the region. 'The 1990s were distinctive in one significant respect: the world was under the impression that a clear and robust consensus existed about what poor countries should do to become more prosperous' (Naim 2000). In the first transition decade, most of the post-communist think tanks acted as institutions of the Washington consensus. The influence of think tanks is one of the reasons why populist movements, which resulted in electoral victories for former communist parties in Lithuania and Poland in 1993 and Hungary and Bulgaria in 1994, did not manage to change the existing policy paradigm.

One of the major roles that the think tanks of the region have played in the politics of transition is to maintain the original prescription coming from the IMF and World Bank as the only legitimate or workable policy paradigm. During this period, think tanks such as CASE in Poland and the Institute for Market Economics in Sofia, alongside other groups, were responsible for preserving the liberal consensus against strong political forces pressing to establish a new populist one. The radical pressure for market solutions emanating from the think tanks was intended to compensate for the weakness or even the absence of pressure for further reforms on the part of local business communities. It was the ability of the think tanks to shape public opinion that secured their influence on the policy-making process. In a situation in which senior policy makers spent hours reading the newspapers rather than memos, policy analysts capitalised on their good relations with the media and established themselves as voices to be heard.

The loyalty of most think tanks to the liberal orthodoxy secured them a place in the policy establishment and made think tanks favorite partners for Western donors and international organisations. Think tanks were not agents of innovative policy thinking or troublemakers in the policy debate; they were guardians of the liberal orthodoxy as the only scientific way to make policies that secure economic prosperity. The reunion of development economics and mainstream economics that took place in the 1990s was the theoretical background for the alignment of think tanks with the donors' paradigm.

It is the management of expert discourse and not in-depth research that has empowered think tanks. In interviews made for this paper, several senior policy makers in Central and Eastern Europe assessed the role of the think tanks in terms contrasting with their self-image. Think tanks see themselves as policy innovators and policy advisors. Policy makers view think tanks mainly as 'communicators', useful appendixes to government press offices.

The debate on the introduction of a currency board in Bulgaria in 1997 is a classic example of the legitimacy of the 'PR view' on policy institutes and their impact on public debate. The hyperinflation in January 1997 earned Bulgaria the status of 'one of the worst-managed countries in Europe'. Society was shaken by a profound political crisis. The public was expecting radical policy solutions. The IMF suggested the introduction of a currency board as the only guarantee for a successful anti-inflationary policy in the existing political environment. But what is a currency board, and how would its introduction affect social and economic life? Neither the political elite nor the public had the answers. Think tanks pretended to have them.

The way Bulgarian think tanks filled the knowledge vacuum in the currency board debate exemplifies the strength and weakness of the post-communist policy institutes. Bulgaria enjoys a highly developed and competitive think tank community. In the early period, six or seven institutes were active in the field of economic policy. Their strategies for informing the public and influencing the debate were identical – translating and popularising literature on currency boards, organising conferences, inviting international experts and writing op-eds. The missing element in this impressive chain of activities was real research. With one notable exception, none of the think tank economists had been working on the problems of currency boards before 1997. The energy invested in rallying for the currency board solution deprived think tanks of time to research the advantages and risks of the debated policy in the Bulgarian political and economic context. The campaign of Bulgarian think tanks in favor of a currency board, a decision that radically reshaped the monetary policy of the country, was not supported by any empirical local research done by the Bulgarian think tank community. Policy institutes started to educate the public five minutes after they had educated themselves.

The currency board example can be used as an illustration of the role of think tanks as agents of policy fashion. Policy fads and fashions are one of the ways in which ideas influence policy making (Hood 1994). The exhaustion of a certain policy paradigm and the process of trivialisation of some policy ideas is a legitimate reason for policy change. Ideas, like clothes, have seasons. The change of one policy paradigm is not necessarily due to the emergence of new problems inconceivable in the old paradigm, or the emergence of new data that question the wisdom of the day. The fashion explanation stresses the fact that the public and especially a democratic public periodically insists on change or a repackaging of the ruling ideas and re-dressing of the policy language.

Think tanks were major agents in the rhetorical revolution that took place in Central and Eastern Europe at the beginning of the 1990s. They were instrumental in cleaning up the ruins of the Marxist paradigm and in overcoming suspicion about the market and private property. Think tanks found the right arguments to convince the public of the failure of the old system. The strange disappearance of the economic and political ideas behind the 'human face of socialism' can be explained only if we underline the radical change in policy language that was promoted by the IMF, the World Bank and think tanks. In order to be heard, the opponents of the reforms were forced to speak the language of the Washington consensus. But speaking the language of the opponent is a recipe for ridiculousness. It is the exhaustion of the Washington fashion that challenges post-communist think tanks today.

Imagining think tanks

The major policy dilemma in the early 1990s was the choice between shock therapy and gradualist policies. This initial strategic policy choice was viewed as decisive for the success of reforms. Ironically, the discovery at the end of the first transition decade is that the controversy over shock therapy versus an evolutionary approach does not help us to understand why some countries are progressing better than others in reforms. Both shock therapists and gradualists can recount their success stories: in the case of the shock therapists, it is Poland; in the case of the gradualists, it is Slovenia and Hungary. Both schools can supply respectable arguments for their disaster cases. But outside the intellectual debates and the 'war of egos', some common-sense conclusions can be drawn.

The common feature of successful countries is not the commonality of the policies adopted but the consistency in policy implementation. The common feature of the failed transitions is the lack of policy consistency. What in our view makes Poland a success story and Russia a horror scenario is the existence of policy consensus in Poland and the absence of policy consensus in Russia. The existence of professional policy deliberation much more than the adopted policy package is the explanation for success. It is the discovery of policy consensus as a critical precondition for the success of reforms that will reformulate the interest in think tanks. It is described elsewhere in this volume as a capacity for 'policy learning' or 'consensual knowledge'. The lesson of the reform decade is that the structure of policy making is a better indicator of economic success than the initial policy choice.

Three other great discoveries that have been made in the past few years shattered the world of the post-communist think tanks and reshaped their mindset and practical behaviour:

- The discovery of globalisation;
- The discovery that the Washington consensus is no longer a consensus; and
- The discovery of the importance of institutions.

The discovery of globalisation

The discovery of globalisation was strange, painful, exciting and unavoidable. In the early years of the transition, post-communist think tanks were preoccupied with the uniqueness of the transformation of Eastern Europe. Post-communism was the theoretical and existential context in which policy institutes have been working. The discovery of globalisation changed the perspective and reformulated the global condition as a condition of reform and transition. The paradigm of catching up with the West, which was widespread in post-communist societies at the beginning of the 1990s, was replaced by 'catching your own chance paradigm', which stresses comparative advantages and innovative approaches. In the words of Thomas Friedman: 'globalisation is not a phenomenon. It is not just some passing trend. Today it is the overreaching international system shaping the domestic politics and foreign relations of virtually every country' (1999: 7). Exposing think tanks to global problems resulted in redefining research areas and applied methodologies, and reassessing the power of networking and exchange of ideas.

Globalisation redefines what is and what is not policy-relevant knowledge. Two decades ago, theoretical speculations like Ulrich Beck's (1992) notion of the 'risk society' were doomed to be arrested in the seminar rooms and intellectual journals. Nowadays, the notion of the 'risk society' has been adopted by the insurance industry, and Beck is invited to lecture to business executives. Globalisation gave new meaning to comparative studies and, as Joseph Stiglitz indicates in Chapter 2 in this volume, reopened the debate: are the best policies best for everybody? The debate on the control of capital flows and the prescription for a currency board in Indonesia following the Asian crisis illustrates the uncertainty with respect to common understandings considered to be universally good policies.

The other side of discovering globalisation was the discovery of global governance. Although this phenomenon is evolving and contested, it gives new meaning to the concept of influence. In the global world, for a think tank to be important it is not enough to be influential with its own government or with its own public. Local think tanks were seduced by the opportunity to exercise influence on a global scale.

The discovery of Washington confusion

The realisation of the non-consensual nature of the Washington consensus came painfully in Central and Eastern Europe. The ideas referred to as the Washington consensus were never undisputed among economists. However, the very success of the phrase indicates that it captured a certain mood in economic circles at the end of 1980s. 'The Washington consensus' became a metaphor for the general turn towards the market as the only system for securing economic prosperity. It was the Asian crisis and the Russian crisis from August 1998 that generated profound doubt regarding the theoretical foundations of the policy ideas preached by the IMF and others.

The other critical argument for revising the Washington consensus in Central and Eastern Europe was public pressure. General support for IMF policies declined dramatically in comparison with the early 1990s. The failure of the transition decade to produce sustainable economic growth and a better standard of living in most of the countries of the region created a desire for new and different policies, or at least for new policy language. The only way to save the pro-market policy consensus was to repackage it. The public was eager for new policies, or at least for new arguments in support of the old policies.

The discovery of institutions

The discovery of the second generation of obstacles to reforms can be conceptualised as the discovery of the institutions. It was also the discovery of a local context. The failure of orthodox liberal policies in countries like Russia forced economists and political scientists to focus their attention on the institutional environment and on the role of the state in implementing market reforms. It was the weak post-communist state and not the 'big state' that emerged as the major obstacle to transforming the economy and society. Transfers of property failed to deliver efficiency and competitiveness. Empirical studies have shown that in a weak institutional environment there is no difference in quality in the performance of privately and publicly owned industrial companies. Legal order and law enforcement were reconceptualised as preconditions and not consequences of the functioning of the market.

Reinventing think tanks

In response to the pressure brought by these discoveries, major shifts in the behavior and strategies of the leading Central and Eastern European think tanks can be predicted: first, a shift to networking and transnational activity, accompanied by the adoption of the latest information technology; second, a shift from their role as paradigm keepers to that of consensus builders; third, a shift in research agendas and renewed interest in local knowledge.

The reinvention of post-communist think tanks as global players, consensus builders and institutes of local knowledge is at the center of the last part of our study, which is a reflection on the possible future of post-communist think tanks and not a report on the present state of affairs. The assumption here is that the study of think tanks should not be divorced from the art of imagining them. Accordingly, the following pages map a vision for the post-communist think tanks in the next decade. Networking, consensus building and local knowledge are the pillars of our imaginary journey in the future of Central and Eastern European policy institutes.

Networking

There are six trivial reasons why think tanks should network. However, there are more than six non-trivial consequences of networking on a global scale. But the trivial reasons first:

1   *Influence* – many of the major problems faced by post-communist Europe today are beyond the powers of national governments. Environmental problems, EU accession, NATO enlargement and a political settlement in Kosovo are all issues requiring regional approaches and regional strategies. Most of the think tanks in Central and Eastern Europe are sensitive about these global issues, and many of them have done a lot of work on European integration and NATO enlargement. Yet, in order to make a difference, policy institutes need partners. It is not enough to come out with a thoughtful policy paper. No matter how well thought-out a single think

tank's paper might be, it will not change the outlook on the Kosovo situation. At best, such a paper could be labeled 'interesting'. Only a joint paper, authored by the most influential institutes in the region, could be viewed not only as interesting but also as important. In order to be influential outside their national borders, think tanks must form coalitions to develop common policy positions.

2   *Common ground* – countries in transition share a common agenda. Most of the policies implemented in Poland or Hungary are debated in Bulgaria and Romania. In this context, think tanks from different parts of the region can be extremely useful to one another. As Stella Ladi notes in Chapter 11 of this volume, a common policy heritage creates considerable potential for knowledge sharing and policy transfers.

3   *Legitimacy* – in some countries, governments tend to ignore the advice coming from independent sources. One strategy to overcome that indifference and neglect is to work in cooperation with well-respected and visible partners. Well-known institutes from the region could be instrumental in promoting their new partners in countries like Macedonia and Albania, where think tanks are still exotic flowers.

4   *Training* – a good policy analyst requires more than an impressive academic background. He or she needs training. Working on joint projects with the best analysts from the region and the West is the best option for training analysts and reforming entire institutes.

5   *Utility* – think tanks not only need to network, they are born to network. Compared with governments and universities, independent policy institutes are in the best position to benefit from networking – they are smaller, more flexible and much more likely to adopt winning managerial and research practices from abroad. Most policy analysts also share a common language: English.

6   *Quality control* – cooperation between institutes with different levels of development will serve to improve the quality of policy products. Institutes like CASE or the Institute for Public Affairs will not associate themselves with low-quality projects.

The non-trivial consequence of networking is the discovery of the regional perspective and the constitution of policy institutes as agents of regional vision. The regionalisation of the policy perspectives of post-communist think tanks can best be illustrated by the example of the establishment of Europe South-East Policy Forum in July 1999. It was followed by the founding of the South East European Policy Information Network, consisting of more than seventy policy institutes from southeast Europe. The network came as a response to the crisis in Kosovo and the need to reconstruct the Balkans. The major challenge of reconstruction was that while a regional approach was promoted as the major paradigm by the Stability Pact adopted by the donor countries, neither governments nor the public were ready for such a development.

The rhetorical support for a regional approach was confronted by hard reality. And the hard reality is that southeast Europe exists as a unified region only from the outside, and only in security terms. Neither the pattern of investment nor the pattern of trade nor the ideologies of the nation-states in the region support the vision of the Balkans as a distinct political, economic and cultural region. The Ljubljana Declaration of more than twenty local think tanks marked the first attempt to create a regional vision for the Balkans and to promote European integration as the only sustainable post-conflict strategy for the region.[4] The declaration was composed around the policy paper developed by the Center for European Policy Studies in Brussels. The media success of the South East European Information Network and the readiness of local think tanks to work in a network regime marked a major break with the early years of transition, when think tanks were eager to communicate with Western policy centers but were sceptical of the advantages of regional cooperation.

The new opportunity for think tanks is to use regional and international networks not simply as intellectual partnerships but as instruments for increasing their policy influence by targeting the international media and international institutions. The new power of NGOs created new clients for the policy research coming out of the think tanks. The early model of government-centered think tanks is being replaced by society-centered think tanks endorsing strategies for coalition building.

Consensus building

The crisis of the Washington consensus as an intellectual and ideological framework represents another pressure for refashioning post-communist think tanks. The failure of the reform policies in many countries and the public criticism of IMF prescriptions have forced think tanks to adopt positions different from those of the first years of change. With first-generation reforms, think tanks were on many occasions critical of the implementation of the policies of the Washington consensus, but they were not looking for different policies. The cure for reforms was declared to be more reforms, not different reforms. Most prominent think tanks still view their policy position as being guardians of orthodoxy, but their strategies have started to change.

Think tank interest in the issues of good governance and transparency are the best illustration of the new wave of problems and agendas considered by the policy institutes. The explosion of anti-corruption research signals three new movements in the research interests of policy institutes: a focus on implementation and not just on policy formation, interest in institutions and a change in rhetoric.

Anti-corruption studies helped the policy institutes to change their already exhausted pro-market rhetoric and rally support for the new generation of reform efforts. In their essence, the key anti-corruption policies prescribed by the post-communist think tanks represent a repackaging of the essential policies from the beginning of the 1990s: deregulation, competition and privatisation. But in discovering corruption, the policy institutes rediscovered the role of the state and its significance in the time of transition. The anti-corruption focus of institutes represents the new importance of policy consensus in the major issues of development. It marked the opening of the think tanks to other NGO groups and strategies for making advocacy coalitions. Coalition 2000 in Bulgaria is a good example of this approach.[5] Anti-corruption campaigns became the meeting point between aspirations for more democracy and the aspiration for opening markets. Investors and democratic activists endorsed each other in the name of fighting corruption.

At the beginning of the 1990s, think tanks conceived their role as being proponents of the best policies. At present, they have a chance to focus on reforming the policy process rather than arguing for the best policy. The environment in Central and Eastern Europe is not particularly favorable for policy deliberations. Political life is highly polarised, and the culture of the rational argument is not the dominant one. European integration and the visible presence of international factors in the policy process put many constraints on the success of policy deliberations. The integration agenda speeds up the legislative process, so the time available for enlightened policy debates is much shorter in Central and Eastern Europe than in the USA or Western Europe. Eastern European countries are adopting much more new legislation than their Western European counterparts. In this hot-house context, the IMF and the World Bank use their power to narrow the range of plausible policy options.

These constraints are not new ones. What has changed is the behaviour of think tanks. At the beginning of the 1990s, most think tanks tried to educate and influence public understanding about the policies and priorities of the IMF. Today, we can see the opposite trend: an attempt on the side of the think tanks to explain the concern of the public to international players, both private and public. This reversal is a promising one. The IMF and the World Bank need not only friendly partners but also knowledgeable critics based in Central and Eastern Europe.

Local knowledge

In *War and Peace*, Tolstoy wrote: 'No battle takes place as those who planned it anticipated. This is the essential condition'. This is an essential condition not only in war but also in day-to-day policy implementation. No policy is implemented as those who planned it anticipated. Local knowledge is the knowledge of why policies that were designed to succeed have failed or are going to fail.

The understanding of why and how certain policies have worked or failed in the local environment is now central to the research of many think tanks. Local knowledge is knowledge of the idiomatic structures of life, and think tanks try to articulate that knowledge. This can be seen mainly in the changes in the research agenda and the move in the direction of local coalition building. In the early years of their existence, economics-oriented think tanks neglected research areas like the informal sector and social capital formation. A fascination with grand universal solutions was responsible for the fact that think tanks position themselves more as commentators than as participants in the policy process. Theoretical papers on fundamental policy choices and inadequate case studies helped to create a name for institutes and generate publicity but presented problems in local application and implementation. The disregard of the local is no longer fashionable.

Think tanks have discovered 'the local'. Knowledge of the policy environment is an essential part of their research. Think tanks are better positioned in this realm of knowledge mainly through their direct involvement in the policy process. In a spectacular way, the functioning of corruption is a demonstration of the power of local knowledge. With corrupt transactions, it is not the biggest bribe that gets the prize. Instead, you should know to whom you should give the money, when to give the money, how to give the money and exactly how much money to give in order to be successful. Think tanks as institutes of local knowledge should share their knowledge of the corrupt system. Wall Street analysts will know what is a reasonable offer for a company going for privatisation. A successful think tank should be able to study the chances of this privatisation deal taking place in accordance with the rules, who are the invisible interested parties, how much this privatisation will cost on the corruption market, and what should be done to sell the enterprise with maximum profit for society. Having this knowledge, think tanks can be experts in the everyday local politics of reform.

Conclusion

Reflecting on the role and performance of the independent policy institutes in Central and Eastern Europe, we can observe important transformations. Post-communist think tanks have entered the process of reinventing themselves. The conditions that made them the fashion of the day are no longer present. Governments have improved their own research capacities, and political parties have invested in policy research. Western financial support is on its way home. The rhetoric of the Washington consensus is exhausted. And words like 'market' and 'reform' have lost their power. But it is the end of old paradigms that present the post-communist think tanks with a new window of opportunity.

In the early years of transformation, think tanks capitalised on their ideological proximity and informal access to the new reform governments in promoting ideas and policy solutions. For a long period, think tanks did not educate the public but simply changed the framework in which post-communist societies debated their problems. All this is history. Think tanks should cross the border of the nation-states and free themselves from their intellectual arrogance in order to initiate global networks and advocacy groups. Going global is the only way to rediscover the art of locality. And rediscovering the local context is the only way for think tanks to make a difference with the power of their knowledge.

Notes

1 Freedom House's directory does not include Russia, Slovenia, Armenia, Georgia and Moldova. It also does not cover the Central Asian republics of the former Soviet Union.
2 For example, Atlantic Club of Bulgaria and the Women in Black movement in Yugoslavia.
3 See the Institute for World Economics in Budapest.
4 Further information can be found at http://www.seein.org
5 Further information can be found at http://www.online.bg/coalition2000/

References

Abelson, D. (1998) 'Policy experts and political pundits: American think tanks and the news media', *NIRA Review*, summer. [http://www.nira.go.jp/publ/review/]

Beck, U. (1992) *Risk Society. Towards a New Modernity*, London: Sage Publications.

Friedman, T. L. (1999) *The Lexus and the Olive Tree*, New York: Farrar, Straus & Giroux.

Freedom House (1999) *Think Tanks in Central and Eastern Europe: A Comprehensive Directory*, Freedom House.

Goodwin, G. (1995) 'The fifth estate: institutions for extending public policy debate in emerging democracies' in G. Goodwin and M. Nacht (eds) *Beyond Government: Extending Public Policy Debate in Emerging Democracies*, Boulder, Colo.: Westview Press.

Haas, P. M. and Haas, E. B. (1995) 'Learning to learn: improving international governance', *Global Governance* 1(3): 255–85.

Hajer, M. (1993) 'Discourse coalition and institutionalisation of practice: the case of acid rains in Great Britain', in F. Fischer and J. Foster (eds) *The Argumentative Turn in Policy Analysis and Planning*, London: UCL Press.

Hall, P. (1990) 'Policy paradigms, experts and the state: the case of macroeconomic policy-making in Britain', in S. Brooks and A.-G. Gagnon (eds) *Social Scientists, Policy, and the State*, New York: Praeger.

Hood, C. (1994) *Explaining Economic Policy Reversals*, Buckingham: Open University Press.

Krastev, I. (1999) 'The liberal estate,' *East Central Europe/Europe Du Centre Est* 26(1).

McGann, J. and Weaver, R. K. (eds) (2000) *Think Tanks and Civil Societies: Catalysts for Ideas and Action*, Somerset, NJ: Transaction Press.

Naím, M. (2000) 'Washington consensus or Washington confusion', *Foreign Policy*, spring: 87–101.

Quigley, K. (1997) *For Democracy's Sake: Foundations and Democracy Assistance in Central Europe*, Washington: Woodrow Wilson Center Press.

Sabatier, P. (1991) 'Political science and public policy', *PS: Political Science and Politics* 24(2): 144–56.

Smith, J. A. (1991) *The Idea Brokers: Think Tanks and the Rise of the New Policy Elite*, New York: Free Press.

Stefancic, J. and Delgado, R. (1996) *No Mercy: How Conservative Think Tanks and Foundations Changed America's Social Agenda*, Philadelphia: Temple University Press.

Stone, D. (1996) *Capturing the Political Imagination: Think Tanks and the Policy Process*, London: Frank Cass.

Struyk, R. J. (1999) *Reconstructive Critics: Think Tanks in Post-Soviet Bloc Democracies*, Washington: Urban Institute Press.

Weaver, R. K. (1989) 'The changing world of think tanks', *PS: Political Science and Politics* 22(2), September: 563–73.

Williamson, J. (1990) 'What Washington means by policy reform', in J. Williamson (ed.) *Latin American Adjustment: How Much Has Happened?* Washington: Institute for International Economics.

9 Influencing government policy making

Simon James

Introduction

This chapter looks at the relationship between think tanks and governments, and particularly at the influence that think tanks can have on government policy. It is written from a slightly peculiar combination of personal perspectives, since I have seen think tanks from three angles. In the 1990s, I had direct experience of their work in Britain, where they had become active and influential over the previous two decades. At various times, I studied and wrote on them from an academic viewpoint (James 1993), briefly did some voluntary research for one of them, and on joining the civil service found myself working in areas (first education, then constitutional reform) that were the subject of their activities.

I 'exported' this experience to the OECD in late 1998 when I joined the staff of its SIGMA programme. The Programme for Support for Improvement and Management in Central and Eastern European Countries – universally known as SIGMA – provides help on the reform of central government in the countries of Central and Eastern Europe.[1] The OECD has shown an occasional interest in think tanks over the years. As I prepared to write this article, I called up the old OECD files and was surprised to discover that they contained early drafts of the well-known seminal articles on think tanks that Professor Yehezkel Dror published in the early 1980s (see notably Dror 1984). These were among the few published outputs of a wider project by the OECD focusing on governments' internal 'thinking capacity'. While the project was time-limited, it is interesting that the OECD saw the potential importance of think tanks a decade before other international organisations (and a pity that its interest was not sustained).[2] SIGMA itself works only with governments, but in the mid-1990s it devoted an issue of its journal *Public Management Forum* to non-governmental organisations, including some useful articles on the value to governments of think tanks and kindred bodies (for example, Kimball 1997). Indeed, it is impossible to work in the field of policy making in Central and Eastern Europe without encountering think tanks that seem as influential, if not more so, than their counterparts in Western Europe, not least because they often come into being with their governments' support and encouragement.

The particular concern of this chapter is with the junction at which think tanks and governments meet, and the influence that the first can have on the second. My premise is that think tanks exist to influence public policy, directly or indirectly. This point is by no means universally accepted. True, a survey undertaken by the Global Development Network in advance of its inaugural 1999 conference found that three-quarters of think tanks surveyed attached high importance to influencing government, but if you look at it another way, the remaining quarter accorded this a low priority. As a paper by the National Institute for Research Advancement of Japan to the inaugural GDN conference (Nagata and Nakamura 1999) pointed out, the effort that think tanks devote to disseminating their findings varies from country to country: very little in Japan, a great deal in the USA. I have trouble understanding what purpose is served by a think tank that does not disseminate its research. This influence can be direct, or can operate at several removes, for example by seeking to influence expert or public opinion. If such think tanks are operating in a vacuum, one might well ask why donors should fund them.

For all that, most think tanks do perceive themselves as being in the business of influencing policy, but the nature of their relationship with government remains an under-explored area. This paper tries to cast some light on this, drawing on personal experience. I first describe the modes and means of influence of thinks tanks as I observed them in the United Kingdom, and I then consider the implications of these for the geographical area in which I now work, Central and Eastern Europe.[3] However, I suspect that there is much in the following observations that will apply to the operation of think tanks throughout the world.

Modes of influence

To my mind, there are three principal modes of think tank influence on public policy: (1) 'atmospheric influence'; (2) 'targeting short- to medium-term agendas'; and (3) 'micro-policy research'. To a greater or lesser degree, these modes of influence are relevant to policy making at the national and sub-national levels of governance, as well as in supranational domains.

Atmospheric influence

Atmospheric influence involves influencing the general climate of thinking about policy and as a result changing the framework of reference of policy makers. This can happen on a number of levels. Occasionally the whole framework is altered. A good example is the long process by which free-market think tanks in the United Kingdom retrieved the concept of the market from obsolescence and reintroduced it to become the dominant political idea of the 1980s (Cockett 1994; Stone 1996). Throughout the 1950s and 1960s, these think tanks were crying in the wilderness, yet in the 1970s their message struck a chord with Mrs Thatcher and her associates, who reoriented their whole pattern of thought towards it. When the Conservative Party came into government in the 1980s it rearranged the entire framework of government policy to match.

Such a universal reordering of the entire pattern of thought is rare: these rearrangements of the political cosmology occur perhaps only two or three times a century. It is also possible for atmospheric change to operate within a discrete policy sphere. For example, consider how thinking has been changed on environmental issues in recent years. Admittedly, the main drivers of these changes have been a combination of scientific investigation and pressure group activity (Mathews 1996), but think tanks and research institutes have played a significant role in a number of Western European and North American countries.

Third, there can be a change of thought on a particular issue. A good example of this was the work carried out by the Policy Studies Institute – one of the longer-established research-oriented British think tanks – on the nature of British unemployment in the 1980s. Previously government and media treatment of 'the unemployed' tended to regard them as an amorphous group, with no distinction more sophisticated than that allowed by such traditional economic classifications as structural and frictional employment. The PSI study offered more subtle insights into the character of unemployment and its different causes and effects. By offering policy makers a better understanding of the problem they faced, it put them in a position to develop more sophisticated and effective remedies.

Whichever of these three levels we look at, there is a tremendous potential for think tanks to participate in, and even lead, the debate that leads to such atmospheric changes, which alter policy makers' framework of thought about a particular issue or range of issues. By altering the boundaries of the politically possible, think tanks potentially change the range of possible policy outcomes.

Influencing the medium- or short-term agenda

At any given time, every national government has an agenda of issues on which it wishes to act (for example, election promises to reform the tax system, or apply for EU membership) and issues on which it is obliged to act whether it wants to or not (for example, to counteract the spread of HIV/AIDS, or legislate to adapt to electronic commerce). There are always forces at work seeking to alter the agenda: to add items, delete items or have a particular issue accorded greater or lesser priority.

This facet of think tank activity has grown enormously in recent decades. To some extent it can be attributed to the growth of 'advocacy' think tanks, which by their nature were created to alter the public agenda, and which to do so have adopted proselytising tactics that the more research-based think tanks have felt obliged to imitate. But, more generally, there seems to have been a (slightly belated) realisation by think tanks of all kinds that dissemination is an essential dimension of their work. In the UK, for example, shrewdly timed papers on savings and pensions reform by free-market think tanks in the 1980s led to legislation on new forms of saving and put the issue of pensions reform on to the British government's agenda (Cockett 1994).

It is no longer enough simply to publish weighty research tomes and wait for their ideas to percolate slowly through the minds of government (or not, as the case may be). Active dissemination of ideas with a view to getting them put into practice is necessary, not least to convince the funders of think tanks that their money is achieving something. Hence, for example, think tanks' greater use of informal meetings with policy makers; testimony to committees of the legislature; participation in conferences; and above all the use of the media to promote research findings. (A useful catalogue of such activities is in Abelson 1998.) The successful use of the media by think tanks tends to feed upon itself: if think tanks provide good copy, media appetite for their output grows and think tanks find it easier to gain media time to air their views, with a consequently higher chance of influencing the public agenda.

Micro-policy research

Think tanks do on occasion go further and also engage in working through the detail of policy: in charting the implications of different courses of action, and in working out some of the intricacies of the changes required. This is not an easy mode of operation for think tanks, for it requires quite detailed knowledge of how a particular area of policy works. This type of approach may therefore tend to be used mainly by think tanks with a narrow and more specialist focus. Two British examples are the Institute for Fiscal Studies, which keeps up a sustained and expert commentary on economic issues, and the Constitution Unit, which carried out a lot of work exploring the detailed implications of the Labour Party's commitments to constitutional reform. The latter's work proved most valuable when the Blair government took office.

However, this approach has also been used successfully by multi-disciplinary think tanks that have found the right expert to write for them. The micro-policy approach can be particularly useful if there is resistance to an initiative from vested interests claiming that it will not work. For example, free-market think tanks in Britain first agitated for the privatisation of certain enterprises in the 1970s and early 1980s, a time when privatisation was not taken seriously by most people. After the privatisation of British Telecom established privatisation as a viable item on the political agenda, think tanks argued for the privatisation of individual enterprises – coal, steel, shipbuilding, the railways – arguing the case for each on its own merits.

There are overlaps between these three modes of operation, and the same think tank may use different modes of operation on different issues. For example, on economic issues, right-wing think tanks in Britain moved from trying to influence the general atmosphere of political thinking in the 1960s and 1970s ('we should privatise') to more specific work on influencing particular aspects of the government's agenda ('specifically, we should privatise the railways') and, on occasion, into micro-policy work in the 1980s and 1990s ('this is how competition between different rail operators could be made to work'). But on social issues, where right-wing ideas made far less impression at this time in Britain, think tanks found themselves far more confined to the 'atmospheric' approach because they could not make the breakthrough that enabled them to move to debate at a more detailed level.

The value of think tanks to governments

Why should governments pay any attention to think tanks? The reasons are numerous.

The research capacities of political parties are often weak. In few countries do parties have the research facilities that would allow them to develop well-considered policies – a lack that is felt particularly by parties in opposition. To some extent, the work of think tanks can fill this gap.

When in government, politicians may find that the civil service machine resists their political ideas. This was certainly so in Britain in the 1970s and early 1980s. The civil service was sceptical of the free-market ideas of the incoming Thatcher government, and its exceptionally strong policy-making capacity did not easily adapt to the more radical mould of thinking that Mrs Thatcher and at least some of her ministers favoured. Hence a reliance on external think tanks to provide some of the raw materials for radical policy making, which the civil service was then asked to refine.

Conversely, it can be that the civil service has a weak policy-making capacity and is therefore unable to undertake the analysis and development work neces-sary to turn ministers' ideas into reality. This is a common problem in Central and Eastern Europe, where the former communist regimes heavily discouraged any attempt at policy analysis or creativity within ministries, which existed solely to execute the decisions of the Party. An analysis by the SIGMA Programme of the policy-making capacities observed:

> Policy preparation within Ministries is often weak. There is no tradition in Ministries in engaging in policy analysis ... Little or no attention is paid to identifying different courses of action and identifying their consequences. At best this leads to sub-optimal policy-making; at worst, it leads to legisla-tion that proves unworkable when it is implemented ... Finance Ministry officials often lack the time or analytical expertise to provide proper budgetary appraisal, and often the broader economic impacts are not exam-ined ... although there are often legal requirements to assess social, environmental and other impacts, these are rarely complied with, partly for lack of time and skills, but mostly because there is no tradition of policy analysis within Ministries and, perhaps in some countries, a reluctance to accept responsibility for the advice offered.

> (James 2000)

To some extent, think tank work can fill the ensuing gap. Most usually this takes the form of accepting a plan devised by a think tank: for example, in 1996 the ruling party in Lithuania used the research and recommendations of the Lithuanian Free Market Institute to design its tax policy (Kimball 1997). Occasionally, however, a task can be taken out of the hands of the civil service and entrusted to a think tank. Examples of this known to the author are:

- An episode in which welfare reform was literally taken out of the hands of the responsible ministries and the policy was devised by a group of outsiders including think tank staff.
- The appointment of think tank staff to a commission of business people established by a prime minister to advise him on removing administrative obstacles to business development.
- The subcontracting to a think tank of the task of carrying out a full review of the remit, structure and staffing of all the ministries and central agencies of one country.

Quigley (1996) has termed this '[demonopolising] government control over the policy making process'. Perhaps 'government' is the wrong word, for in all three instances cited, the minister in charge of the policy set the parameters for the think tank's work and retained the final decision on the think tank's recommendations. But certainly think tanks have been used to remove policy formulation from the hands of the civil service. Not that civil servants in Central and Eastern Europe will necessarily react to such actions as violently as Western European civil servants. The weakness of policy analysis in those countries is to some extent a deliberate choice by ministry staff. Often there is a potent legal culture that tends to see policy problems as mere issues of regulation and legal drafting; there is a refusal to engage with policy substance. This often combines with an inability to grasp the distinction between political activity (in the party sense) and policy analysis (in the sense understood in Western Europe). Officials are often relegated, or often insist on relegating themselves, to administrative tasks, while any analytical work – because it is seen as 'political' – is referred up to a higher political level.

Think tanks have the supreme advantage, from a politician's point of view, of being 'deniable'. They can float ideas in which politicians may be interested but which they are uncertain about voicing publicly themselves. If public reaction is good, politicians can take up the idea; if not, they can repudiate or ignore it. Indeed, the most influential of British free-market think tanks in the 1970s – the Centre for Policy Studies, created by Margaret Thatcher and her associates before she became Conservative leader – enjoyed precisely that kind of relationship with her when she entered government. Its head described think tanks as outriders who, if they win the preliminary skirmish of ideas, allow politicians to move on to new ground (Sherman 1984).

Think tanks' relations with governments will always be delicate. Think tanks exist to influence policy makers, therefore they must maintain good relations with the government of the day, and a substantial portion of their output needs to address the government's current concerns. At the same time, independence of thought is their *sine qua non*; if they say nothing different or new, and if they do not sometimes highlight important but neglected issues, nobody has any reason to listen to them. Consequently, they must tread the fine line between, on the one hand, maintaining their independence in setting their own agenda and in determining the content of their advice, and on the other hand, tailoring their work to make it attractive and interesting to policy makers.

The means of influence

There are essentially two means of influence open to a think tank: public and private. The first uses the skills of public relations, the second the skills of government lobbying. All think tanks use both approaches, but the degree to which they rely on one rather than the other varies greatly.

The public approach usually follows a standard pattern. The think tank prepares a publication – usually a pamphlet by an expert or groups of experts – that sets out the idea the think tank wishes to propagate. This is publicised initially through press releases, press conferences and interviews and followed through by such media as press articles that summarise the arguments in the pamphlet; seminars to discuss its contents; providing experts from the think tank to speak on the issue on television programmes and at conferences, and so on. The US Agency for International Development's representative in Hungary has publicly advised think tanks that one of the skills they need to succeed is use of the media: 'Persistence and high visibility ensure that issues are constantly before the public' (Cornell 1996). If successful, this establishes the think tank as an influential (or at least newsworthy) source of expertise on the topic. The difficulty is that unless the idea meets with some response from policy makers it may die away. So think tanks have to become adept at finding different ways of propagating the same idea.

Such a public approach is, in the end, a scattergun technique. It is a good way of broaching a topic, but a more targeted approach is needed to engineer change. That is where the private approach comes in. It consists of targeting particular decision makers and selling the idea to them. Think tanks need to use the full range of lobbying tactics: identifying their main decision makers; finding out what their preoccupations and interests are; discovering their attitude towards the issue the think tank is promoting; submitting to them a short, reasoned case in support of the idea; and finding opportunities to meet them and press the idea on them.

Several points about these two means of influence are worth stressing. First, and of crucial importance, when arguing for an issue, there is no substitute for a reasoned argument backed up by evidence. Appealing to the political instincts of ministers is a sure way of catching their attention, but relying solely on this approach is not sustainable in the long term. It will occasionally succeed – it did in Britain in the case of the poll tax – but in the long term it is very likely to fail (as the poll tax ultimately did). One of the reasons that free-market think tanks caught the attention of Conservative governments in the 1980s and 1990s was that their often strident pamphlets coincided with the gut feelings of ministers. In many cases, their publications were long on assertion and short on evidence, and when examined in detail by ministers and their civil servants it quite frequently turned out that the assertions were not supported by the bulk of available evidence, or that their recommendations were unworkable, or both. The arguments of think tanks do not have to be underpinned by a wealth of detailed research, but they do need to be based on a solid foundation of evidence.

Second, it is important to pay attention to feasibility. Many policy ideas that look good on paper crash soon after take-off because they are not workable in practice (again, the poll tax comes to mind, but there are examples in every country). A think tank will get nowhere if it puts up ideas that will not work in practice. This is a particular need if the think tank is engaging in the 'micro-policy' approach, but it applies to all think tank outputs. At the same time, a think tank should avoid being drawn into the trap of engaging itself in the implementation of a policy, in the same way that it should avoid being drawn into doing the work of the civil service. It has neither the resources nor the expertise to undertake work on implementation, and such trespassing in a field that is rightly the work of government ministries can only lead to conflict and disappointment. However, this need not prevent it engaging in monitoring or evaluation of the policy as it is implemented.

Third, it is a great mistake to focus lobbying activities solely on the minister in charge of a ministry. Engaging the attention of the political head is important, and probably essential to gaining a foothold for the idea within the government. He or she will have the most important influence on a decision yet will also be extremely busy and will have little time to follow through the ideas. The framework for a policy discussion in the government will be set by less senior figures, by assistant ministers and the staff who make up ministers' immediate entourage. A great deal will depend on the attitude of the ministry's civil servants, who do a lot of the work to develop and implement the idea. Needless to say, the degree to which civil servants are actively involved in policy formulation varies from country to country and, while in the UK it is higher than in most, a think tank cannot afford to ignore ministry line staff in any democratic country. Any presentation of an idea should be addressed to all of these levels, and the fact that the civil servants will be examining the issue more from a technical and practical viewpoint only reinforces the need to present a clearly argued case firmly rooted in evidence.

All three of these points are well illustrated by the case, mentioned above, of the Lithuanian Free Market Institute's work on tax reform:

> After conducting extensive research, LFMI documented that one of the largest barriers to economic growth in Lithuania was its inhibiting tax system. To draw attention to this issue, LFMI invited leading domestic and international tax experts, government officials, parliamentarians and

journalists to a December 1995 conference focusing on the Lithuanian tax system.

During the conference, the participating government officials and parliamentarians were introduced to possible policy alternatives that could improve the effectiveness of the country's tax structure. LFMI capitalised on this new awareness by submitting, to the appropriate government offices, a comprehensive tax reform proposal that would, among other things, replace indirect taxation with direct taxation.

In the months following the conference, one of the participating government officials, Mindaugas Stankevicius, became Lithuania's Prime Minister. While developing his party's tax reform programme, he sought LFMI's advice and guidance about implementing some of the ideas voiced by LFMI at the conference and in their proposal.

The extensive research undertaken by LFMI provided the ruling party with well-documented, trustworthy data that could be used to further their political and economic goals. The co-operation between the ruling party and LFMI was not based on party affiliation, but rather on LFMI's innovative approach to solving problems inherent in Lithuania's tax system.

(Kimball 1997)

In short, the most efficacious approach for a think tank appears to be a 'triple-track' approach: that is, getting the issue into the public eye and keeping it there; using political contacts to arouse interest and response within the government; and making sure that all levels affected by the issue within the ministry are given a clear and rational statement of the case. The balance of effort between these three types of activity will depend on the issue, the personalities involved, the public response to the think tank's proposals and the degree to which the think tank can present its thinking as being on the same wavelength as that of the government.

Implications for Central and Eastern Europe

Much of the foregoing is drawn from my experience in the UK, but most of it applies to the countries of Central and Eastern Europe. However, there are obvious differences, including several advantages that think tanks in those countries have over their Western counterparts.

One of these advantages is precisely that experience in the West during the past two decades has proved that think tanks can have considerable influence. This has encouraged governments and international donors to fund them in Central and Eastern Europe. How many of these organisations now exist is open to question. A 1997 survey by Freedom House in Budapest identified 106 in eleven countries (Kimball 1997). Research by James McGann, more recent and covering more countries, identifies 342 (McGann 2000). Much turns on your definition of a think tank (a notoriously intractable question), but beyond question they are numerous, and many are funded from abroad.

A second advantage is the discovery by foundations and development agencies that think tanks can be relatively inexpensive. As recently as the early 1980s, in the studies commissioned by the OECD referred to above, Yehezkel Dror assumed that the necessary critical mass for a think tank was twenty to twenty-five staff. However, subsequent experience shows that a think tank needs far fewer staff – those in Central and Eastern Europe today typically have between five and ten. In part this is due to advances in information technology, but it probably owes more to the discovery that a think tank can usually draw on a wide circle of sympathisers to offer expert advice, and especially to write or comment on publications. The use of such a 'penumbra' of advisors has been a marked feature of think tank development in the United Kingdom – perhaps more so than in the United States, which has tended to rely more on large in-house salaried staffs. This makes them an attractive investment for donors, and – in theory at least – should make it easier for think tanks to attract core funding to finance their operations. They thus avoid the problem faced by many Western institutes, which have to rely on research contracts to pay their way and so have limited control of their own research agenda.

Quite apart from this purely practical issue, there is a tremendous opportunity for think tanks created by the ideological vacuum left by the revolutions of 1989. It is fair to say that they were caused more by the implosion of one idea, communism, than by the expansion of any other. While Western ideas have moved into the gap – liberal democracy, market economics, European unification – there is no single, simple, dominant theme. Indeed, the interplay of these three ideas can be particularly complex and unstable in a country in transition from communism. The rediscovery of a free-market imperative gave Thatcherite think tanks a simple song to sing in the 1970s. Today, in contrast, their counterparts in Central and Eastern Europe face far greater intellectual challenges in fashioning new strategic policy options. In that respect, their task is similar to, but far more difficult than, the task faced by left-leaning think tanks in Western Europe trying to define the nebulous 'third way'.

The weakness of the structures for policy debate in Central and Eastern Europe also opens up great potential for think tanks to influence public policy – in aggregate, probably more so than in Western Europe or North America. This weakness is due to the relatively deficient policy-making capacities of the civil services of many Central and Eastern European countries mentioned above. It is also due to the relative poverty in many of these countries of alternative sources of policy ideas and criticism, such as universities, and to the still underdeveloped state of civil society in many countries.

Because government capacities for policy analysis in Central and Eastern Europe are weak, think tanks need to promote not just new ideas but new ways of thinking and a higher quality of policy debate. This needs to include:

- Better policy analysis by ministries: for example, encouraging the examining of a range of policy options and the implications of each before initiating legislation. In contrast to the situation in the UK in the 1980s, when think tanks set out to challenge the civil service, in Central and Eastern Europe today the task is more to build it up.

- The involvement of a wider range of actors in policy debate. This is a facet of the generally accepted need to foster the development of civil society in Central and Eastern Europe. The position of think tanks in policy debates puts them in a good position to assist.
- The use of experience from other countries. This has long been a weakness in the West: examining ideas from abroad is comparatively rare. The westward orientation of post-communist politics in Central and Eastern Europe (encouraged by the funding of think tanks from Western sources) encourages a global approach to policy research.

Inevitably, the opportunities listed above bring problems with them. First, it is doubtful whether Central and Eastern Europe can sustain the present number of think tanks. Many have come into existence in the artificial circumstances of easily available international funding. It is a truism of international aid that donors tend to have relatively short time horizons. This money will start to dry up as the attention of international donors moves elsewhere. Most immediately, there is likely to be a rundown of funding in central and northeastern Europe as donors concentrate their efforts on the Balkans in the aftermath of the Kosovo crisis. The probable consequence would be a shake-out in the think tank world: a number of organisations will simply prove unviable. In one sense this could be a good thing: as Ivan Krastev points out in Chapter 8, many think tanks have attained influence not because of the quality of their work but because of the weakness of other actors in the policy-making sphere. Unfortunately, one cannot be certain that those who will go to the wall will be those whose work is of the lowest quality. The shake-out may come before some institutes generating good work have been able to consolidate their positions in their countries' policy-making landscape. And there is a possibility that those overseas donors willing to maintain funding may be prompted more by ideological motives – for example, promotion of bodies zealous about the free market – than by concern for the quality of a particular think tank's output.

Second, in the 'market of ideas' of Central and Eastern Europe, market mechanisms are underdeveloped. In particular, think tanks are likely to experience ownership problems in their relations with donors and with the government. With donors, because they inevitably have some agenda of their own, which can create tensions, a problem explored by Raymond Struyk in his recent study of think tanks in post-Soviet countries (1999). With the government, because ministers and civil servants will have little experience of dealing with think tanks. These policy actors may not know how to act as a customer for a think tank's work: they may have unrealistic expectations of what it can achieve; they may not know how to commission work effectively (writing a specification is quite an art); and they may not know how to make the best use of the output of think tanks once received. These problems will be compounded if the government actually helped to set up the think tank in the first place, as has happened in several cases. This is supported by empirical research undertaken by Struyk, who notes a striking difference between how policy makers perceive the influence of think tanks in interviews he conducted. Armenian policy makers were quite negative about think tanks, those in Bulgaria and Hungary were more neutral about their roles, whereas Russian policy makers were more positive.

Linked to this is a third difficulty, the danger that the small size of the policy-making elite in many countries may force the staff of think tanks into close proximity with the government whether they like it or not. Of the nineteen countries of Central and Eastern Europe, nine have fewer than 5 million inhabitants. This, combined with the shortage of analytical skills needed for policy development, makes it likely that governments will seek to enrol leading figures in think tanks as advisors, either formally or informally. This exacerbates the usual problem, described above, of keeping the right distance between government and think tank.

A fourth problem is that of the danger that the think tank, even if politically neutral (not all are), will be seen as politically engaged. Inevitably, part of the role of a think tank is to criticise. In all countries, some politicians react better to criticism than others. And in countries where civil society is still developing, there may initially be an inability to grasp that criticism of a government can be a constructive, not destructive, exercise. This problem may be magnified by the fact that because parliaments are more pro-active in Central and Eastern Europe, think tanks are likely to be drawn into a more open dialogue with them. Indeed, at least one think tank has entered into a formal agreement with a parliament to provide comments on draft laws promoted by the government. This can serve to raise the think tank's political profile in a way that the government may not appreciate.

Fifth, there is a danger in drawing too freely on examples from other countries. This can be a valuable and economical way of improving the quality of public policy. Governments rarely have the time to do this. In contrast, think tanks, can usefully make it part of the added value that they bring to policy debates. As Stone (2000) puts it:

> Their potential importance to the process is their concentrated ability to diffuse ideas by (1) acting as a clearing-house for information; (2) their involvement in the advocacy of ideas; (3) their well-developed networks – domestically into the political parties, bureaucracy, media, and academe; and (4) their intellectual and scholarly base providing expertise on specialised policy issues.

Greater ease of communication, especially the Internet, has greatly facilitated the exchange of ideas between think tanks in different countries and continents – an innovation like the Global Development Network is particularly helpful for this purpose. The countries of Central and Eastern Europe have also tapped into their diaspora of expatriates in other countries. Yet there are dangers in adopting ideas from abroad uncritically. In particular:

- Beware of adapting ideas from other countries that have not been trialed there. It is a valid criticism of many of the free-market ideas proposed by think tanks in Britain in the 1980s that, although they originated in the United States, they had not actually been put into practice there (for such a critique, see Marmor and Plowden 1991).
- Beware of transplanting ideas from abroad without adjusting them to local circumstances. The wholesale adoption of the 'agency' concept in the delivery of public services, often on the advice of proselytisers from the West, without adapting them to the local legal and political cultural mechanisms, has in some cases caused serious problems in Eastern Europe.
- Beware of adopting ideas from abroad without having the necessary infrastructure in place to support them. As Ivan Krastev indicates in Chapter 8, some of the privatisations in Central and Eastern Europe took place before adequate safeguards against abuse had been put in place, with unfortunate results.

Many of these points are dealt with by Joseph Stiglitz in Chapter 2. I echo his warnings on the perils of transplanting policy and agree that in this context, one of the most valuable tasks that think tanks can perform is not just to identify good ideas from abroad that can be transplanted to their own countries – a commendably economical approach – but also to examine them to see how well they worked elsewhere and what adaptations are needed to ensure that they transfer successfully to a different country. But I will add one slight note of dissent. Stiglitz' warning that care needs to be taken in transplanting ideas, and his effective horticultural metaphor – *nemawashi* – is a long overdue correction to a carefree 'one size fits all, one flavour cures all' approach. In the former Soviet bloc it has led to the equivalent of walnut trees being replanted in beds of concrete, not to mention telegraph poles being planted in herbaceous borders.

Yet there is an opposing danger: the cry that goes up in countries in transition that these ideas may be all very well in Western countries, 'but our country is different'. Sometimes the belief is genuine; sometimes it is the defensive reflex action of those with vested interests in the present state of affairs. The problem is familiar to those who lived through public sector reform in 1980s Britain, where the armed forces, the police, the social services, the lawyers and the medical profession all resisted change on the grounds that 'we are different'. To which the proper, and eventually effective, reply was: 'You are not different. Special, yes. Different, no. And although these changes will be adapted to your needs and particular circumstances, they will be implemented'. The difference when the same reaction arises in countries in transition is that their newly regained sovereignty can easily act as an additional barrier to reform. A national government can exercise coercive power over its own domestic interest groups; it is less easy for international organisations to engineer change through the persuasive-coercive power of conditions attached to a loan (or in the case of Eastern European countries, of the conditions attached to joining the EU). In short, the need to adapt change to suit the local climate, and to enable local ownership of that change, should not be allowed to become an excuse for endless prevarication and evasion of change. That is no remark in the abstract; it is based on this author's personal experience of blocked reforms in Central and Eastern Europe.

Sub-national and supranational activities of think tanks

This paper has concentrated solely on the impact of think tanks at the national level, but there is no reason, in principle, why they should not operate equally effectively at either sub-national or international level. The general impression from the Global Development Network conference was that activity at the sub-national level is not very common (a proposed panel on the subject was abandoned during planning due to lack of active interest). There are probably three reasons for this. First, since funding for think tanks is limited, their activity tends to focus on what is seen as the crucial decision-making level, which in most countries is the national level. Second, if the purpose of think tanks is to influence public policy, they will flourish at sub-national level only if there is a corre-sponding level of government with significant powers. Third, regional think tanks are likely to emerge only if there is a substantial regional economic base to sustain them. (There is a link between the existence of such regional economic centres and a federal system, but that link is neither simple nor automatic.) Italy, for example, has the majority of its big think tanks located outside Rome, in the major economic centres of Turin, Milan, Bologna and Naples (Radaelli and Martini 1998). This is in spite of the absence of a federal system and the fact that Italy's regional tier of government is of recent creation and is still finding its role.

These three factors tend to combine to ensure that regional think tanks are unlikely to emerge in small countries, and likely to be found only in larger coun-tries with (1) wealth and (2) a system of federal or strong regional government. So among the few countries where think tank activity is discernible at sub-national level are Germany, Switzerland, the USA and Canada, which have federal systems of government and decentralised funding structures. It is notice-able that in the United Kingdom regional think tanks started to emerge only in response to the extensive devolution of power to Scotland and Wales. The creation of the Scottish Council Foundation was explicitly a response to the potential that devolution created for allowing a distinctive line of policy in Scotland, while devolution to Wales reinvigorated the Institute of Welsh Affairs.

However, when think tanks are located away from the national capital, their focus may be national in part or in whole. Germany has long had think tanks located throughout the country in, among other places, Munich, Frankfurt, Cologne/Bonn, Stuttgart, the Ruhr and the Hamburg–Kiel area, and most have dealt with a mixture of nationwide and *Land*-related issues. Consequently, not all relocated to Berlin when the capital – and the government apparatus – moved there from Bonn. As Thunert has pointed out, this versatility on the part of think tanks must to some extent be due to the nature of German federalism: a federal system of sixteen states (most governed by coalitions), a tradition of corporatism and consensus orientation, and a complex and interlocking system of federal decision making in which decisions are often taken jointly by several levels of government, provide think tanks with multiple points of access to decision makers (Thunert 2000). But there are other examples: the Italian think tanks mentioned above, although mostly located outside Rome, focus mainly on the national level. In Europe particularly, the increasing blurring of frontiers between regional, national and international levels of government are likely to edge think tanks in other countries in the same direction and away from an assumption that think tanks must automatically position themselves in the capital city and target their work primarily on the national government.[4]

As far as Central and Eastern Europe is concerned, however, the development of sub-national think tanks seems unlikely. None of these countries is federal, and the creation of regional tiers of government has been undertaken to a great extent to provide a mechanism for receiving EU regional funds. Most of these countries are small, both geographically and demographically. In most, the political system is based very much on the capital city, and they lack strong economic sub-centres. The principal exception is Poland, large in both area and population, increasingly prosperous and with substantial economic centres outside the capital. It boasts at least one substantial think tank outside Warsaw – the Gdansk Institute for Market Economics – and it will be interesting to see whether the creation of a stronger tier of regional government in 1999 will stimulate the development of sub-national think tanks, perhaps based on universities.

Think tank activity at international level seems likely to develop in two ways. One is that think tanks may find that they are drawn into dealings with international organisations. This is most likely to be true in Central and Eastern Europe, where international organisations – notably the World Bank, the IMF and UNDP – are often more active than in Western countries. These organisations usually operate in areas of primary concern to think tanks, notably economic.

Another supranational player that think tanks are likely to target is the European Commission. A recent survey (Sherrington 2000) shows that, while supranational think tanks focusing their attention on EU institutions are still few in number, many think tanks in member states focus at least part of their energies on influencing the European Commission (with which the prerogative of initiating policy in most areas lies). Sherrington attributes this not only to the obvious factors of the extension of the EU's competencies and the impact of EU actions on member states but also to the Commission's willingness to seek the input of think tanks in agenda setting and policy formulation. It seems very likely that their Eastern European counterparts will start trying to develop the same relationship with Brussels. Since candidate countries, on accession to the EU, have to adopt the entire corpus of European law as it then exists, and since none will accede to the EU for at least several years, they have a vital interest in how all aspects of EU law develop between now and their accession (indeed, new developments could materially affect their ability to fulfil those laws and so join the EU).

A second possibility is the development of collaboration between think tanks on a regional basis. Much informal collaboration already exists. There are cooperative ventures between think tanks in different countries of similar outlook: joint research projects, joint publications and networks of think tanks. Some of these networks are *ad hoc*, some well established, such as the Trans-European Policy Studies Association, which promotes collaborative research between think tanks from all fifteen EU member countries, and the European Information Network on International Relations and Area Studies, which operates a technical information exchange network involving most of the leading European institutes dealing in international and strategic studies (for details and more examples, see Sherrington 2000 and Thunert 2000). Similar practices are developing in Central and Eastern Europe. The GDN conference heard of work by the Center for Social and Economic Research of Poland in building an *ad hoc* network of think tanks in Eastern Europe (Blaszczyk 1999). In 1998, think tanks from seven Balkan countries launched a joint project to identify conditions for long-term stability and growth in the region (Stanchev 2000).

This kind of cooperation is usually informal and a bit haphazard. This is not a criticism, since networking can be stifled by over-organisation. However, the international collaboration between think tanks in Southeast Asia, described in Chapter 10 by Helen Nesadurai and Diane Stone, suggests that more structured collaboration can yield substantial results. This is an important lesson for southeast Europe given the recent creation of an institutionalised framework for cooperation in the shape of the Stability Pact fostered by the EU to bring peace and order to the Balkans. Although the broad aims of the pact and the political framework created to sustain it command general support, its promoters have struggled to give it substance in the shape of practical economic and social initiatives. One possible contribution towards filling the gap is to draw on the combined efforts of think tanks in the region, and the Center for Liberal Studies in Bulgaria seized the initiative in 1999 with a paper proposing a 'vision community' of thinkers from the region to prepare an agenda for civil society to underpin the pact (Center for Liberal Studies 1999). Ivan Krastev in Chapter 8 describes the creation in parallel of the South-East European Policy Information Network, drawing together seventy think tanks from ten countries, which has opened a dialogue with the coordinator of the Stability Pact, Bodo Hombach.

The advantage of think tanks in such activities is that they are in the most literal sense 'irresponsible'. That is, they possess an intellectual freedom of manoeuvre that governments do not. A think tank can float an idea or think aloud without committing anybody: at worst, it risks being ignored. In contrast, any initiative by a government will be seen as forming part of its overall diplomatic strategy and for that reason will never be seen objectively. So it would be difficult for a government to float the idea speculatively, for instance, of the creation of a free-trade area with neighbouring governments. A think tank, on the other hand, can do so without inhibition and without appearing to threaten anyone's interests (provided that the think tank is seen as being independent of its home government). In this sense, think tanks have a potential to act as agents of policy innovation in a way that governments cannot.

In two fields at least, think tanks in Central and Eastern Europe are likely to be active on the international scene. One is the Stability Pact. The other is contact with the European Commission. The drive for accession is so strong in most countries of Central and Eastern Europe, and it is so important a factor in their domestic politics, that think tanks are likely to engage in this field. Indeed, a number of think tanks have been created specifically to work in this field, and the recently created European Institutes in Bulgaria and Romania, established with their governments' encouragement, have lost no time in putting themselves in contact with Brussels.

Think tanks are now a part of the policy-making landscape of many if not most countries. They can exercise considerable leverage from a small base, and they have considerable potential to influence public policy for the better. If that potential is to be realised, more attention has to be paid to their relations with government. While the observations in this paper are drawn only from direct experience in the UK and indirect observations in Central and Eastern Europe, they constitute, I hope, at least one step towards opening up this neglected area of enquiry.

Notes

1   The term 'Central and Eastern Europe' covers all countries on the continent of Europe that are seeking membership of the European Union, plus the ex-Yugoslav republics.
2   OECD/SIGMA work with think tanks has been sporadic. In the early 1980s, there was a project by the Technical Assistance group (now the Public Management Service, to which SIGMA is attached) that led to the commissioning of the Dror article. Although one staff member – Bob Bonwitt, currently head of SIGMA – continued a personal interest in the subject and maintained contacts, nothing systematic resulted.
3   Unavoidably, my use of examples is confined by obligations of confidentiality as a UK civil servant.
4   I am grateful to Dr Martin Thunert of Hamburg University for his advice on sub-national think tanks.

References

Abelson, D. (1998) 'Think tanks in the United States', in D. Stone, A. Denham and M. Garnett (eds) *Think Tanks Across Nations. A Comparative Approach*, Manchester: Manchester University Press.

Blaszczyk, B. (1999) 'Building CASE: the way from a small institute to a regional framework', paper presented at the Global Development Network Conference, 5–8 December, Bonn.

Center for Liberal Studies (1999) 'Project paper "Blue Bird": an agenda for civil society in Eastern Europe', paper circulated to international NGOs, Sofia: Center for Liberal Studies.

Cockett, R. (1994) *Thinking the Unthinkable: Think-tanks and the Economic Counter-revolution, 1931–1983*, London: HarperCollins.

Cornell, T. (1996) 'Ideas into action: think tanks and democracy', *Economic Reform Today* 3 (special issue): 2–4.

Dror, Y. (1984) 'Required breakthroughs in think tanks', *Policy Sciences* 16: 199–225.

James, S. (1993) 'The idea brokers: the impact of think tanks on British government', *Public Administration* 71(4), winter: 491–506.

James, S. (2000) 'A capable centre of government supports European aspirations', *Public Management Forum* 6(1), January/February: 10–11.

Kimball, J. (1997) 'NGOs make an important contribution to policy development', *Public Management Forum* 3(3), May/June: 8–9.

Marmor, T. and Plowden, W. (1991) 'Spreading the sickness', *The Times Higher Education Supplement*, 25 October: 17.

Mathews, J. T. (1996) 'Creating an independent institute for policy research on global issues: the World Resources Institute', in J. Telgarsky and M. Ueno (eds) *Think Tanks in a Democratic Society: An Alternative Voice*, Washington: Urban Institute Press.

McGann, J. (2000) 'Introduction', in J. G. McGann and R. K. Weaver (eds) *Think Tanks and Civil Societies: Catalysts for Ideas and Action*, Somerset, NJ: Transaction Press.

Nagata, N. and Nakamura, M. (1999) 'Overview of Japanese think tanks: dilemmas of funding and expectations to policy research', paper presented at the Global Development Network Conference, Bonn, 5–8 December.

Quigley, K. F. F. (1996) 'Think tanks in newly democratic Eastern Europe' in J. Telgarsky and M. Ueno (eds) *Think Tanks in a Democratic Society: An Alternative Voice*, Washington: Urban Institute Press.

Radaelli, C. and Martini, A. (1998) 'Think tanks: the Italian case' in D. Stone, A. Denham and M. Garnett (eds) *Think Tanks Across Nations. A Comparative Approach*, Manchester: Manchester University Press.

Sherman, A. (1984) 'Why we asked the unasked questions', *The Times*, 1 September: 12.

Sherrington, P. (2000) 'Shaping the policy agenda: think tank activity in the European Union', *Global Society* 14(2): 173–89.

Stanchev, K. (2000) 'Back to normal?' *NGO News*, winter: 3.

Stone, D. (1996) *Capturing the Political Imagination: Think Tanks and the Policy Process*, London: Frank Cass.

Stone, D. (2000) 'Non-governmental policy transfer: the strategies of independent policy institutes', *Governance* 13(1): 45–70.

Struyk, R. J. (1999) *Reconstructive Critics, Think Tanks in Post-Soviet Bloc Democracies*, Washington: Urban Institute Press.

Thunert, M. (2000) 'Players beyond borders? German think tanks as catalysts of internationalisation', *Global Society* 14(2): 191–211.

Part IV

Knowledge across borders

10 Southeast Asian research institutes and regional cooperation

Helen E. S. Nesadurai and Diane Stone

Introduction

Think tanks, or policy research institutes, have long acted as policy entrepreneurs. First, through their advocacy of preferred policy positions, think tanks have played a key part in policy thinking in national and international affairs by seeking to set agendas, define problems and establish the language of policy. Second, these organisations potentially contribute to governance by supplying information and expertise, and by encouraging exchange between official and other private actors. Third, in global and regional politics think tanks can act as agents of second-track diplomacy. In particular, the leading think tanks of ASEAN[1] countries, which will be the main focus of this paper, have been key initiators in the creation of new formal intergovernmental arrangements involving the wider Asia-Pacific region. Accordingly, this chapter adopts a network frame of analysis. Not only does this kind of analysis recognise the role of informal actors in decision-making processes, it also accommodates the idea that think tanks can be characterised as 'agents of change' that provide a propeller for policy learning and innovative policies.

The focus is on elite or mainstream institutes that have good working relationships with their governments. Some of their network arrangements have come to be regarded as significant precursors to governmental involvement in regional intergovernmental associations such as Asia Pacific Economic Cooperation (APEC) and, in the field of security, the ASEAN Regional Forum (ARF; Khong 1995). Although the focus here is on economic cooperation, there are important organisational and individual relationships overlapping into the security field, most particularly but not exclusively through ASEAN's Institutes for Strategic and International Studies (ASEAN–ISIS). A broader research community of think tanks, university centres and business actors has been involved in non-governmental efforts to promote economic cooperation through regional bodies such as the Pacific Trade and Development Conference (PAFTAD) and the Pacific Economic Cooperation Council (PECC).

These think tanks have been embedded in networks at three interrelated levels: first, they operate in policy networks within their national constituencies; second, they have formed their own networks, such as ASEAN–ISIS; and third, think tanks operate within regional and international policy networks. We concentrate on the second and third levels of networking. These networks are particularly effective at the regional level given the weak degree of institutionalisation in Asian regional cooperation, an important aspect of which appears to be a cultural aversion to formal institutional arrangements and a reflection of an Asian style of governance and diplomacy.

Networks and Southeast Asian think tanks

Most think tanks in Southeast Asia have played a role at the earlier stages of regional cooperative efforts, in agenda setting, where these organisations perform three important tasks. First, think tanks act as *innovators* by providing new policy ideas about economic cooperation. Second, think tanks *diffuse* these norms and understandings; they can start the ball rolling for a 'habit of dialogue'. Third, through their *networking*, joint research and other collaborative ventures intra-regionally, and for some through their involvement in the political processes of their home countries, think tanks can help to shape the political choices made by states. To date, most analysis has concentrated on the more tangible institution-building exercises and the disputes of business and government actors concerning APEC, with the research community tending to be portrayed as playing a subsidiary role. This is not unusual. Because think tanks are considered relatively autonomous non-governmental organisations operating at the margins of politics, they have not been accorded a significant influence in policy making.

Yet an examination of the debates, discussion and research into ideas about Asia-Pacific economic and security cooperation that preceded attempts at institutionalisation focuses analytical attention on scholars, think tanks and others in the research community. The latter were engaged in a long-term activity to set domestic and regional agendas in favour of regional economic and security cooperation. This research community has many institutional bases, but in terms of setting the agenda they consolidated in regional non-governmental organisations. This is not to suggest an uncontested or consensual pattern of research or debate. Significant divisions exist between scholars, institutions and nations. Notwithstanding ongoing scholarly debates and intellectual divisions, the body of policy-related research conducted by a number of think tanks from the ASEAN states and East Asian countries, combined with their policy entrepreneurship, has contributed to wider political understanding about the possible benefits of cooperation.

Network approaches

It is a trend to talk about the 'material power of ideas' (Jacobsen 1995: 284). An ideas-oriented approach would appear well suited to an analysis of think tanks. However, it is not clear that ideas have an independent impact on policy. Instead, certain ideas are given clarity, amplification and force via organisations such as think tanks. Yet think tanks are not neutral organisations. They reflect and diffuse a variety of interests. They are a point of intersection for the interests of the state, and business and intellectual elites, and at the regional level they are participants in a research community that is one component of a tripartite alliance alongside actors from business and government. As such, the ideas that think tanks deal with are inflected with the motives of vested interest. Think tanks are not isolated from broader interests but are interconnected and require support for their ideational work. In terms of think tank influence, it suggests that 'the more powerful the sponsors of ideas, the more powerful the ideas' (*ibid.*: 295). As such, network approaches are useful in placing think tanks in a web of interdependencies.

Three network approaches – policy communities, advocacy coalitions and epistemic communities – are outlined. They help, first, to highlight and interpret the role of Southeast Asian think tanks, and, second, to show how networks in the Asian regional context are not static but evolve in complex ways to facilitate learning that prompts new institutional developments. Börzel (1999: 254) suggests that 'the capacity of policy networks for overcoming collective action problems can only be accounted for if policy networks are conceptualised as arenas of communicative action'. The argument here is that think tanks are potentially catalysts for communicative action in policy networks.

Network arrangements assist in the achievement of collective aims in a variety of ways. Networks help to build trust and to provide opportunities for communication that can lead to the development of linkages that promote coordination between actors. A policy network is 'a set of relatively stable relationships which are of non-hierarchical and interdependent nature linking a variety of actors who share common interests with regard to a policy and who exchange resources to pursue these shared interests acknowledging that cooperation is the best way to achieve common goals' (*ibid.*: 253).

One of the most well-established perspectives in the network literature is that of 'policy community' (Kingdon 1984). Policy communities are stable networks of policy actors from both inside and outside government that are highly integrated into the policy-making process. These communities are said to emerge and consolidate around specific policy fields or subsystems such as education policy, tax policy or security policy and revolve around relevant institutions such as specific ministries or government agencies. Think tanks (or their scholars), along with relevant interests, are likely to be accorded 'insider' status if they share the central values and attitudes of the policy community. Participants within a policy community are embedded in series of relationships and dependencies that make the style and structure of a policy community differ from one policy sector to another. Think tanks potentially have important information and analytic resources that they can exchange with other participants in a policy community. This approach assumes that participants in a community act strategically in the pursuit of self-interest and engage in bargaining. However, there are a number of limitations with the policy community approach to understanding think tank involvement in regional community building in the Asia-Pacific region. Institutions are almost absent at the regional level and do not provide a pole around which a community can consolidate. Furthermore, the

issues and actors involved in regional affairs overlap and interact. The boundaries between what could potentially be described as policy communities are very
indistinct. Finally, this model also has difficulty explaining the impact of political
discourse on policy making and in shaping perceptions.

The 'advocacy coalition' approach incorporates ideas about policy communities but places greater emphasis on the view that policy research and analysis has
a long-term enlightenment function in altering policy paradigms. This approach
highlights the role of beliefs, values and ideas as a neglected dimension of policy
making. Within policy subsystems, advocacy coalitions are distinguished from
one another by their beliefs and resources. Importantly, this approach argues that
agenda setting is dominated by elite opinion. The impact of public opinion on
policy agendas is far more circumscribed than in the policy community model.
In this regard, the advocacy coalition model is more relevant to an analysis of
Asian think tanks and policy elites. Of further importance is the concept of
policy-oriented learning within and between advocacy coalitions. Policy-oriented
learning involves 'relatively enduring alterations of thought or behavioural intentions that result from experience and which are concerned with the attainment
or revision of the precepts of the belief system of individuals or collectivities'
(Sabatier and Jenkins-Smith 1993: 42).

The epistemic community concept more directly attempts to specify the
conditions under which ideas generated by (social) scientists acquire political
impact (Haas 1992). The model focuses on the specific role in the policy process
of knowledge or experts who share norms, causal beliefs and political projects
and who seek change in specific areas of policy. By contrast, the policy community model places greater stress on the interplay of interests. Epistemic
communities share consensual knowledge. This is generated from common
causal methods or professional judgement and common notions of validity,
which are usually expressed through a common vocabulary. Consensual knowledge is 'the sum of technical information and the theories surrounding it that
command sufficient agreement among interested actors at a given time to serve
as a guide to public policy' (*ibid.*). Some groups of neo-classical economists,
cetologists and atmospheric scientists, among others, have developed consensual
knowledge within specific policy fields to form epistemic communities. Knowledge
is a central aspect of power in this perspective. Epistemic communities flow
through expert organisations, where the technocratic policy expertise of think
tank policy experts is aligned with the interests of political and economic elites.
Consequently, think tank analysis, research programmes and dialogues represent
part of a wider struggle to control the terms of political debate.

All these network concepts include interest groups, politicians and bureaucrats but give significant consideration to academic policy analysts, think tanks,
intellectuals and other experts. Another common feature of the three network
approaches is the concern with ideas, beliefs and consensual knowledge. That is,
networks allow for learning and new realisations or reinterpretations of self-
interest among network participants. In particular, learning and re-evaluation of
actor preferences occurs through 'communicative action' or 'arguing', whereby

the preferences of network participants change. Indeed, what is interesting about policy networks 'is that they allow its members to shift from strategic interaction (bargaining) based on the maximisation of self-interests, to communicative inter-action (arguing) based on mutual trust and problem-solving' (Börzel 1999: 254). This notion of learning and 'arguing' through networks represents a useful framework for explaining the dynamics of regional cooperation in Southeast Asia and the wider Asia-Pacific, much of which has been founded on a 'habit of dialogue' fostered by think tanks.

There are limitations with network analysis. As has been said of the epistemic community literature, but which also applies to most of the other network approaches, the approach is 'a model of elites by elites for elites' (Jacobsen 1995: 303). For example, in the advocacy coalition model, non-elites have 'neither the expertise, nor the time, nor the inclination to be active participants in the policy subsystem' (Sabatier and Jenkins-Smith 1993: 223). The general public and broader civil society are lost from analytical sight. While this is of concern for the scholar of democracy, it is perhaps a fair reflection of policy-making realities in Southeast Asia.

Southeast Asian think tank development

Formal independence is a characteristic emphasised in the literature concerning Western think tanks. Thus think tanks are said to be independent and private organisations. Connections to government, companies or other interests are evident, but cultural conventions prevail regarding acceptable levels of funding dependence or collaboration. Independence provides legitimacy. By maintaining their distance from political and business interests, policy institutes supposedly have greater ability to 'think the unthinkable'. By contrast, to some Western observers, many Asian think tanks are considered to have an unhealthily close relationship with government. Asian think tanks tend to be 'regime-enhancing' rather than 'regime-critical' (Yamamoto and Hubbard 1995: 45). The kind of understanding that they tend to promote is an elite view that does not disrupt the position of incumbent regimes. Some observers even claim that these bodies are 'state-directed' (Jayasuriya 1994). The importance of think tanks to the state lies in their capacity to amplify messages that come from the top down to the rest of society.

In parts of Asia, the rights of citizens to organise, lobby and protest – such as by contributing to the establishment of an alternative think tank – cannot be taken for granted. In countries where non-government initiatives can easily be regarded as anti-government, 'research institutions … are very vulnerable to governmental intervention in the form of approval/disapproval of projects and severance of financial support' (Noda 1995a: 374). Such organisations, where they exist, often cannot afford to challenge state prerogatives. Indeed, it can be very difficult for new organisations to acquire credibility and recognition in soci-eties where oppositional bodies are viewed with hostility. Instead, it is often the case that think tanks, and non-governmental organisations (NGOs) in general, are organised and funded by the state. Many of the leading Asian think tanks are 'governmentally organised' (GONGOs) and are ever mindful of government controls and constraints. In these late industrialising societies, the boundaries between the state, the market and civil society are blurred to such an extent that it is difficult for interests to develop autonomously within civil society. Conditions of control and circumscribed academic freedoms are apparent in the Southeast Asian context, where think tanks need to court government acceptance. However, there are significant differences between regimes in the region.

Singapore does not have many think tanks. While they are constituted as organisations legally independent from government, Singaporean think tanks have close relationships with the National University of Singapore (NUS) and government, usually through directors with previous or concurrent bureaucratic or party political experience. The Institute of South East Asian Studies (ISEAS) is one of the oldest (established 1968 by an act of parliament) and best-known Singaporean think tanks. It is an important regional institution as a research centre for scholars and specialists interested in Southeast Asia from a time when human resources in this field were underdeveloped. Long considered to be one of the best research institutes on Southeast Asian issues, it continues to attract top scholars. The Singapore Institute of International Affairs (SIIA), established on the initiative of academics from the NUS, is a member of the ASEAN–ISIS network of think tanks. Another prominent institute at the NUS is the Institute of Policy Studies (IPS). The Institute of Defence and Strategic Studies (IDSS) is the latest think tank in Singapore. It was established in July 1996 as a research and teaching institute within the Nanyang Technological University, and its activities extend to regional security issues.

In Indonesia, the Centre for Strategic and International Studies (CSIS) is the oldest and still one of the most influential think tanks in the country. It was once closely aligned with the Suharto presidency, although the relationship cooled markedly in Suharto's final years when a number of CSIS scholars became critical of the regime. While CSIS was a centre for nationalist economic thinking in the 1970s, 'it has since swung around and become a focus for liberal economic policy research and serves as the co-ordinating body for Indonesia's participation in the Pacific Economic Cooperation Conference' (MacIntyre 1995: 164). Jusuf Wanandi is the leading security specialist at CSIS and a pivotal figure in promoting economic and security cooperation in the Asia-Pacific region. He is also considered to be a policy entrepreneur of exceptional ability. Not only is he viewed as the 'gateway' to the security and foreign policy elites of Indonesia but he is also well connected in the USA, Japan, Australia, China and Europe. There are a number of other Indonesian think tanks, such as the Centre for Policy and Implementation Studies (CPIS) and the Indonesian Institute of Sciences (or to give it its Indonesian acronym, LIPI), but they have not played such a strong regional role as CSIS.

The 1990s witnessed a small boom in think tank growth in Malaysia (Khoo 1998). Nevertheless, the channel for policy influence is very narrow and 'limited to informal and personal relationships between intellectuals and government leaders and policy makers', restricting think tank access to a few institutes (Noda

1995b: 409). The Institute of Strategic and International Studies (ISIS) in Kuala Lumpur was established in 1983 and is Malaysia's most prestigious think tank. Its current executive chair and former director-general, Noordin Sopiee, has been influential as a speech writer and policy advisor to Prime Minister Mahathir.[2] ISIS Malaysia's annual Asia-Pacific Roundtable is one important networking forum in which scholars, business persons, journalists, public officials and even political leaders come together once a year in Kuala Lumpur to engage in dialogue, information sharing and scholarly exchange on matters of critical interest to the Asia-Pacific region.

Other notable think tanks in Malaysia include the Malaysian Strategic Research Centre (MSRC), inaugurated in September 1993. The Malaysian Institute of Economic Research (MIER) was established in 1985 and focuses its research and other activities on economics, and financial and business issues. Its work is closely related to the interests and concerns of the private business sector through its economic forecasting research. The Institute of Islamic Understanding (IKIM) was created in 1992, and its primary objective was the 'elaboration of the theoretical and theological basis of an Islamic work ethic in the context of perceived cultural barriers among Muslims to the achievement of Malaysia's rapid development targets' (Noda 1995b: 414).

In the Philippines, the universities have been the natural reservoirs of research talent and advisory capability (Liguton 1991). While think tanks during the Marcos years focused largely on domestic policy concerns, since 1986, several think tanks linked to the Philippines government have emerged whose policy focus is with the external global and regional environment. Among the most widely recognised of these post-Marcos government think tanks are the Centre for International Relations and Strategic Studies of the Foreign Service Institute (CIRSS–FSI) and the Office for Strategic and Special Studies of the Armed Forces of the Philippines (AFP–OSSS). By contrast, the Philippine Institute of Development Studies (PIDS) is less focused on national security and has a stronger orientation towards economic development.

The post-Marcos years also saw the emergence (and re-emergence) of a variety of non-government think tanks, some of them continuing their Marcos years tradition of anti-government, anti-establishment credentials by engaging in protest movements and solidarity networks across the Asia-Pacific region and dissociating themselves from the formal policy process (Kraft 1999). Others, like the Centre for Research and Communications (CRC), have become directly involved in trying to influence public policy. The CRC was established in 1967 as an independent institution and has grown to become a large body with over 200 full-time staff members. It has focused on issues concerning Philippine political and economic development as well as on Asia-Pacific issues. Among newer research institutes characterised by their increasing cooperation with the government is the Institute of Strategic and Development Studies (ISDS), headed by Professor Carolina Hernandez. The ISDS is an independent institute founded in 1991 by a group of academics connected to the University of the Philippines.

Hernandez has tied the institution into ASEAN–ISIS and in this capacity has contributed directly to Philippine foreign and defence policy discussions.

In Thailand, the dominance of the bureaucracy has left little space for independent policy institutes. The older institutes have usually been affiliated to a university and hence classified as governmental. The only complementary body to organisations such as ISEAS in Singapore, ISIS in Malaysia or CSIS in Indonesia is the Institute of Security and International Studies, an academic centre based at Chulalongkorn University. While it is a university body, it has considerable autonomy and functions like a think tank, particularly given that most of its funding is garnered from foreign foundation grants with supplementary funding from government and the university. The two other prominent think tanks in Thailand are the Thailand Development Research Institute (TDRI) and Thailand Environment Institute (TEI). TDRI was the first independent think tank in Thailand, and its primary focus is on national social and economic development issues, although the institute has also worked on regional issues. The TDRI was established in 1984 with Canadian development assistance and receives a large part of its funding from external sources through project consultancy work (Yongkittikul 1996).

This provides a thumbnail sketch rather than a comprehensive picture of think tanks in Southeast Asia. There is a significant level of personal and institutional interaction between the majority of institutes mentioned. However, it must also be remembered that these organisations operate independently, and not all are in the same networks. It is also clear that there are scholar-practitioners who have played important interlocutory roles at the interface of both national and regional research and policy communities. They often play the pivotal role of 'research broker' between the intellectual and research community on the one hand and the political and bureaucratic decision-making world on the other. The network literature has a tendency to analyse networks as a group objectively originating ideas. Individual personalities are important, however, particularly in the absence of strong regional institutions.

Regional think tank dialogues

The ASEAN–ISIS network was formally launched in June 1988, although CSIS initiated the ASEAN–ISIS network as early as 1984 (Hernandez 1997). It was founded by think tanks in the core ASEAN countries, namely CSIS Indonesia, ISIS Malaysia, SIIA of Singapore and ISIS Thailand. An individual, Professor Carolina Hernandez, rather than an organisation, was the Philippine founding member of ASEAN–ISIS. In 1991, the newly created ISDS under the directorship of Hernandez became the Philippine member of ASEAN–ISIS. In 1995, with the anticipated entry of Vietnam as a full member of ASEAN, the Institute for International Relations (IIR) in Hanoi became the sixth member of ASEAN–ISIS, while in 1997, the Cambodian Institute for Cooperation and Peace (CICP) joined as the group's seventh member.

ASEAN–ISIS is registered with the ASEAN secretariat as an ASEAN NGO, while its charter mandates that only research institutes based in ASEAN member countries may join ASEAN–ISIS. Since no counterpart research institute has been established in Brunei, an ASEAN member, officials from Brunei's Ministry of Foreign Affairs participate in ASEAN–ISIS activities, although in a 'private' rather than official capacity, as do members of the Institute of Foreign Affairs from the Ministry of Foreign Affairs in Laos. ASEAN–ISIS also maintains an extensive network of institutional linkages with leading think tanks outside ASEAN in Asia-Pacific countries like Australia, Canada, China, Japan, New Zealand, South Korea and the United States, as well as with countries outside the Asia-Pacific region like India (Hernandez 1997). The main objectives of ASEAN–ISIS are:

- To strengthen and increase regional cooperation in the development of research;
- To increase the effectiveness and efficiency of research by intensified communication and coordination; and
- To contribute to ASEAN cooperation by promoting public knowledge and understanding of problems and issues faced by the ASEAN communities.

ASEAN–ISIS was not the first think tank dialogue in Southeast Asia, and it is not the last. However, it is one of the most prominent dialogue structures that has institutionalised with a strong regional presence and, more importantly, political recognition. While it focuses on security and international affairs, the network does address issues of Asia-Pacific economic cooperation, especially through its sponsorship of the Asia-Pacific Roundtable held annually in Kuala Lumpur, where these issues are discussed. Nevertheless, as discussed in the next section, many Southeast Asian think tanks had been participating in Pacific-wide policy networks individually well before the formation of the ASEAN–ISIS network and continue to do so as separate institutes.

There are well-established avenues for research collaboration, exchange and joint projects between Asian think tanks, and between them and think tanks outside the region. Most interaction is of a scholarly, if policy-focused, character. These scholarly interactions provide a solid base and a diverse series of networks that establish familiarity and some loyalty among participants establishing the foundations for a 'habit of dialogue'. More importantly, a number of leading Asian think tanks have played a pro-active policy entrepreneurship role at the regional level and have had significant impact in promoting ideas about regional cooperation. These pre-eminent Southeast Asian think tanks act collectively as a transnational non-governmental group of organisations in regional agenda setting and participate heavily in second-track diplomacy processes.

Political and economic cooperation and the research community

In the Asia-Pacific region there are well-established processes of second-track diplomacy surrounding issues of security and economic cooperation. Second-track diplomacy is not state-centred and incorporates a more diverse range of actors than bureaucrats and politicians. Official diplomats share the stage with and make use of the growing cast of non-state actors on the world stage. As outlined in Chapter 7, track-two diplomacy entails activities or discussions involving academics and intellectuals, journalists, business elites and others as well as officials 'acting in their private capacity'. However, the value and impact of track-two activity is not unambiguous, and arguments have been made for both the positive and negative value of second-track processes.

On the positive side, informal diplomacy involves think tanks playing a facilitating role. To an extent, they can act as the 'honest broker' inviting all interested parties to sit down behind closed doors to address a particular problem or proposal. They provide 'a middle ground' where new forms of cooperation or approaches to regional conflicts can be explored in an 'off-the-record setting'. Such an activity is useful to governments if the think tank is a prominent organisation of which foreigners have heard, and more importantly, if it can draw upon a network of distinguished states-people, business leaders, diplomats, military officers and scholars. Informal dialogue is also valuable at times when for whatever reason, official dialogue has stalled or official relations are strained. On the negative side, governments can use the track-two process and think tanks for the purposes of public symbolism. Non-officials are given the impression that their advice and analysis is useful, although this could be illusory. At worst, the various think tank gatherings may offer little more than an amenable social and intellectual exercise for participants. If this were the case, however, such arrangements would not persist. Instead, the pace of informal dialogue has accelerated. Furthermore, track-two activity has preceded and complemented official interest in security, economic and political cooperation in the Asia-Pacific region.

Think tanks, Pacific policy networks and economic cooperation

Ideas about Pacific economic cooperation have not found their way on to the regional policy agenda by chance. The evolution of the Pacific economic idea has been a long process of negotiation and education (Woods 1991). Three bodies in particular stand out for their efforts in promoting the idea of economic cooperation and the concept of an Asian-Pacific region or community – PAFTAD, PECC and the Pacific Basin Economic Council (PBEC). PAFTAD, PECC, PBEC and other processes of regional interaction provided the locus for the reinforcement of shared norms about the virtue of economic cooperation. Each of these bodies has a varying history of the degree of governmental and non-governmental participation and organisation in them, but these regional non-governmental organisations are not think tanks. However, the involvement of key think tanks in their establishment and ongoing activities has been central to their influence in spreading ideas and educating interests (Higgott 1996). Think tank involvement in these regional organisations was as policy entrepreneurs.

Their early involvement in discussions about economic cooperation placed them in strategic positions to educate other participants and interested parties.

In particular, the ideas underpinning Asia Pacific Economic Cooperation (APEC) long preceded its actual establishment. The agenda-setting process behind the institutionalisation of APEC represents years of information gathering and sharing, policy consultation and regional consensus-building activities that occurred outside government. Indeed, one senior participant in this community, Stuart Harris (1994) argues that the emergence of an intergovernmental organisation for economic cooperation was only possible after lengthy and sustained dialogue on economic cooperation at a non-governmental level. Indeed, much of the current APEC agenda has come from the PECC process. For instance, the notion of 'open regionalism' that underpins APEC was first articulated by PECC in the 1980s. It was a novel concept, since regional groupings or preferential trading associations tended to discriminate between insiders and outsiders during this period. The 'open regionalism' concept allowed APEC members to reconcile their participation in APEC, an economic cooperation association between countries in the Asia-Pacific region, while allowing them to maintain open markets to all other countries. It helped to allay the fears of APEC member countries that did not want APEC to become a discriminatory, inward-looking trade bloc and wished to continue to maintain open markets on a global rather than Asia-Pacific basis.

PAFTAD is one of the oldest NGOs operating in the area of regional economic cooperation. Its first conference took place in 1968 and was organised by the Japanese Economic Research Centre (JERC). The Japanese foreign minister at the time was Saburo Okita, who was also president of JERC. PAFTAD has long been 'the intellectual driving force of the cooperation movement … [claiming] to understand the political realities confronting economic policy makers' (Woods 1991: 313). It has combined scholarly research and technical expertise with policy-oriented research relevant to cooperative interstate relations in the region. PAFTAD has been more academic in style than PBEC, which was also formed in 1968 as an extension of the Australia–Japan Business Cooperation Committee. PBEC is more closely associated with business and lacks a separate policy analysis capacity, but it draws on the expertise of think tanks, academics and others.

The Pacific Economic Cooperation Conference, later Council (PECC), was yet another initiative of the Japanese and Australians in 1980. It is run by an international steering committee that overlaps with both PAFTAD and PBEC. The East–West Center in Hawaii played an important role in the early stages of PECC organisation by providing a focus for US involvement. Other key institutions for national organisation of PECC activities included JERC, institutes at the Australian National University, and the Asiatic Research Centre at Korea University, along with the Korea Development Institute. In Southeast Asia, the regional think tanks were the main organising forces.

PAFTAD, PECC and PBEC were important as venues for early technical discussions about the prospects for regional cooperation. The research, analysis and publications undertaken under the auspices of these three regional associations helped to form a body of consensual knowledge about the value of economic cooperation. However, these processes were private and informal, lacking official standing. Consequently, the actors and agreements they made were dependent upon the 'consent, endorsement and commitment, often including financial commitment, of governments' (Harris 1994: 390). These processes could not be implemented without government support. Yet there was government involvement. Foreign ministry or other officials were represented at PECC and participated in PAFTAD meetings or as observers at PBEC meetings (*ibid.*: 391). Furthermore, the national committees were the focus of activity and the link to government.

After building the 'habit of dialogue' over decades, the economic cooperation movement consolidated within APEC. Founded in 1989, APEC is currently made up of twenty-one member economies.[3] APEC can be seen as an Asia-Pacific region-wide exercise in economic dialogue that aspires to become the vehicle for setting regional economic policy direction for the twenty-first century. APEC is an official exercise in regional dialogue, confidence building, information sharing, transparency and 'voice' for the region in the wider global trade debates. While it has developed into a consensus-based community devoted to free trade and investment and economic and technological cooperation, it is not a stable arrangement and has lost some direction it had prior to the Asian financial crisis.

Southeast Asian think tanks and ASEAN/Southeast Asian regionalism

Much of the scholarly research on think tanks and second-track diplomacy has focused largely on their role in promoting regional security and economic cooperation in the wider Asia-Pacific region. Through Pacific-wide organisations (PECC, PAFTAD, PBEC) and Southeast Asian networks (ASEAN–ISIS), think tanks have been important actors in promoting learning through dialogue and information sharing within a wider community of political, official and corporate actors. In turn, this has facilitated the eventual formal, although limited, institutionalisation of regional economic and security relations through APEC and the ARF.

Less studied, however, is a similar form of process within Southeast Asia that began in the mid- and late 1980s involving think tanks from ASEAN countries with their counterparts in mainland Southeast Asian countries that were not then members of ASEAN. Think tanks from the ASEAN countries, including but not limited to the ASEAN–ISIS network, began to interact with scholars, policy makers and political leaders from the non-ASEAN Southeast Asian countries of Vietnam, Laos, Cambodia and Myanmar from the middle of the 1980s. This form of networking occurred regularly and in a variety of forums and dialogues covering both economic and security issues. Most importantly, these interactions took place well before the formal expansion of ASEAN to include

Vietnam in 1995, Laos and Myanmar in 1997 and Cambodia in 1999. These processes also began at a time when official links between the ASEAN countries and the communist countries and Myanmar were tenuous. Think tanks, in these instances, functioned less as agenda setters than as facilitators of social learning and identity building. The dialogues and networking activities they initiated provided forums where opinion formers, decision makers, leaders of social movements, members of social and business networks, intellectuals, and experts interacted in establishing shared understandings or in introducing new members to the community of shared understanding.

The series of conferences and dialogue sessions convened by ISIS Malaysia from the late 1980s brought together scholars, policy makers and bureaucrats, and business persons from all ten Southeast Asian countries. The Southeast Asian Roundtables on Economic Development (SEA-RED), first organised in 1989, discussed a variety of economic issues of relevance to Southeast Asia, while the Southeast Asian Forum (SEAF) focused on Southeast Asian security issues. The first SEAF was held in 1988. From the mid-1990s, both these meetings were held under the auspices of ASEAN–ISIS and convened in a different ASEAN country each year. Funding usually came from external agencies, including the Canadian International Development Agency (CIDA), the Japanese government, and foundations from Germany and the USA.

The SEA-RED meetings were especially notable as they brought together elites from the capitalist and communist/transition countries of Southeast Asia to discuss economic development issues. An examination of the conference agenda through the years indicates that discussions essentially focused on the development experiences of the capitalist ASEAN countries through the 1970s and especially the 1980s, with a strong focus on how the ASEAN countries reformed their economies from the mid-1980s. The issues discussed ranged from the role of foreign investment in the growth of the ASEAN countries, the role of government in industrial development, private-sector-led development, public–private interactions in development, economic cooperation and regional integration, and macroeconomic stabilisation. More recently, the SEA-RED discussions have concentrated on globalisation issues and responses to the financial crisis. Participants from countries like Vietnam, Laos and Cambodia found the reform experiences of the ASEAN countries to be particularly relevant, as their comments during discussion sessions indicated.[4] Through such institutionalised, informal processes of interaction, learning was promoted between the capitalist and communist countries of Southeast Asia, with these processes continuing in the 1990s when the latter countries engaged in economic transformation. The process of discussion and dialogue enabled the communist/transition countries to learn from the experiences of the ASEAN countries and was especially enlightening as both sets of countries shared similar concerns with internal stability and cohesion, and regime and state security.

The SEAF series of meetings was significant for three reasons. First, they provided information on the roles and responsibilities of ASEAN membership. This, in turn, facilitated official learning of what it means to be an ASEAN member. It was through such dialogue and networking that elites from Vietnam, Cambodia, Laos and Myanmar were introduced to the ASEAN style of diplomacy and what that meant. Second, the SEAF series is significant since debate and discussions on the concept of 'One Southeast Asia' first took place in these informal or non-official networks, although public officials often participated in these sessions in a personal capacity. The 'One Southeast Asia' project – ASEAN's project of enlargement, which was finally realised in April 1999 – was initially discussed by members from all ten countries of Southeast Asia at a 1993 SEAF meeting. Such dialogue was significant because it took place even before official discussions had begun on the matter between ASEAN countries and prospective new members, namely Vietnam, Laos, Cambodia and Myanmar. Third, the SEAF meetings paralleled the tentative steps being taken at the official level at Indochina–ASEAN reconciliation during the late 1980s and early 1990s. These second-track diplomacy meetings were important because the participants from Vietnam, Laos, Cambodia and Myanmar were public officials, policy makers and present and future political leaders participating in their 'private' capacities. Through these informal processes, the foundations were laid to facilitate regional cooperation and the expansion of ASEAN towards 'One Southeast Asia'.

Interactions such as these through the SEA-RED and SEAF sessions helped to increase the knowledge that participants had about each other's purposes, as well as of each other's interpretations of society, politics, economics and culture. This was especially salient when ASEAN's capitalist members met the communist/transition countries of Southeast Asia. They allowed a common base of perceptions and expectations to be established and shared. Most importantly, these processes of networking helped to diffuse the ideas, norms and principles of ASEAN regionalism to the political elite of the non-ASEAN countries through their think tanks. To the extent that these interpretations are increasingly shared and disseminated across countries, the foundations are laid for the development of a collective regional identity (Hettne and Soderbaum 1999: 13).

Recent dialogue activity

The APEC process generated a new round of networking activities. It includes the APEC eminent persons group, the Pacific Business Forum (PBF) and the APEC study centres (see Morrison and Evans 1995 for a discussion). All initiatives involve the production or dissemination of expert knowledge of an epistemic-like community. Richard Higgott argues that evidence of the influence of this community may be ascertained from the composition of the now-disbanded eminent persons group of experts, which produced three major reports for APEC. Seven of the eleven members were or had been professors of economics, many of them are associated with think tanks, and all had, in one form or another, been involved in government at senior levels and with PECC (Higgott 1996). Similarly, the PBF (also disbanded to become the APEC Business Advisory Council) brought in the think tank community through Ambassador Tommy Koh from Singapore, who was at the time director of IPS.

The study centres are based in educational institutions and occasionally in think tanks such as ISEAS in Singapore and the Korean Institute for International Economic Policy in Korea. Other research is conducted under APEC auspices in conjunction with PECC and APEC study centres in the APEC expert working groups and committees. This is not to suggest that an epistemic community operates in these locations. It may be more accurate, given the political divisions and policy debates broadcast within APEC, that a number of different advocacy coalitions are competing over the most appropriate future for APEC.

Furthermore, there are many other dialogue initiatives and workshops in the region also seeking to build networks, promote cooperation and facilitate research, educational and information exchange. Seeking signs of a convergence of thought – of consensual knowledge – among a multiplicity of uncoordinated dialogue and networks is much more difficult and uncertain compared with the innovative and unique arrangements represented by SEA-RED/SEAF and PECC, PAFTAD and PBEC. Following a Japan Center for International Exchange (JCIE) meeting – the Tokyo Forum in 1995, which brought together regional policy research institutes to discuss, yet again, means of strengthening the regional movement – two leading figures, Charles Morrison from the East–West Center in Hawaii and Paul Evans, then based at the Joint Centre for Asia Pacific Studies, expressed concern about dialogue initiated without strong research foundations and networks without leadership, coherence and good prospects of sustainability. Nevertheless, regional and international network activity continues apace with JCIE now convening the annual Global ThinkNet meetings of think tank directors.

Similarly, the Asian Development Forum (ADF) was convened in March 1998 by the World Bank and the Asian Development Bank with the support of the Philippines government and PIDS. The second meeting was in June 2000. ADF incorporates a wider constellation of actors than think tanks, although they are specifically included as 'development agents'. It is one of many of a series of conferences and workshops conducted in the region. The niche occupied by the Forum is to build development capacity in East Asia by (1) disseminating knowledge about best practice in development policy and strategy and (2) strengthening links within the development community of East Asia, which comprises international, government, private sector, academic and non-governmental groups. The ADF parallels (even replicates) much of what has preceded through PAFTAD, PBEC and PECC and other APEC meetings. Nevertheless, while the development banks continue to support the Forum it will remain an amenable exercise for regional participants to meet old friends and strike new deals. For some participants, the ADF also provides a route of access to the recently initiated GDN.

Yet another instance of track-two dialogue is convened through ASEAN–ISIS and the Konrad Adenauer Stiftung (KAS 2000). The ASEAN–EU think tank dialogue was first convened in November 1999 and sponsored by KAS and ISDS in the Philippines. The meeting sought to address a 'redefined' ASEAN–EU relationship. It emerged from a concern among ASEAN–ISIS members that Europe was losing interest in ASEAN in the wake of the Asian financial crisis and political tensions that had developed between ASEAN and the EU over the enlargement of ASEAN and the contentious issue of human rights.

Think tanks and formal institutional arrangements

The implications of emerging multilateral venues for regional think tank activity are twofold. First, track-two activities have grown in tandem with formal institutional arrangements. They have not been squeezed out by official actors. In some instances, their track-two role has been enlarged in that they have been called upon to provide research and analysis or policy suggestions for track-one officials who are too busy to devote full attention to developments. This is especially apparent in the security field, where the Council for Security Co-operation in the Asia-Pacific was formed to help to coordinate track-two and other security dialogues. Previously, non-governmental activity propelled economic cooperation initiatives. That is, PAFTAD, PECC and PBEC preceded APEC.

A second implication of increased official interest in multilateral institutions is that the capacity of think tanks to shape agendas potentially diminishes. Increasing official involvement in regional activities undermines this capacity. In tandem with themes developed by Ivan Krastev in Chapter 8, think tanks are less able to act as policy innovators. This was the experience of PECC in the first few years after APEC's formation. While PECC leaders managed to convince APEC's leaders and officials to pursue a close and symbiotic relationship with PECC, this relationship was awkward at times with government attention predictably shifting toward APEC (Woods 1995: 815). Nevertheless, PECC, PAFTAD and PBEC have managed to remain relevant. As official government involvement becomes more pronounced, the think tanks of these track-two networks are called upon not as innovators but in a more passive technical role as information providers and analysts. Their second-track role remains important but in the sense of playing an important interlocutory role in domestic and regional policy communities through monitoring of security and economic developments, providing technical assistance and participation in advisory procedures. PECC, PAFTAD and PBEC perform this function for APEC. In 1999, for instance, senior APEC officials called on PECC to conduct an independent assessment of APEC members' individual action plans for trade and investment liberalisation that they had agreed to implement. PECC will also submit its findings on trade in services arrangements in APEC and its report on impediments to trade and investment liberalisation in the region to APEC.[5]

The impact and influence of the multilateral think tank meetings can be overstated. They do not represent or mirror official thinking. Think tank meetings, workshops and conferences are not a substitute for political decision making. Furthermore, the track-two process has not been characterised by consensus or a uniformity of opinion. There are significant differences between official and non-official participants regarding the importance and potential impact of track-

two diplomacy and substantial debate over practical issues to institute cooperation. For the ASEAN participants, the purpose of dialogue is to 'build
confidence and trust through incremental steps, starting with personal relationships' (Kerr 1994: 406). Others want to pursue a 'harder' version of regionalism
founded on rules, laws and institutions. In fact, this is probably one reason why
ASEAN–ISIS has been less conspicuous as a second-track network actor in the
Asia-Pacific economic cooperation process. The ASEAN–ISIS member think
tanks differ in their ideas and opinions on the kind of Asia-Pacific economic
cooperation that should be pursued.

Nevertheless, non-governmental activity through regional dialogue indicates a
desire on the part of politically significant policy actors to avoid anything that
could jeopardise security and economic development in the region. Policy advice
can be either accepted or ignored by officials but still serve to provide a sounding
board for new ideas and a basis for the development of consensual knowledge
and common experiences.

Conclusion

Think tanks have played an important role in conceptualising and promoting
regional economic and political cooperation through organisations such as
PECC, PAFTAD and PBEC. Through these networks, think tanks have been
pro-active in promoting learning within a wider community of official and
corporate actors. Social learning has taken place through efforts to establish a
'habit of dialogue' via track-two diplomacy. Accordingly, the activities of
Southeast Asian think tanks provide a good case of how network arrangements
can facilitate the assimilation and education of interests towards cooperative
endeavours. This 'communicative action' has been an important dynamic in the
creation of new institutional arrangements in the region.

It is the epistemic community approach that has captured most attention from
regionally focused scholars (e.g. Kahler 1995: 31). An 'epistemic-like community' of
neo-classical economists and free trade acolytes is said to revolve around APEC
(Higgott 1994). APEC and a market-led conception of the Asia-Pacific region is
supported by cooperation between a group of academics (mainly economists), business people and government officials. The group operates within a set of formal,
semi-formal and informal institutions and networks centred around PBEC,
PAFTAD, PECC, PBF and APEC. These organisations and informal processes of
regional interaction provide the locus for the reinforcement of shared cooperative
norms and the development of consensual knowledge.

The epistemic community approach fits well with developments in Asia-
Pacific cooperation where intellectual elites have interacted with policy makers.
However, as ideas of economic and security cooperation coalesce into new
regimes or institutions, a 'policy community' in which political and economic
interests are more pronounced may develop. It is thus important not to lose sight
of the utility of the other network concepts. Networks are not static but are
constantly evolving and disaggregating in complex ways. At one time, a group of

actors in a specific policy field may make up a tight, coherent epistemic community, but this community may gradually dissolve into a looser kind of network if the ideas fail to capture political attention. Similarly, the type of network in operation differs from one policy area to another, or across domestic and regional levels. Epistemic communities may be more apparent at the regional level, whereas policy communities are likely to be predominant at the domestic level, where institutions such as ministries and government agencies dominate and interests are well established.

Furthermore, the different network concepts highlight different features and characteristics of communicative action or modes of learning. Think tanks have acted as policy entrepreneurs in their advocacy of the norms and values of regional cooperation and community building. It is the role of policy entrepreneurs in wider policy networks that is the key to understanding the development of the regional economic and security dialogues of the last decade. State policy makers work with incomplete information, and the role of these policy entrepreneurs in mitigating their information deficits is important. But more important is the 'habit of dialogue' or the processes of 'arguing' that have allowed state actors to redefine their policy interests in light of the ideas of regional cooperation articulated by members from the academic, research institute and corporate communities and via their informal participation in non-governmental forums.

Notes

1   ASEAN is the Association of Southeast Asian Nations established in 1967 by Indonesia, Malaysia, the Philippines, Singapore and Thailand. Brunei joined the organisation in 1984 on its independence from Britain, while Vietnam, Laos, Myanmar and Cambodia joined in the 1990s. By April 1999, ASEAN included all ten countries of Southeast Asia.
2   Noordin Sopiee wears many hats. He is or has been chairman of PECC, director-general of the Malaysia PBEC Committee, chairman of the East Asia Centre for Economic Cooperation, the Malaysian representative on the eminent persons group of APEC, the Malaysian representative on the CSCAP steering committee and convener of the Commission for a New Asia. He was also a former group chief editor of the government-owned newspaper *The New Straits Times*.
3   APEC's members are Australia, Canada, the United States, New Zealand, Mexico, Chile, Peru, Japan, China, Hong Kong, Taiwan, South Korea, Papua New Guinea, Brunei, Indonesia, Malaysia, the Philippines, Singapore, Thailand, Vietnam and Russia. Russia, Vietnam and Peru are the most recent members, admitted in 1998.
4   Complete conference proceedings of SEA-RED and SEAF are available in the library of ISIS Malaysia in Kuala Lumpur.
5   See 'PECC Statement to the APEC SOM III, 12–13 August 1999, Rotorua, New Zealand', delivered by PECC director-general Dr Mignon Chan. Accessed at http://www.pecc.net/apecsom3_9908.htm on 4 November 1999.

References

Börzel, T. (1999) 'Organizing Babylon – on the different conceptions of policy networks', *Public Administration* 76, summer: 253–73.

Haas, P. (1992) 'Introduction: epistemic communities and international policy coordination', *International Organization* 46(1): 1–35.

Harris, S. (1994) 'Policy networks and economic cooperation: policy coordination in the Asia Pacific', *Pacific Review* 7(4): 381–95.

Hernandez, C. (1997) 'Governments and NGOs in the search for peace: The ASEAN–ISIS and CSCAP experience', paper prepared for the Alternative Systems Conference 'Focus on the Global South', Bangkok, 27–30 March. Accessed on 2 November 1999 at http://www.focusweb.org/focus/pd/sec/hernandez.html.

Hettne, B. and Soderbaum, F. (1999) 'Theorising the rise of regionness', paper presented at the After the Global Crisis: What Next for Regionalism Conference, Coventry, UK: Centre for the Study of Globalisation and Regionalisation, University of Warwick, 16–18 September.

Higgott, R. (1994) 'Introduction: ideas, policy networks and international policy coordination in the Asia-Pacific', *The Pacific Review* 7(4): 367–80.

Higgott, R. (1996) 'Free trade and open regionalism: towards an Asian international trade strategy', paper presented at the Europe in the Asia Pacific Conference, May 28–31.

Jacobsen, J. K. (1995) 'Much ado about ideas: the cognitive factor in economic policy', *World Politics* 47: 283–310.

Jayasuriya, K. (1994) 'Singapore: the politics of regional definition', *The Pacific Review* 7(4): 411–20.

Kahler, M. (1995) 'Institution building in the Pacific', in A. Mack and J. Ravenhill (eds) *Pacific Cooperation: Building Economic and Security Regimes in the Asia-Pacific Region*, Sydney: Allen & Unwin.

Kerr, P. (1994) 'The security dialogue in the Asia-Pacific', *The Pacific Review* 7(4): 397–409.

Khong Y. F. (1995) 'Evolving regional security and economic institutions', *Southeast Asian Affairs 1995*, Singapore: Institute of Southeast Asian Studies.

Khoo S.-M. (1998) 'Think tanks and intellectual participation in Malaysian discourses of development', in D. Stone, A. Denham and M. Garnett (eds) *Think Tanks Across Nations: A Comparative Approach*, Manchester: Manchester University Press.

Kingdon, J. (1984) *Agendas, Alternatives and Public Policies*, Boston: Little, Brown.

Konrad Adenauer Stiftung (KAS) (2000) Summary statement, 'Asia and Europe: redefining the partnership in the next millennium.' First ASEAN–EU Think Tank Dialogue, 27–28 November 1999, EDSA Shangri-La Hotel, Mandaluyong City, Philippines.

Kraft, H. J. (1999) 'A look at think tanks in the Philippines', *NIRA Review*. Accessed at http://www.nira.go.jp/publ/review/99winter/kraft.html.

Liguton, J. P. T. (1991) 'Think tanks' response to governance amidst changing political setting and growing globalization: the Philippine case', in J. W. Langford and K. L. Brownsey (eds) *Think Tanks and Governance in the Asia-Pacific Region*, Canada: Institute for Research on Public Policy.

MacIntyre, A. (1995) 'Ideas and experts: Indonesian approaches to economic security cooperation in the Asia-Pacific', *The Pacific Review* 8(1): 159–72.

Morrison, C. and Evans, P. (1995) 'Enhancing cooperation among policy research institutions in Asia Pacific', JCIE papers no. 18, Japan: Japan Center for International Exchange.

Noda, M. (1995a) 'Policy-oriented research institutions in Indonesia from the viewpoint of Asia Pacific intellectual cooperation', in T. Yamamoto (ed.) *Emerging Civil Society in the Asia Pacific Community*, Singapore: ISEAS; and Japan: Japan Center for International Exchange.

Noda, M. (1995b) 'Research institutions in Malaysia: from the perspective of the under-pinnings of the Asia Pacific community', in T. Yamamoto (ed.) *Emerging Civil Society in the Asia Pacific Community*, Singapore: ISEAS; and Japan: Japan Centre for International Exchange.

Sabatier, P. and Jenkins-Smith, H. C. (eds) (1993) *Policy Change and Learning: An Advocacy Coalition Approach*, Boulder, Colo.: Westview Press.

Woods, L. T. (1991) 'Non-governmental organizations and Pacific cooperation: back to the future?' *The Pacific Review* 4(4): 312–21.

Woods, L. T. (1995) 'Learning from NGO proponents of Asia-Pacific regionalism', *Asian Survey* XXXV(9): 812–27.

Yamamoto, T. and Hubbard, S. (1995) 'Conference report', in T. Yamamoto (ed.) *Emerging Civil Society in the Asia Pacific Community*, Singapore: Institute of Southeast Asian Studies; and Japan: Japan Centre for International Exchange.

Yongkittikul, T. (1996) 'The role of independent research institutes in policymaking: the Thailand Development Research Institute', in J. Telgarsky and M. Ueno (eds) *Think Tanks in a Democratic Society: An Alternative Voice*, Washington: Urban Institute Press.

11 Globalisation, think tanks and policy transfer

Stella Ladi

Introduction

There is growing academic interest in the processes of policy transfer and in the phenomenon of globalisation, but little work has been done to link the two. Joseph Stiglitz in Chapter 2 refers to processes of globalisation and the importance of global scanning for policy ideas, but he does not explore the causes of the existing situation and the actual mechanisms of policy transfer. The investigation of this intellectual gap constitutes the subject of this chapter and the basis for an empirical research project exploring the relationship between these phenomena and focusing on the stages of policy transfer. The chapter concentrates on the role of think tanks as agents of policy transfer through a study of the role of a European think tank, the International Dialogues Foundation (IDF).

The argument is organised into two parts. In the first part, 'globalisation' and its relationship with the concepts of policy convergence and/or divergence is discussed, and an attempt is made to integrate them with the policy transfer literature. Think tanks are then defined and their role in a policy transfer network assessed. The second part of the paper engages in empirical analysis and is divided into two sections. The first section provides a contextual introduction to the IDF and its political environment. The youth employment conference that was organised by the IDF and aimed at the exchange of ideas on youth employment policy projects and the first steps towards the implementation of its outcomes are then outlined. The succeeding section applies the 'policy transfer network' framework to the IDF. This discussion provides some useful insights for think tanks and research institutes interested in policy transfer by providing an analysis of avenues for and constraints to policy transfer when 'scanning globally' for policy ideas and practices.

Globalisation and policy transfer

'Globalisation' is a term that is widely used in social science literature, although each discipline emphasises different aspects of the phenomenon. In economics, the focus is upon the global integration of markets. In international relations and political science, however, analysis centres on the role of the state and emerging forms of governance. Some see the state as withering away and being replaced by new forms in the organisation of human society (Held 1996). Others claim that there is nothing new in the process and that the state is not withering away (Hirst and Thompson 1996). Among them, one can find writers (e.g., Anderson 1995: 65–106) arguing that we are facing a phenomenon of regionalisation, not globalisation. Other writers (e.g., Cerny 1997) claim that the state is not withering away but that its functions and structures are changing in a more globalised world.

The terms 'globalisation', 'internationalisation' and 'transnationalisation' are often used interchangeably in the literature. Internationalisation can be used in the same way as globalisation, but it can also refer to a previous 'stage' of globalisation. Hirst and Thompson (1996) argue that economies are highly internationalised but not globalised. Transnationalisation is also an elusive concept. McGrew (1992), for example, asserts that 'transnational relations describe those networks, associations or interactions, which cut across national societies, creating linkages between individuals, groups, organisations and communities within different nation-states', and he differentiates them from trans-governmental relations. For the purpose of this paper, the term 'globalisation' is used in the way that Cerny defines it:

> Globalisation is quite simply the sum total of the wide range of political, economic and social processes of transnationalisation and internationalisation taking place in the world today.
>
> (1997: 123)

A useful way to disaggregate the phenomenon of globalisation is to analyse it in terms of convergence and/or divergence. The question of whether different societies are converging or diverging is not a new one. Contemporary discussion, which began in the 1960s, was normatively driven and was not directed towards an interpretation of reality (Tinbergen 1959). The concepts of convergence and divergence were associated with the processes of industrialisation (Kerr *et al.* 1973) and later with the processes of modernisation (Inkeles 1981). The question of convergence and divergence has recently reappeared, but this time the framework has shifted from industrialisation and modernisation to internationalisation and globalisation (Cerny 1996; Berger and Dore 1996; Unger and Van Waarden 1995). *Policy convergence* (and consequently policy divergence) are understood in Bennett's (1991: 215–33) terms to include a vast spectrum of outcomes, such as convergence of policy goals, content, instruments, outcomes and styles. One pathway to the analysis of actual mechanisms of policy convergence/divergence is to study the relationship between policy transfer and globalisation.

Policy transfer as a general framework has been developed by Dolowitz and Marsh (1996) to include concepts such as policy diffusion, emulation, policy learning and lesson drawing. Policy transfer is a 'process in which knowledge about policies, administrative arrangements, institutions and ideas in one political setting (past or present) is used in the development of policies, administrative arrangements, institutions and ideas in another political setting' (Dolowitz and Marsh 2000: 5). In this regard, it is a more detailed and nuanced concept of the methods of 'global scanning'. The actors involved in policy transfer processes are various and can be independent of the state, as is the case, for example, with think tanks. The importance of the different actors involved in policy transfer is an empirical question.

A discussion of the link between globalisation and policy transfer is provided by Evans and Davies (1999), for whom the question of policy transfer is a question of structure and agency. Policy transfer should therefore be discussed within the broader framework of globalisation in order to link this meso-level transfer process to the macro-level. The processes of globalisation act as a facilitator of policy transfer because they increase the opportunities for policy transfer. At the same time, however, policy transfer facilitates processes of globalisation in regional structures such as the European Union (EU), where such transfer is a frequent occurrence. Regionalisation is understood as an aspect of the convergence and divergence dimensions of globalisation, so structures such as the European Union can also be seen as another dimension of globalisation. If globalisation is understood as both convergence and divergence, the processes of globalisation can be investigated empirically through the study of convergence and divergence.

Cerny (1997) describes globalisation as a complex process, practice and discourse that is responsible for both convergence and divergence. Convergence can be seen, for example, in the manner in which the European states are organised in the global economy in areas such as economic fiscal policy. For example, there is a dynamic among European states towards tax harmonisation. At the same time, divergence can be observed in that not all states react in the same way to the pressures and/or discourse of globalisation. For example, the way a state reacts depends on its history and its level of economic development. If Unger and Van Waarden's (1995) argument that policy learning is one of the mechanisms through which convergence occurs is expanded, then policy transfer can be seen as one of many mechanisms through which globalisation occurs. For instance, it can be seen in terms of the development of information and communication networks (Cantwell 1992) or in terms of global economic integration. It is apparent when governments seek common solutions to common problems such as the transfer of the ideas and practices labelled as the 'new public management' (Dunleavy 1994).

Thus policy transfer may be viewed as a consequence of globalisation. However, it may also be viewed as a process of globalisation itself in that the dissemination of ideas and programmes between countries and between supranational institutions may be leading to a convergence of the political and economic landscape. It might be argued that such convergent landscapes then provide opportunities for further policy transfers, resulting in a virtuous or a vicious circle of cause and effect. On the other hand, if negative or partial lessons are drawn (Rose 1993; Dolowitz and Marsh 1996), then non-transfers may conceivably result in policy divergence. This argument parallels some of the themes outlined in Chapter 2 by Joseph Stiglitz when he writes about 'global best practice' and how it needs to be modified in order to suit local conditions. This chapter, however, places a special emphasis on the way in which think tanks act as agents of policy transfer in a globalised environment. Their role can be understood better through the lens of the globalisation literature, where transnational relations and the spread of ideas are more broadly discussed.

Think tanks as policy transfer agents

In the policy transfer literature, the dissemination of ideas and the diffusion of knowledge are important issues, and agents such as think tanks play a central role. In this chapter, the term 'think tank' is used to describe organisations that are distinct from government and that have as an objective the provision of advice on a diverse range of policy issues through the use of cognitive and elite mobilisation. Stone (1996: 14–16) developed some criteria to identify think tanks in the American and British political systems. Although these criteria do not fit the policy research institutes to be found in other developed, transitional and developing countries perfectly, they provide a general guide to the characteristics of think tanks. These criteria are as follows:

- *Organisational independence and permanence* – this means that they usually have a charitable or non-profit status and that they are independent of governmental or corporate interests. At the same time, they have a permanent presence. Independence cannot easily be defined and for this and other reasons is also difficult to observe. Furthermore, it is necessary to establish whether by independence we mean administrative independence (McGann 1995: 3), intellectual independence (James 1993: 493–4) or financial independence (Stone and Garnett 1998: 4). We usually observe partial independence, and it is very difficult to find organisations that can claim total independence. For example, it is possible, for an organisation that cannot claim administrative independence because it is funded by the government to be intellectually more independent than a private organisation that is financially dependent on a political party or corporation.
- *The self-determination of the research agenda* – it is interesting to note that even if organisations state that they are independent, it is likely that funding criteria will influence their agenda and sometimes even their findings (Gray 1978: 181–2).
- *Policy focus* – this refers to the objective of bringing knowledge and policy making together where possible by informing and influencing the policy process.
- *Public purpose* – think tanks usually claim that their goal is to conduct research in order to inform the public and the government how to improve public policy.

- *The expertise and professionalism of research staff* – this is the intellectual resource of institutes but also a source of their authority and the basis for legitimising their findings.
- *The organisational yield of the institutes* – this is research, analysis and advice that comes in the form of various publications, or of activities like conferences, seminars and workshops.

With these characteristics, many think tanks represent 'third-sector' organisations. The third sector has traditionally been seen as a positive aid to society, but Salamon (1995) identifies three misapprehensions about this sector:

- The 'myth of pure virtue', which expects non-governmental organisations to be very flexible and not to face organisational problems such as bureaucratisation;
- The 'myth of voluntarism', which sees the third sector as relying mainly on volunteers, with roots in civil society where relationships with the state potentially create a conflict of interests; and
- The 'myth of immaculate conception', which conceptualises the third sector as something completely new without any historical or ideological roots.

To the above we have to add that third-sector organisations are very often expected to be more efficient and to have more know-how and on-the-ground experience than other organisations (Aquina 1992: 57–74). Finally, when we focus upon the advocacy organisations of the third sector, they are often seen as representing the public interest rather than narrow economic interests (Jenkins 1987: 296). As Smith (1977: 254) argues, scholars consider independence to be the most important factor in policy analysis, because governments are too busy, academia is too narrow, and industry wants to sell. To a greater or lesser degree, these assumptions underpin the GDN view of 'local research institutes'. In this chapter, it is argued that think tanks choose to resemble third-sector organisations in order to gain the good reputation that these organisations have acquired. But as Salamon (1995) indicates, most of these virtues are mythical. This is something that we should remember when we discuss think tanks and their role in the transfer of ideas if we assume them to act as independent agents within our political systems.

The role of think tanks in society has been described in different ways. Smith (1994) sees them as the solution to problems arising out of the decline of political parties in liberal democracies and the general change in the political environment. However, Cornford's (1990) understanding of think tanks as brokers and mediators seems more plausible. Think tanks do not set out to replace political parties. Their main function is to accommodate the system by acting as mediators, and by offering their knowledge resources in order to improve policies. The relationship between think tanks and knowledge communities is discussed next: knowledge is one of their main resources.

Knowledge communities, think tanks and processes of policy transfer

Knowledge is one of the main tools available to think tanks when they endeavour to influence public policy. The discussion of the relationship between knowledge, power and public policy is old and diverse. Gagnon (1990: 1–18) distinguishes three different pathways in the literature. The first discusses the relationship between knowledge and power as part of a rationalistic paradigm, where the state, seeking help, turns to 'scientists'. The second traces an indirect relationship between knowledge and power, where knowledge is diffused and influences power as part of a 'common wisdom'. The third understands knowledge and power as organically related and attempts to explain the emergence of power centres outside the state such as might be found in think tanks, foundations, the law fraternity and consultancy firms. All three explanations can be valid and interrelated, which means that if a case study demonstrates that the state turns to 'scientists' for knowledge, this does not mean that knowledge cannot be diffused informally or that knowledge and power are not organically related.

Think tanks are possessors of knowledge, and this can place them at the centre of policy developments requiring expert advice and technical information. A tool for understanding the role of think tanks in the spread of policy ideas is the concept of 'policy transfer networks' (Evans and Davies 1999). This approach ties together network concepts – especially Marsh and Rhodes' (1992) idea of a policy community as well as that of 'epistemic communities' (Haas 1989) and 'advocacy coalitions' (Sabatier and Jenkins-Smith 1997) – to the policy transfer phenomenon. To varying degrees, these network concepts incorporate knowledge and learning as an independent force in policy reforms. Epistemic communities are networks of experts attempting to influence policy change (Haas 1989: 16). However, the concentration on knowledge elites possessing (social) scientific expertise neglects the role of other kinds of agent, for example groups without any kind of special knowledge representing oppressed people. The advocacy coalition approach has a similar emphasis on the role of ideas, cognition and learning as factors central to policy change, but it more directly stresses political dynamics and the role of politicians and bureaucrats in providing opportunities or building barriers to knowledge providers in policy development. This network is not restricted to possessors of scientific knowledge, as in the case of epistemic communities. A policy community account recognises the knowledge resources of the agents but stresses the economic and political interests of diverse participants. Accordingly, the character of a policy transfer network is not necessarily static but may evolve at various stages of transfer where members of the network come from diverse backgrounds. These network approaches provide analytical tools to connect third-sector organisations like think tanks to political and economic interests. They also signify that 'learning' and consensus building in networks are important components in policy transfer (Bennett and Howlett 1992).

Evans and Davies (1999) provide an illustrative sequence of stages for a voluntary policy transfer process and another sequence, with slight differences, for coercive transfer. The role of think tanks is discussed within this framework. The reason why this sequence is useful is twofold. First, it provides a framework for the exploration of the role of an agent in processes of policy transfer. In particular, the policy transfer network framework helps the researcher to organise and systematise the analysis of the role of think tanks in the policy transfer process. Second, at a more practical level, it can be useful for a think tank that engages in a process of policy transfer to assess its activity in relation to this framework in order to understand the potential impact of its effort to influence policy change. Table 11.1 summarises the stages of the transfer process at which a think tank – or a coalition of institutes – can become involved. It is a heuristic device that is useful for the investigation of processes of policy transfer but is not designed to provide prescriptive operational guidelines for think tanks.

The first stage includes the *recognition* of the existence of a problem in a particular policy area that requires action to instigate change. The assessment that there is a problem and the decision that some action should be taken are usually made by politicians or bureaucrats. It potentially stimulates the emergence of a policy transfer network if solutions to the problem cannot be found locally. The role of think tanks in the recognition stage can be significant if they manage to influence the way in which the problem is defined and persuade decision makers of the necessity to act. The role of Paremvasi, a Greek knowledge institution, in persuading the Greek government of the need to introduce an ombudsman (a structure evident in many other political systems) as a means of supervising Greek public administration is a good example. Paremvasi persuaded the government to consider this policy change through publications in daily newspapers and through the organisation of open discussion meetings between members of the government, the major opposition parties and Paremvasi (Paremvasi 1998).

The next step for the key agents is the *search* for new ideas. This will happen if decision makers or private groups feel that existing ideas are not satisfactory explanations of or solutions to a policy problem. A government might play a very active role in encouraging the search for reform ideas within its own bureaucratic structure as well as by outside bodies. In processes of coercive transfer, the main difference is that there are agents who try to impose the transfer, such as through conditions on loans provided by international organisations. An example of a search activity is provided by German organisation e3, which coordinated Headways, a project that involved bringing together twenty-eight local environment-related projects from EU countries 'to promote exchange of experience, good practice and know-how in selected priority fields of environment policy at Community level' (e3 1998: 5). Paremvasi followed a different search strategy by using the academic knowledge of its members regarding how the institution of the ombudsman functions in other European countries.

Table 11.1 The emergence and development of a policy transfer network

The process of transfer	The role of government and other decision makers	Potential roles of think tanks as agents of policy transfer
1. Recognition	Recognition of the existence of a policy problem due to crisis or unforeseen events or pathologies in policy implementation.	Analysis of policy trends; expert recognition of emerging problems; warnings and advice about prevention or the need for policy change in expert community, journals, etc.
2. Search	The absence of immediate solutions prompts a search for agents that can help in the definition and solution of the problem.	Independent investigation of potential solutions, which can include research into other political systems.
3. Contact	Contact through the search with other agents that can help with the solution of the problem.	Attempt to become involved in the solution to the problem by lobbying, expert commentary, seeking position on government bodies or funding.
4. Emergence of information feeder network	Monitoring of participants in the information feeder network to decide which agents will be included in the transfer process.	Think tanks are acting as information clearing houses or resource centres; concentration of expertise; develop reputation for reliable information and knowledge on policy issue.
5. Cognition, reception and emergence of a transfer network	Final decision on individuals or organisations to be included in the policy transfer network and interact with decision makers through commissions of inquiry, policy task forces, etc.	Think tanks recognised as sharing commitment to common value system and incorporated into the policy transfer network. Incorporation into this relatively elite activity also depends on think tank knowledge resources.
6. Elite and cognitive mobilisation	Observation of the elite and cognitive mobilisation organised by the think tank. Suggest agents that could be included. Fund study trips overseas, initiate research programmes or sponsor international conferences.	Think tanks assist in coalition building and seek funding to generate and spread more information about the policy problem: they search for ideas within and outside their political system in a more consistent fashion. Think tanks also act as 'gate-keepers'.
7. Interaction	Decision makers participate in events/publications organised by network participants. Establish advisory boards.	Think tanks help to convene and build consensus in the network through conferences, websites, journals, newsletters and closed meetings.

The process of transfer	The role of government and other decision makers	Potential roles of think tanks as agents of policy transfer
8. Evaluation	Decision makers evaluate the alternative suggestions made by the policy transfer network.	Think tanks help in the assessment of cross-national evidence. They often advocate certain solutions.
9. Decision	Decision makers decide to adopt a policy or programme.	Think tanks have limited or no role in formal decision making.
10. Implementation	The selected policy/programme is being implemented.	Think tanks monitor and evaluate the implementation of policy, provide feedback to government, advise on how the transfer can be modified to match local circumstances.

Source: Adapted from Evans and Davies 1999.

At the *contact* stage, think tanks could become important actors in transfer processes if they possess – or they say that they possess – relevant knowledge resources or contacts with other knowledge elites (Stone 1996: 14–16) that other agents of transfer require. Through their research networks and studies of other political systems, think tanks can provide detailed information about policy and practices elsewhere. This can be demonstrated by presenting their knowledge resources in *an information feeder network* through public mechanisms such as conference organisation and building formal links with other organisations. Other means of presenting think tanks' knowledge resources include the use of information technology and the creation of new websites or their involvement in domestic and transnational policy networks. If a government or international organisation that has recognised the problem and the need for policy transfer in the first place is satisfied by the capacity for cognitive and elite mobilisation that the think tank demonstrates, it may lead to the *cognition, reception and emergence stages* of the policy transfer network. That is, a network moves from an informal arrangement to a more formalised process with official engagement.

The entrance of the think tank into the network does not depend so much on its innovative ideas but rather upon whether or not it shares a common value system with the government or international organisation that wants the policy transfer to occur. At this point, the policy transfer network acts as a barrier to the entry of ideas and programmes that are opposed to its value system (Evans and Davies 1999). In the case of the 'Headways' project, after a process of presentation of available information through the publication of a book including the twenty-eight case studies, the cognition, reception and emergence stage of a policy transfer network occurred. The participants in this network included the EU and bureaucrats from various national governments as well as other interested individuals from universities, businesses and research institutes.

The Danish approach was identified as the 'best practice', and a project named Ecotrans, which aims to transfer elements of the Danish project to eastern Germany, Greece and the UK has evolved. Funding for Headways and Ecotrans has come from the European Commission, signifying a close match between the value systems of the organisations involved and that of the European Union (UnderstandingBus 1998).

Interaction is of particular importance in the case of an agent of transfer such as a think tank. The think tank will organise forums for the exchange of ideas between the relevant actors in order to find and advocate 'best practice' and proceed with the policy transfer. After this, *evaluation* begins with the members of the policy transfer network deciding upon the more detailed objects, degree and prerequisites of the transfer. The final *decision* on the transfer depends upon the broader processes of policy change (Wolman 1992). The role of the think tank (and any other private organisation) at this stage is rather limited, as they have already attempted to persuade policy makers of the value of their proposals during the previous stages. Of political necessity, the policy decision is made by politicians or bureaucrats.

Finally, in order to have a complete picture of policy transfer, the *implementation* of the adopted policies or programmes should be considered. Even at this last stage of the transfer, think tanks can be significant actors because they can offer their expertise during the establishment and implementation of policies or programmes. An active role in the implementation of the ombudsman institution in Greece was played by Paremvasi when Professor Diamandouros, one of the founding members of Paremvasi, was selected as the first individual to hold the key post of ombudsman (Paremvasi 1998). Implementation is another stage at which ideas, policies and practices from elsewhere can be modified and adapted to local conditions through the learning process. The following section discusses in more detail the role of the IDF in the transfer of youth employment policy projects and ideas between European and Middle East/North Africa.

The IDF and youth employment policy

The International Dialogues Foundation (IDF) is an independent Dutch non-governmental organisation. It is supported by voluntary advisors, and its finances are derived from project-related grants. Its decision-making body is the general board, which has recently developed an international character by including members from various European and Middle Eastern/North African countries. Its key areas of activity include the organisation of conferences and the publication of documents and reports, which mainly concern the dialogue between Islam and the West (IDF 1998a: 1). As its name suggests, the IDF's main aim is to increase dialogue and understanding between European and Arab countries in order to allow further cooperation between the two worlds. This section concentrates on the projects that the IDF has developed for the youth target group. The first European youth conference was held in 1995 and was entitled 'Intercreation: Islamic Youth in Europe'. Convened in Istanbul, the conference addressed general questions concerning Islamic and Western societies. A common call from the participants was for the next conference to be more practical.

The IDF's profile conforms to the criteria for think tanks outlined earlier. First, it is an independent organisation and has been in existence for ten years. Its independent status can be deduced from the nature of its funding sources, which include not only the EU and the Dutch government but also apolitical private organisations. Second, while the IDF is to some extent restricted by the policies of the EU and of the Dutch government, it is able to maintain its own research agenda. The project coordinator of IDF, Edu Willemse (1998b), states: 'a) we are independent and b) we keep in mind the criteria and the policy lines of our donors'. The third characteristic is that the IDF attempts to influence, at least indirectly, the policy process. As both Edu Willemse (1998b) and IDF director Peter Idenburg (1998) remark, they do not expect to influence policy directly, but they think that policy makers at least read the IDF's reports because this provides them with a new perspective on certain issues. Fourth, public purpose forms a crucial part of its rhetoric in the sense that dialogue is viewed as the main way of promoting public awareness of issues such as Europe–Arab relations. Fifth, its advisory board consists of a professional elite. Additionally, the IDF possesses a good network of communications, which is in a sense even more important than the possession of knowledge because it facilitates the acquisition of knowledge, even from outside the organisation. Finally, the IDF acts through publications and conferences.

The IDF works within the Dutch political system and the EU. Its cooperation with Arab countries such as Egypt, Morocco and Jordan means that it is also aware of the political and social systems of these countries. The specific IDF project that is discussed in this section concerns youth unemployment, and in order to understand its role and its potential influence on the policy transfer of youth employment projects it will be necessary to discuss the environment within which it works.

The EU, because of its goals of a common market and of increasing mobility of workers, has taken action in the field of employment policy with the establishment of the European Social Fund. In 1994, a new employment initiative was approved composed of four main strands: 'Horizon', 'NOW', 'Youthstart' and 'Integra'.[1] For funding allocations, these projects have to fulfil three main criteria: innovation, transnationality and multiple effect. 'The objective of transnationality is to facilitate the transfer of expertise and dissemination of good practice between the Member States' (Department of Enterprise, Trade and Employment 1998). This mission statement suggests that the EU is keen to promote policy transfers that will enhance policy convergence. Another element is EU activity in the Mediterranean region. Since 1991, the EU has adopted a new Mediterranean policy with two central objectives: to develop economic ties between the EU and the Mediterranean region, and to promote cooperation between the Mediterranean countries (EU 1998). The EU encourages the participation of NGOs in these activities, and the IDF has certainly taken advantage of the opportunities created through these policy initiatives because they are directly related to its aim of achieving greater Europe–Arab cooperation.

The Netherlands has one of the lowest rates of unemployment in Europe. However, it still has a large number of long-term unemployed people, especially among unskilled workers and immigrants. Both the EU and the Dutch government were inclined to search for solutions to youth unemployment problems and were keen to include immigrants from Middle Eastern/North African countries in any initiatives. These objectives provided the IDF with a policy environment conducive to the transfer of youth employment projects between organisations and countries.

The youth employment conference and its aftermath

The youth employment conference organised by the IDF took place in mid-March 1998 and had as a theme 'Employment for Migrant Youth in Europe and Youth in the Emigration Countries'. The conference investigated 'youth employment projects … in order to find under which circumstances these projects could also be set up in other participating countries' (IDF 1998b). The conference was organised in two parts; the first part focused on migrant youth in the EU and the second on Middle Eastern/North African countries, from where many immigrants originate. The aim of the conference was twofold: to build alliances between the participating organisations and to exchange experiences on how to set up youth employment projects.

The conference was sponsored by a range of bodies, primarily the EU but also the Dutch Ministry for Foreign Affairs, the Dutch European Cultural Foundation, the Dutch Commission for Sustainable Development and Cooperation and the Robert Bosch Foundation. The conference took an original approach to the problem of youth unemployment because instead of starting from above and from what the politicians had to say about these problems, it began with youth organisations from both the EU and the Middle Eastern/North African countries. In short, the conference sought to articulate and broadcast what Stiglitz would call 'local knowledge'.

Participants at the conference came from a diversity of backgrounds. There were representatives from political youth organisations, immigrant organisations and NGOs, and a number of civil servants and entrepreneurs from both European and Middle Eastern/North African countries (IDF 1998c). The conference organised six workshops, the aim of which was to prepare draft proposals for new projects based on proposals presented by the coordinators of the workshops. Like GDN99, a second aim was to build networks by establishing contacts between the participating organisations. Proposed projects must be organised by a variety of participating countries, depending on whether they are European or Euro-Mediterranean projects (IDF 1998d: 2). The six workshops held during the conference were 'Continuous Learning', 'Start-Up – Migrant Entrepreneurs in Europe', 'Youth Employment Assistance Company', 'Young Entrepreneurs', 'Work for Students and Academics' and 'The Bridge Building Function of New Media'.

At the conference, the IDF was designated the organiser of a permanent European youth platform for employment in order to facilitate communication between organisations and the implementation of agreed projects. The IDF has proposed a steering committee that includes members from EU and Middle Eastern/North African countries who belong to a range of organisations (IDF 1998e). The tasks of the steering committee are to keep the network of organisations in contact, to look at the progress of the programmes adopted for implementation and to organise the third conference in spring 2000 (Willemse 1998b).

The youth employment policy transfer network

IDF programmes represent a case of indirect coercive policy transfer. On the one hand, organisations were free to participate and to form or reject partnerships and projects during the conference, but on the other hand the nature of the projects adopted was largely influenced by the funding priorities of the EU and its concern for Euro-Mediterranean cooperation. As was noted during interviews with participants, mainly ideas have so far been transferred. Nevertheless, a start has been made on the transfer of some projects. These projects emerged from the 'Continuous Learning' and 'Young Entrepreneurs' workshops, and their success is to be evaluated at the next conference in Egypt. The degree of transfer is also difficult to identify before the implementation of a project. In this respect, the degree of transfer that has so far occurred can be described as 'inspiration'. These ideas are likely to be adapted and synthesised depending on each country's individual characteristics (Willemars 1998).

The sequence of policy transfer that was described earlier allows us to explore the role of the IDF in a more organised way. In the *recognition* stage, the IDF did not play an important role. Both the EU and the Dutch government recognised the existence of the unemployment problem through the EU's employment initiative of 1994, and the EU also recognised the need for cooperation with Mediterranean countries through the Barcelona Declaration of 1995. In other words, international agreements instituted a dynamic for policy transfer. Initially, the EU *searched* indirectly for relevant agents through the establishment of funding programmes such as Youth for Europe. The IDF took advantage of this new policy direction to take action in the field of youth employment policy and of Mediterranean cooperation. The IDF *contacted* the EU and the Dutch government in order to obtain funding, but the IDF presented its past work and applied for the funding without organising an *information feeder* network.

The *cognition, reception and emergence of a transfer network* occurred when the IDF persuaded the EU and the Dutch government that it was capable of action in the two specific fields of youth unemployment and Europe–Arab dialogue. Obtaining funding for the organisation of the conference provided the impetus for the policy transfer network to emerge. *Elite and cognitive mobilisation* began with the IDF's mobilisation of its contacts with governmental bodies and non-governmental institutions in both European and Middle Eastern/North African countries in order to find suitable organisations for the policy transfer process. *Interaction* took place during the conference, where youth organisations, and EU and Dutch government representatives met. *Evaluation* started at the same time but is still in progress, as the transfer of projects has not been completed. The EU, the Dutch government and the governments of the participant countries are expected to play a significant role in determining whether the projects will finally be adopted. However, the transfer of ideas is not dependent on government decisions.

The youth employment policy transfer network that has been initiated by the IDF is still in progress, consequently monitoring of project *implementation* is incomplete. The most developed project at present is 'Continuous Learning'. The model was presented by the Dutch Youth Organisation of the National Federation of Christian Trade Unions (CNV), and a version of the programme is expected to be adopted by a Portuguese and a German organisation. Funding has been provided by the EU. At the moment, there is no Middle Eastern/North African participation, but efforts are being made by the IDF to expand the project (IDF 2000). The second project that is being transferred is 'Young Entrepreneurs'. Two models were presented in respect of this, one from a Dutch organisation and one from an Egyptian organisation. Cooperation has already started between the Dutch organisation and a German one for the transfer of the model. The Egyptian organisation is not participating actively at the moment, mainly because of the administrative constraints that it faces in initiating such a venture. Finally, an example of a project that has not worked at all is the 'Work for Student and Academics', which was designed to promote employment opportunities for graduates and academics in Palestine. It has not been implemented as a consequence of the complicated political situation in Palestine.

The main constraints upon policy transfer are twofold: first, the proximity of the cultural environments of the actors involved as well as the social and political problems faced by Middle Eastern/North African countries. It was easier for European countries to exchange projects between themselves rather than with Middle Eastern/North African countries. In the EU, established structures and a dynamic for harmonisation are in place to facilitate transfers. By contrast, there are fewer avenues for dialogue for the Middle Eastern/North African countries to draw upon. A second constraint was the organisational and technological ability of the Middle Eastern/North African countries wishing to adopt a programme. This was particularly so in respect of an Internet project, which aimed at the establishment of a communications network between the various organisations through the Internet. There was an attempt to create a web page and to organise a virtual conference through the Internet, but the lack of advanced technology in the Middle Eastern/North African countries resulted in the failure of this project. At the moment, an electronic mailing list exists for the exchange of ideas and for advice regarding further applications to the EU for funding, but it has not been as successful as the GDN mailing lists.

Policy transfer prospects

The IDF case study provides some evidence to suggest that in some cases policy transfer will lead to policy convergence and in others to policy divergence. Policy convergence is likely to occur between countries that are close culturally and ideologically, while policy divergence is likely in cases of cultural and ideological diversity. From the coalitions that have been formed to date, policy transfer will occur, at least in the first place, between EU countries. For example, the project on vocational training that came out of the 'Continuous Learning' workshop in Bonn, which is funded by the EU and is the most advanced project, involves cooperation between a Dutch, a German and a Portuguese organisation (IDF 2000). There is no example at the moment of close cooperation between a Middle Eastern/North African and a European organisation that could indicate a tendency towards divergence or convergence. At this stage, no concrete conclusions can be drawn about policy convergence with regard to its role in educing further policy transfers. Notwithstanding this, it can also be said that the creation of a permanent youth platform for employment, and the plan to organise a third conference in 2000 in Egypt, are likely to promote further policy transfer. The fact that the next conference is going to take place in a Middle Eastern/North African country indicates a more concerted attempt to promote policy transfer to the Arab world.

The study of the IDF indicates that think tanks can be key agents in the dissemination of ideas and thus of policy transfer in the international domain. At this stage of IDF activities and project development, there is clear evidence of a transfer of ideas, and it is arguable that this will provide opportunities for further policy transfer to occur, especially the transfer of concrete programmes. Participants were open to new ideas, and it was much easier for them to take them on board than to take up concrete projects. To adopt a new project needs the cooperation of a number of institutions in their countries, political support and the allocation of funding.

The policy transfer network approach (Evans and Davies 1999) allowed us to explore the IDF case study in a more organised way. Apart from its value in directing the exploration and understanding of processes of policy transfer, it also has some practical value for think tanks, which are increasingly forced to engage in processes of policy transfer because of their participation in international networks such as the GDN and in response to wider processes of globalisation. Increasingly, funding allocation depends on whether international partnerships are created. The policy transfer network model allows think tanks to systematise the assessment of the processes of policy transfer in which they participate. For example, the policy transfer network approach suggests that the inclusion of an organisation in a policy transfer network depends not only on its innovative ideas but also on the sharing of a common value system with the decision makers. Accordingly, while most think tanks are third-sector organisations and independent intellectual mediators, their connections with political and economic interests cannot be denied. Think tank networking to facilitate the spread of ideas and substantive policy transfer can best be assessed by drawing on this assumption.

The policy transfer network approach needs to be combined with the globalisation literature in order to explain why think tanks engage in processes of policy transfer. As was discussed earlier, globalisation is the cause of an increase in processes of policy transfer, while policy transfer is one of the mechanisms of globalisation. This means that policy transfer is responsible for the intensification of globalisation. Think tanks, like most institutions, are feeling pressure to respond to this process. Their possession of knowledge resources and ideas makes it easy for them to engage in the spread of ideas and in policy transfer. However, it is important to be aware of whether they become agents of voluntary, indirect coercive or coercive transfer. Nedley (2000) argues that there is very little policy transfer from the global South to the global North and that this constrains the success of policy transfer and has implications for the nature of the transfer.

Although there was an attempt by the IDF and its partners to achieve policy transfer from the South to the North, it has not succeeded due to political, social, cultural and technological constraints. In assessing the IDF case study, it could be argued that the whole project would have been more successful if there was more policy transfer from the South to the North, which would make the whole process more balanced. The IDF is aware of this dilemma, which is one reason why the next conference is being organised in a Middle Eastern/North African country. At a more practical level, it should be noted that a conference on its own is not enough to promote policy transfer. A series of informal meetings and visits has to follow as well as intensified communication through the use of information technology. The IDF is now in the process of using these methods.

Knowledge and expertise are critical 'commodities' that think tanks have to offer in policy transfer processes. Equally important is their ability to point out where knowledge can be found by using their networking ability. Common knowledge and common attitudes to policy change are the forces that bring the members of knowledge communities together – whether these be epistemic, advocacy or policy communities – and comparison and learning about policy practices in different countries and jurisdictions can establish a dynamic for policy transfer. The EU and the Dutch government exhibited a rational approach to knowledge by turning to experts for assistance on the development of youth employment policies. However, an organic conception of the knowledge and power nexus also recognises that the international transfer of knowledge and policy ideas can occur independently of the state carried by think tanks, NGOs, foundations and others. Is knowledge the most powerful tool of political actors in a globalised environment? Or is it just rhetoric used to justify political decisions? This chapter has suggested that knowledge has power in itself, but a genuine desire for policy change is also necessary for policy transfer to occur.

Note

1   For more information on this topic, consult http://europa.eu.int/en...blic/overview.

References

Anderson, J. (1995) 'The exaggerated death of the nation-state', in J. Anderson, C. Brook and A. Cochrane (eds) *A Global World? Re-ordering Political Space*, Oxford: Oxford University Press and the Open University, 65–106.

Aquina, H. (1992) 'A partnership between government and voluntary organisations: changing relationships in Dutch society', in B. Gidron, R. Kramer and L. Salamon (eds) *Government and the Third Sector*, San Francisco: Jossey-Bass, 57–74.

Bennett, C. and Howlett, M. (1992) 'The lessons of learning: reconciling theories of policy learning and policy change', *Policy Sciences* 25: 275–94.

Bennett, C. (1991) 'Review article: what is policy convergence and what causes it?' *British Journal of Political Science* 21: 215–33.

Berger, S. and Dore, R. (eds) (1996) *National Diversity and Global Capitalism*, Ithaca, NY; and London: Cornell University Press.

Cantwell, J. (1992) 'The internationalisation of technological activity and its implications for competitiveness', in O. Granstand, L. Hakanson and S. Sjolander (eds) *Technology Management and International Business*, Chichester: Wiley.

Cerny, P. G. (1997) 'Globalization and politics', *Swiss Political Science Review* 3(4): 122–8.

Cerny, P.G. (1996) 'Globalization and other stories: The search for a new paradigm for international relations', *International Journal*, 51(4): 617–37.

Cornford, J. (1990) 'Performing fleas: reflections from a think tank', *Policy Studies* 11(4): 22–30.

Department of Enterprise, Trade and Employment, Ireland (1998) Employment Initiative website http://entemp.ie/

Dolowitz, D. and Marsh, D. (1996) 'Who learns from whom?' *Political Studies* XLVI: 343–57.

Dolowitz, D. and Marsh, D. (2000) 'Learning from abroad: the role of policy transfer in contemporary policy-making', *Governance* 13(1): 5–24.

Dunleavy, P. (1994) 'The globalization of public services production: can government be "best in world"?' *Public Policy and Administration* 9(2): 36–65.

e3 (1998) *Headways Opening Employment Opportunities for Unemployed People in the Environmental Sector*, Berlin.

Evans, M. and Davies, J. (1999) 'Understanding policy transfer: a multi-level, multi-disciplinary perspective', *Public Administration* 77(2): 361–86.

EU (1998) 'European Social Fund: an overview of the programming period 1994–1999', March (http://europa.eu.int/en... blic/overview/chap1.htm).

Gagnon, A.-G. (1990) 'The influence of social scientists on public policy', in S. Brooks and A.-G. Gagnon (eds) *Social Scientists, Policy and the State*, New York: Praeger, 1–18.

Gray, C. (1978) '"Think tanks' and public policy', *International Journal* 33(1): 177–94.

Haas, P. M. (1989) 'Do regimes matter? Epistemic communities and evolving policies to control Mediterranean pollution', *International Organisation* 43(33): 377–403.

Held, D. (1996) *Models of Democracy*, Cambridge: Polity Press.

Hirst, P. and Thompson, G. (1996) *Globalization in Question*, Cambridge: Polity Press.

Idenburg, P. (1998) interview with Director of the IDF, 2 July, the Netherlands.

Inkeles, A. (1981) 'Convergence and divergence in industrial societies' in M. Attir, B. Holzner and Z. Suda (eds) *Directions of Change*, Boulder, Colo.: Westview Press, 3–38.

International Dialogues Foundation (IDF) (1998a) programme of activities, February, The Hague: IDF.

International Dialogues Foundation (IDF) (1998b) *IDF Newsletter*, 29 January, The Hague: IDF.

International Dialogues Foundation (IDF) (1998c) *List of Participants*, 10 March, The Hague: IDF.

International Dialogues Foundation (IDF) (1998d) *Workshop Procedures & Rules of Plenary Parliament Session*, 5 March, The Hague: IDF.

International Dialogues Foundation (IDF) (1998e) *Open European Youth Platform for Employment – Draft Member List for the Steering Committee*, May, The Hague: IDF.

International Dialogues Foundation (IDF) (2000) *Report of the Telephone Meeting of 10th December 1999*, The Hague: IDF.

James, S. (1993) 'The idea brokers: the impact of think-tanks on British government', *Public Administration* 71: 491–506.

Jenkins, C. (1987) 'Nonprofit organisations and policy advocacy', in W. Powell (ed.) *The Nonprofit Sector*, New Haven, Conn.; and London: Yale University Press, 296–318.

Kerr, C., Dunlop, J., Harbison, F. and Myers, C. (1973) *Industrialism and Industrial Man*, Middlesex: Penguin Books.

Marsh, D. and Rhodes, R. (1992) *Policy Networks in British Government*, Oxford: Clarendon Press.

McGann, J. (1995) *The Competition for Dollars, Scholars and Influence in the Public Policy Research Industry*, Lanham: University Press of America.

McGrew, A. G. (1992) 'Conceptualizing Global Politics', in A. McGrew and P. Lewis (eds) *Global Politics*, Cambridge: Polity Press.

Nedley, A. (2000) 'Policy transfer and the developing country experience gap: taking a southern perspective', paper presented in the ESRC research seminar 'Studying Policy Transfer', University of York.

Paremvasi (1998) *Ombudsman as the Central Goal for Paremvasi*, Athens: Paremvasi.

Rose, R. (1993) *Lesson Drawing in Public Policy: a Guide to Learning across Time and Space*, London: Chatham House.

Sabatier, A. and Jenkins-Smith, H. (1997) 'The advocacy coalition framework: an assessment', paper presented at the Department of Political Science, University of Amsterdam.

Salamon, L. (1995) *Partners in Public Service*, Baltimore: Johns Hopkins University Press.

Smith, B. (1977) 'The non-governmental policy analysis organisation', *Public Administration Review* 3: 253–8.

Smith, T. (1994) 'Post-modern politics and the case for constitutional renewal', *Political Quarterly*: 128–37.

Stone, D. (1996) *Capturing the Political Imagination: Think Tanks and the Policy Process*, London: Frank Cass.

Stone, D. and Garnett, M. (1998) 'Think-Tanks, Policy Advice and Government', in D. Stone, A. Denham and M. Garnett (eds) *Think-Tanks Across Nations: A Comparative Approach*, Manchester and New York: Manchester University Press, 1–20.

Tinbergen, J. (1959) *The Theory of the Optimum Regime*, Amsterdam: North Holland.

UnderstandingBus (1998) subsidy application to the EU-Commission GD V, Berlin.

Unger, B. and Van Waarden, F. (eds) (1995) *Convergence or Diversity?* Aldershot: Avebury.

Willemars, V. (1998) interview with the grants officer of the European Cultural Foundation, 30 June, Amsterdam.

Willemse, E. (1998a) interview with the project coordinator and coordinator of the IDF conference in Bonn, 15 March, the Netherlands: IDF.

Willemse, E. (1998b) interview with the project coordinator and coordinator of the IDF conference, 2 July, Leiden, the Netherlands: IDF.

Wolman, H. (1992) 'Understanding cross national policy transfers: the case of Britain and the US', *Governance* 5(1): 27–45.

12 Think tanks and the ecology of policy inquiry

Evert Lindquist

Introduction

The Global Development Network initiative is an ambitious and far-reaching attempt to link knowledge to public policy. More particularly, it conceives of think tanks as critical knowledge generators or brokers in the policy-making process. In the discussions preceding and during the conference, many concerns were expressed about the future development of the GDN. This included questions about the capacities of think tanks, about which institutions might control the policy and research agenda, about whether the activities of the GDN might be dominated by a single discipline, and about the appropriate governance arrangements and activities for the network.

Most of the exchanges on these matters, not surprisingly, have been infused by the traditional contours of development debates, with a focus on North–South and other regional differences, different kinds of knowledge and the growing demand by donors that think tank organisations demonstrate influence and effectiveness. While posing and answering these questions from a development perspective is ultimately critical to the success of the enterprise, for this observer there has been insufficient recognition that more fundamental and generic issues are at play. It is thus important to locate how the debates about the GDN fit into broader formulations about the role of think tanks, and, even more generally, about the knowledge-into-policy process. Broader perspectives should assist in providing more clarity about how to elaborate the GDN initiative.

This chapter seeks to put the challenges and concerns associated with the GDN in perspective, and to identify some models and proposals for structuring the network. Those who are debating the GDN's future need to understand that many of the issues at stake – whether and how to make think tanks and social science research more relevant; the sheer diversity of think tanks in terms of values and activities; and the best ways to link governments and think tanks – are not, for the most part, unique to the think tanks, governments and international organisations grappling with the challenges confronting developing and transitional countries. To be sure, there are important differences and sensitivities to acknowledge when designing the GDN that flow from the challenges associated with developing and transitional countries. However, these considerations should be separated from the larger and enduring questions about the role of think tanks and social science knowledge in the policy-making process.

This chapter begins with a brief review of the literature on policy making, knowledge utilisation and the role of think tanks. I then counter the generic notion of 'think tanks' with a more diverse image of the range of their possible activities and modes of influence. The third part shows that think tanks are best understood as part of a larger 'ecology' of organisations or policy networks committed to policy inquiry, which should condition expectations about influence. Given that the question of managing networks of think tanks and other experts outside government is crucial to the GDN, I introduce two models from the Canadian experience: the Policy Research Initiative and the Canadian Environmental Network, and conclude with some proposals for the GDN.

Generally, this paper argues that the problem of connecting decision makers with producers of policy-relevant inquiry has long been a challenge. Think tanks – because they tend not to be encumbered by bureaucracy or university norms – are regarded as logical candidates to bridge the gap between them. However, I argue that not only do think tanks have diverse objectives but they also have numerous competitors with overlapping mandates and often more resources or access to decision makers than do think tanks. Furthermore, there are multiple types of influence on policy making. As a result, it is difficult to discern influence and effectiveness in the short term and, in the long term, it would be better for donors to sustain the 'ecology' that supports and uses think tank inquiry. Consequently, I also propose that the GDN initiative focuses on facilitating interaction with annual conferences, continues to elaborate its website and considers establishing issue-related caucuses in addition to strengthening regional organisations.

Knowledge, policy making and think tanks

The GDN initiative flows from a perceived acute need for policy-relevant knowledge to support decision making and restructuring in developing and transitional countries, to build public sector capacities and to strengthen civil society. The breadth of these challenges is such that a range of academic and professional disciplines ought to be engaged. Think tanks are perceived as important linchpins between the worlds of knowledge and of decision making, which embrace the work of national governments and international organisations. However, at the same time that their utility is recognised, there is increasing demand on the part of donors and recipients for think tanks to demonstrate their effectiveness.

These aspirations are not new. The goal of bringing academic knowledge and insight to bear on solving social and economic problems materialised well over a century ago when social science research first started to emerge and accelerated as disciplines such as economics, politics, law, sociology and administration developed stronger footholds in universities, particularly in North America. Several foundations furthered the development of these disciplines, and some of the earliest think tanks, such as the Brookings Institution, emerged during this time. Brookings, for example, sought to improve government practices such as budgeting and administrative reform, and later to influence economic policy (Critchlow 1985; Smith 1991; Abelson 1996). Later, universities and think tanks proliferated and expanded in the post-Second World War era. By the end of the twentieth century, not only had hundreds of think tanks large and small emerged in North America, but they were proliferating rapidly around the world (Langford and Brownsey 1991; Stone *et al.* 1998; McGann and Weaver 2000).

Despite the increase in potentially policy-relevant institutions and inquiry, the more perplexing question that has long worried observers is whether decision makers receive useful information from these sources to deal with the challenges they confront. Although social science reputedly informed the design of many of the Great Society programmes in the USA during the 1960s, a literature emerged during the 1970s and 1980s questioning the quality of that advice, the usefulness of such research to inform particular policy decisions, and how social science research actually achieved its influence (Lynn 1978). The problem was originally framed in terms of bridging two distinct cultures: one comprised of decision makers seeking practical, reliable solutions to cope with a multitude of vexing problems; and the other of professors seeking to expand the boundaries of their respective disciplines while developing and maintaining the respect of colleagues according to academic norms (Caplan 1979; Lindquist 1990: 28–30). One of the conclusions of this literature was that social science research rarely had a direct effect on decision making. Rather, influence was achieved indirectly through 'enlightenment,' 'percolation' and 'knowledge creep' by steadily influencing the views of decision makers and their advisors on problems through new concepts and evidence (Weiss 1977; 1980). The solution touted for improving the 'uncertain connection' (Lynn 1978) between decision makers and academics was to expand the 'brokerage' function between the two cultures (see Figure 12.1).

The emergence and proliferation of think tanks can thus be seen as an organisational expression of a long-held critique of both social science research and the ability of governments to reach out to secure policy-relevant insights. On the one hand, think tanks are ostensibly liberated from the political and bureaucratic constraints and transactions of governments, and on the other, they are not bound by academic disciplinary norms. The archetypal think tank can be characterised as having:

- A commitment to practical problem solving and policy relevance;
- A willingness to pursue multi-disciplinary work (although many are very specialised and draw on generalist expertise or from very few disciplines);
- A focus on policy alternatives and the future, and a receptivity to new ideas;
- An ability to mobilise quickly to advance new ideas; and
- A strong emphasis on communication and marketing to decision makers and the media.

Whether most think tanks live up to the archetype is an entirely different question, one that will be addressed later.

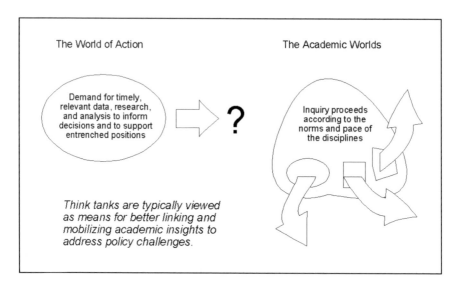

The World of Action

The Academic Worlds

Demand for timely, relevant data, research, and analysis to inform decisions and to support entrenched positions

?

Inquiry proceeds according to the norms and pace of the disciplines

Think tanks are typically viewed as means for better linking and mobilizing academic insights to address policy challenges.

Figure 12.1 The two-community formulation

Early in the twenty-first century, not only do these arguments stand for having think tanks in the policy process but they have also gathered force in the information age. Governments around the world are buffeted by rapidly changing economic and social environments, as well as the opportunities and competitive threats afforded by new technology, which require new frameworks to guide policy and governance. The need for organisations, like think tanks, that can adapt quickly, mobilise expertise and respond with new policy ideas has increased dramatically. Moreover, the barriers to creating and sustaining think tanks have been greatly reduced, permitted by the advent of more flexible labour markets and information and communications technologies. Even more intriguing is the widespread consensus that for countries to respond successfully to these challenges requires strengthening the capacities not only of governments but also of civil societies. Though not an entirely new idea, think tanks are increasingly seen as crucial links between, on the one hand, non-governmental organisations, communities and citizens, and on the other hand, decision makers in governments and international organisations. Governments and non-governmental interests alike know that it makes sense to actively monitor, exchange knowledge and ideas, and sometimes mobilise with counterparts in other jurisdictions with similar interests. Think tanks are crucial nodes in these international networks because they are relatively liberated from the constraints and commitments of national governments. In short, the opportunities for think tanks have expanded greatly during the last few decades.

These developments have been complemented by new perspectives on how policy making works, and the role of think tanks and experts more generally. Rather than see a relatively few interests in control of policy levers and debates, observers are more likely to identify networks of actors from inside and outside government – policy communities – and include among them counterparts at the sub-national and international levels (Pross 1986; Coleman and Skogstad; Jordan 1990). Expertise is more likely to be seen as being decoupled from institutions and not solely the domain of the most powerful government and private sector organisations. Indeed, often the most sought-after experts will be mobile and entrepreneurial, often developing attachments and exerting influence through several institutions simultaneously or over the course of a career (Heclo 1978; Lindquist 1992). More generally, expertise is not seen as 'objective knowledge' but as 'contested information'. Rather than moderate political and policy debates, experts may exacerbate conflict and serve on behalf of different 'advocacy coalitions' (Sabatier and Jenkins-Smith 1993; Lindquist 1992). Decision making is now cast in less deterministic terms and in a more random and chaotic vein, influenced as much by chance and other policy domains as by power. Policy entrepreneurs such as political leaders, administrators and experts find ways of making opportunities more likely to happen or position themselves well to take advantage of them when they do occur (Kingdon 1984; Baumgartner and Jones 1993). Given that policy making is so complex and fluid, it is generally agreed that it makes sense to take a long view on the question of influence on decisions, perhaps requiring a decade or two.

I have cast the diffusion of expertise, the more unpredictable nature of policy making, the need for brokering knowledge between policy makers and researchers and the concomitant expansion of opportunities for think tanks as secular trends. But it is important to emphasise that how these trends play themselves out depends on the particular governing institutions and political traditions in each country. Governments have varying degrees of comfort with independent research that challenges the premises and approaches to policy development. In countries with authoritarian governments and less developed civil societies, financial support for think tanks and other independent organisations to undertake policy inquiry may be very limited, and their leaders may have to adopt indirect strategies of influence or to take personal risks in advancing informed views. What is surprising, however, has been the proliferation of university, non-profit and state-based think tanks around the world during the last quarter of a century (Langford and Brownsey 1991; Stone *et al.* 1998; McGann and Weaver 2000). This suggests that the pressures on countries to interpret policy developments, to learn from other jurisdictions and to identify alternative courses of action to deal with rapidly changing governance challenges – however constrained or open the political discourse in each jurisdiction – are widely shared around the world.

What do think tanks really do? Can it be measured?

It is often presumed that think tanks have, as a core function, the production and dissemination of policy research, and that their activities are interdisciplinary. However, think tanks are incredibly diverse with respect to their mandates and activities (see Figure 12.2). When combined with the more encompassing models of policy making described above, it is apparent that think tanks can exert influence in many different ways.

It is first worth noting that many think tanks do not have as a primary objective the production of policy research, let alone multi-disciplinary research. Supporting such research usually involves a substantial outlay of resources and a significant lead time. Think tanks are more likely to support policy analysis, which relies on available data and research for insight and arguments, identifies alternatives and requires less time to produce. Some think tanks may collect and store data from different sources, undertake surveys and develop policy indicators, but most rely on government statistics for their work. Some think tanks may carve out broad policy domains to monitor and assess, while others may specialise in relatively narrow policy niches. Some think tanks may rely on generalist expertise, or that of one or two disciplines, such as economics or political science, to inform their inquiry. Some think tanks may try to influence political and bureaucratic leaders, while others may choose to inform students, the public or other groups. More generally, rather than emphasise either data collection, research or analysis, some think tanks may strive to bring individuals and organisations together to debate issues, or to serve as clearing houses for information with websites and resource centres.

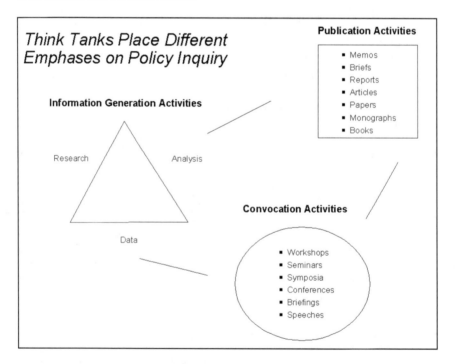

Figure 12.2 Think tanks place different emphases on policy inquiry

The very diversity of think tanks suggests caution about making generalisations within sectors and across countries. The very complex and fickle nature of policy-making processes, with so many forces at play, should give pause to anyone who seeks to ascribe 'influence' definitively to a particular think tank at any given time. Even though 'performance measurement' and 'results-oriented management' are fashionable in most OECD countries, it seems clear that invoking uniform indicators – such as the amount of media coverage, the number of Nobel Prize winners and CEOs sitting on advisory and governing boards, the number of publications and events held each year, and even financial health – may not fully or accurately reflect the extent of influence of think tanks. Quality, as opposed to quantity, is difficult to determine – and in the policy world, much depends on the eyes of the beholder in terms of values, methodology, level of analysis and intended audience. What one think tank considers 'success' may not interest other think tanks and their supporters. Further complicating these assessments is the different governing environment in which think tanks and their staff must operate; gauging influence in an authoritarian system as opposed to a more liberal and democratic system is a very different, but no less complicated, task. There may be a great incentive in authoritarian systems for think tank leaders not to claim 'success' or influence in the manner of their counterparts operating in more open political contexts.

Indeed, think tanks may be valuable for some simply because they exist, serving as beacons to a larger constituency of interests. Or they may offer relatively comfortable sites for dialogue and debate between staff, members and invited guests and provide a ready source of commentary for the media, thus supporting more informed public debate. It is often hard to determine how such contributions influence thinking, but there could be significant, cumulative effects over time. In some cases, think tanks may be of great value less because they are sources of breakthrough ideas and policy proposals and more because they offer retrospective and prospective coherence in a rapidly changing world, functioning as portals for information from other jurisdictions. They also stand as institutions that nurture and showcase new talent, perhaps exposing new staff to the realities of policy making and preparing them for subsequent positions in the public, private and non-profit sectors.

Think tanks are not alone: the three-community framework

The electronic discussions before GDN99 revealed considerable concern among participants about whether think tanks actually exert influence and whether they have access to sufficient resources and talent to produce work of relevance to decision makers. Others debated the question of whether think tanks ought to serve governments, donors and other international organisations, business associations, special interests, or citizens and communities. Many participants worried about how receptive governments in more authoritarian systems might be to policy inquiry that challenged their policies and governance styles. Related to this was the question of whether funding organisations, if willing to supply the necessary resources for think tanks (regardless of substantive and ideological orientations), would inordinately skew research priorities and recommendations.

Anxiety about think tanks and their relationship to potential and existing funders, and in whose interest they work, has long vexed even the best-endowed think tanks in North America and Europe, not to mention the vast majority of smaller and more precarious think tanks around the world. As I have argued elsewhere, the question about the extent of influence can only be answered in relative terms; it requires a thorough understanding of the institutional terrain in which think tanks work before an informed assessment can be ventured (Lindquist 1993). Indeed, think tanks are not alone: many other organisations are involved in policy inquiry and have similar aspirations of relevance. I refer to these actors collectively as a 'third community' involved in the knowledge-into-policy process, providing an array of different organisational 'sites' for producing policy inquiry and which constitute important links between decision makers and academics (Lindquist 1990). This framework is portrayed in Figure 12.3.

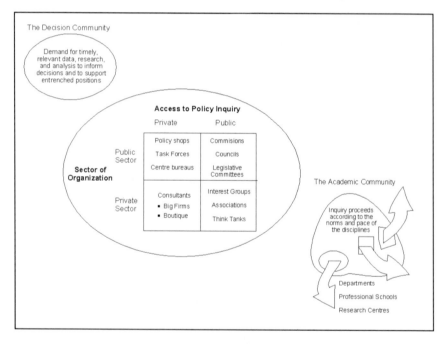

Figure 12.3 The third community and the network of policy actors

Each site is generally guided by different incentives and constraints, along with the unique mandates of specific organisations. However, broad distinctions can be made not only about governmental or non-governmental status but also about whether organisations are engaged in 'private' or 'public' inquiry. *Private* inquiry involves producing information with an aspiration of relevance, but it is forwarded for the *exclusive* use (however temporary) of the policy makers who commissioned the work. Actors inside and outside the government regularly undertaking such work include central agency bureaux, department policy shops, internal and cross-departmental task forces and committees, and consultants with clients at the political or top levels of the public service. *Public* inquiry refers to policy inquiry that is specifically intended for public consumption on completion of the work. It may or may not be sponsored by the public or private sector, and it embraces the work of external task forces, government commissions, peak interest associations and think tanks. This also includes the work of professors and academic centres with a policy bent: these bodies often administer sizeable grants and undertake policy-relevant work, and they thus constitute *de facto* think tanks. Indeed, in many countries, government grants councils encourage academics to undertake more policy-relevant research and other activities.

This framework has several implications for the GDN initiative. First, it cautions governments, international organisations and donors alike to have realistic expectations about the impact of knowledge and the influence of think tanks on decision makers and the policy-making process. Think tanks compete with a panoply of actors, many of whom have more substantial resources and better access to decision makers. Indeed, encouraging the proliferation of think tanks (particularly small ones) may serve only to increase the cacophony of policy voices without meaningfully increasing policy capacity in a sector. Furthermore, it may reduce the credibility of non-governmental voices in the eyes of decision makers, since without value-added contributions, think tanks will seem little more than special interest groups furthering certain values. However, I want to be clear that this does not mean that think tanks of all sizes cannot make important contributions to policy debates or exert influence on final decisions; rather, we should acknowledge that even think tanks of any scale may seem small compared with government and private sector organisations. Moreover, this framework reminds us that influence is often achieved over time, sometimes many years, in indirect and subtle ways through the movement of people across organisational boundaries and the seepage or spill-over of ideas into different institutional arenas.

The second major implication is related to the last point. The three-community framework shows how think tanks are part of a larger 'ecology' of organisations and individuals that comprise the knowledge-into-policy process. No matter how large the think tank, it will rely heavily on 'inputs' from elsewhere in policy networks. Most think tanks trade on the involvement of notables from the media, the private sector and the political and senior administrative cadres of government to attend events and to sit on advisory councils. Think tanks could not survive without academics and other experts to produce significant studies, and they usually depend on universities as important 'farm systems' for new recruits (Lindquist and Desveaux 1998). In other words, building healthy and sustainable think tanks requires a broader strategic perspective. It must encompass support for universities in their traditional academic mode as disciplinary training grounds and research enterprises, as well as more policy-relevant activities.

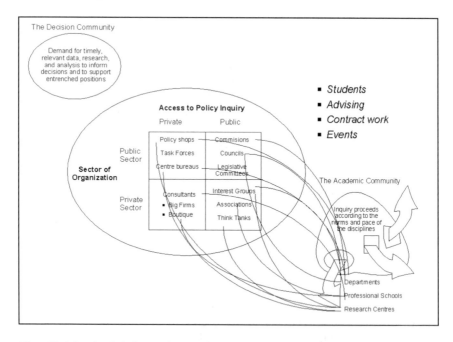

Figure 12.4 Academic influence is pervasive and subtle in the third community

This leads to a final 'ecological' point. Even if international organisations and donors succeed in nurturing think tank and academic policy inquiry, and in fostering better connections with their counterparts around the world, they need to determine whether or not there is sufficient capacity among government and non-governmental actors in the network to receive and make use of this information. At one level, there may be political or ideological barriers to openly acknowledge and discuss the work of outside organisations. However, as noted in Chapter 6, the problem can be more deeply rooted in that governments may have insufficient internal expertise or resources to interpret such work properly, convey its relevance to policy makers and pursue or support a productive discussion and follow-up research activities. Supporting think tanks and academics to pursue policy inquiry may be a futile exercise without addressing the important question of state capacity.

Governments and policy networks: some models to consider

The question of whether, how and to what extent governments, international organisations and foundations should support and structure their relationships with think tanks should be considered against a much larger canvas. Lest one believe that this unfairly removes think tanks from the forefront of the analysis, let me simply assert this is precisely the vantage point that all potential funders take when thinking about making strategic investments in any kind of policy inquiry. Governments need to weigh the costs and benefits of supporting think tanks against the ability of other institutions capable of undertaking policy inquiry, such as its own array of central and departmental policy shops, task forces, commissions, consultants, academics and university research centres. Donors increasingly evince interest in knowing whether think tanks, even if they undertake good work, can be expected to exert some influence on the policy-making process. In short, many funders are increasingly strategic about how they support policy inquiry.

These decisions have been made against the backdrop of the new realities of the information era, no matter what the precise distribution of analytical capabilities in each society. The strides in communication technology have greatly reduced the cost of establishing think tanks and continue to allow for the dispersal of more expertise outside the arms of government. Web-based dissemination of information lowers the barriers for obtaining data, analysis and research from around the world – governments have lost their monopoly and sometimes their comparative advantage in securing such information. There is greater recognition that policy problems do not respect artificial boundaries, not only within governments but also across sectors and jurisdictions.

Moreover, economic, technological and social change is proceeding so quickly and in such fundamental ways that political and bureaucratic leaders in developed and developing nations alike have reversed their condescending view of academics and critical policy inquiry. They have quickly recognised the value of such inquiry in assisting them to recognise and anticipate new challenges (that is, they now see the legitimacy of asking the 'big questions') and to develop workable and sometimes creative responses. Increasingly, political and bureaucratic leaders need to understand how to manage networks, which permit collaboration and the exchange of information, even though these ideas and research findings may be contested (Lindquist 1992; Sabatier and Jenkins-Smith 1993; Lindquist 1998).

Let me be even more provocative and suggest that the demand for such advice is sufficiently strong that it may have become difficult for think tanks and universities to supply this kind of knowledge without compromising their core tasks. Indeed, enlightened observers and leaders also realise that absorbing think tanks and academics too closely into their webs of influence might serve to strangle the very creativity that produces insights or knowledge that might unexpectedly be relevant to emerging policy problems (March and Sevon 1988; Lindquist and Desveaux 1998). It is not just a question of whether or how governments seek to control the production of policy inquiry for instrumental purposes but also how governments or donors may inadvertently affect the longer-term health of think tanks, academic centres and the larger networks they participate in.

I have already argued (see Fig. 12.4) that acknowledging the context in which think tanks work leads, at the very least, to a larger set of questions about how to make good strategic investments, because alternative investments must be weighed. How useful will the sponsored research, analysis, data or event be? Will the work be completed in a reasonable time frame? Can confidentiality be maintained for a period of time? Can they get access to work that otherwise might not get done? Do they need to get a public message out that reflects internal concerns? But a focus on creativity and surprise leads one to an even broader *non-instrumental* criterion for evaluating options for support, as well as options for how best to nurture or enrich policy networks and epistemic communities.

My thinking on these matters is shaped by two recent Canadian examples of organising interactions with networks of academics, think tanks and non-governmental organisations. These experiences, I believe, are pertinent to the GDN debate because they provide examples of top-down and bottom-up approaches to organising the interactions between governments and networks of non-governmental organisations. Moreover, neither involved huge outlays of funds – in each case, the primary focus was on leveraging resources and building communities of interest on policy issues. There is space only to sketch out the nature of these initiatives.

The Policy Research Initiative of the government of Canada

During the mid-1990s, there was growing concern about the policy capacity in Canada's federal public service. The secretary to the cabinet created two task forces led by deputy ministers, one on strengthening policy capacity and the other on managing horizontal issues. These were commissioned to probe the extent of the problem in the public service and to propose solutions (see Canada 1996a, b). Generally, it was concluded that internal capacity had to be strengthened, but to grapple fully with the complex problems confronting the country required leveraging the expertise residing in think tanks, non-profit organisations and universities. To do so, it was also recognised that the government had to improve its 'receptor' capacity; that is, to identify, receive and interpret information emanating from think tanks and other organisations and to more systematically interact and exchange ideas with outside analysts and researchers.

This led in 1996 to the Policy Research Initiative, which sought to increase the capacity of policy units across the public service and to strengthen connections with external research organisations. A functional community (or network) of assistant/deputy members responsible for policy analysis across the public service was established to explore issues pertaining to recruitment, training and development, and to work laterally on policy issues. A Policy Research Secretariat (PRS) was formed to support the exercise. Four networks of officials produced reports surveying the state of understanding and policy challenges in the areas of global change, growth, social cohesion and human development and then went on to identify gaps in knowledge. This exercise informed transition planning and the priorities of the second government of Prime Minister Jean Chretien. The PRS also created a superb website – it is a real resource that provides hyperlinks to scores of policy institutions inside and outside Canada, regularly announces policy-relevant events and reports and points visitors to 'tools' or 'resources' that would be useful for policy analysts.

Since its inception, the PRS has held regional round tables, consultations and two national policy conferences with think tanks, academics and some non-governmental organisations with research interests. It has taken advantage of an annual round of national academic meetings (the Congress of Humanities and Social Sciences) to facilitate additional meetings with government officials and to institute briefings for members of parliament on social science research findings. It has also led to collaboration with the Social Sciences and Humanities Research Council of Canada (the primary sponsor of academic research) on the Trends Project, which provided funding for several clusters of academics to explore eight topics. It has also served to accelerate the data liberation initiative between the Council and Statistics Canada, which seeks to give academic and other researchers quicker and greater access to data that would otherwise be inaccessible or too expensive to obtain.

The Canadian Environmental Network

The Canadian Environmental Network (CEN) was formed in the late 1970s by non-governmental environmental groups in order to facilitate and to coordinate their interactions with the federal Department of Environment (Environment Canada). The CEN is a loose clustering of hundreds of non-governmental environmental groups, large and small. It has a small national secretariat, which supports eleven regional networks of its members, fourteen caucuses organised around specific environmental issues and two working groups on specific initiatives. Even though the CEN is not comprised of think tanks, it provides a fascinating organisational model that the GDN would do well to consider.

The CEN emphatically states that it does not take positions on issues; its purpose is primarily to facilitate communication between its members and the interactions of its members with Environment Canada on a coordinated basis. The CEN provides a process for selecting delegates for meetings and for consultations inside and outside the country, and it maintains links with its counterparts in other jurisdictions. The secretariat maintains a database and the website, and it publishes newsletters. The CEN describes itself as a 'non-advocacy network,' an interesting posture given the fact that environmental groups are noted for their skill in and commitment to advocacy.

It is for these reasons that transparency, neutrality and cooperation are essential to the CEN. It operates in a decentralised manner; regional and affiliated networks deal with issues, a particularly important matter in a federal jurisdiction. Caucuses and working groups can be created when members identify a specific issue that needs to be pursued; they must seek formal recognition from the national steering committee and identify at least one chair and secure sufficient national representation to ensure a good mix for government and other consultations. The subjects of caucuses and working groups include the atmosphere, biotechnology, ecological pest management, environmental assessment, environmental education, energy, forests, health and sustainability, mining, the oceans, toxic waste, water, youth, an overhaul of the Fisheries Act and the harmonisation of regulations across jurisdictions. Effectively, though, the caucuses and working groups are self-organising and often work with non-environmental groups with similar interests. They receive modest support from the national steering committee to maintain what are typically volunteer activities. However, caucuses can mobilise to secure additional resources from government or the private sector to pursue issues in more detail.

The activities of the CEN have to be put in perspective – it is effectively a means for environmental groups to streamline and coordinate interactions with the federal government. Environment Canada funds all sorts of policy inquiry for science-based and policy-related research and analysis, a good portion of which would flow to think tanks, universities and environmental groups alike. Such funding would dwarf the resources committed to supporting CEN activities.

Implications for the GDN: a modest proposal

The Policy Research Initiative and the Canadian Environmental Network stand as interesting examples of, respectively, top-down and bottom-up approaches to managing the interface between governments and networks of non-governmental organisations. There are undoubtedly similar initiatives from other jurisdictions and sectors that could also serve as models to be considered by those seeking to elaborate the GDN. There are several lessons worth considering:

- Small secretariats can achieve a lot; a network does not have to create 'heavy' bureaucracies to facilitate interaction and information exchange.
- A premium should be attached to facilitating communication and the exchange of ideas between actors within and across policy networks – in other words, finding efficient ways to move insights across institutional and sectoral divides.
- There is a larger 'ecology' of interests and capacities that are connected to policy inquiry and political action. Cultivating knowledge networks involves more than nurturing think tanks and should also encompass supporting university researchers and other knowledge institutions.
- Networks and issues will evolve over time, so a key objective should be to sponsor continuous interaction and to enrich lines of communication on new topics of interest.
- Astute network management is about respecting different organisational, substantive and ideological orientations of members.
- Governments, international organisations and other private sponsors should have the right to fund initiatives, but members of the network also have the right to secure funding and mobilise on other initiatives.

In short, there is no reason why the more instrumental inclinations of governments and the self-organising tendencies of non-governmental actors cannot be simultaneously achieved by astute and transparent network management.

The overarching lesson is not to 'over-organise' or 'over-formalise' emerging networks, which only serves to undermine the distinctive flexibility of this organisational approach. Rather, the goal should be to find ways to expand the network and to encourage participants to communicate regularly, to exchange information and to mobilise on matters of concern to their members, and always to leave open the possibility of unpredicted issues and initiatives. However, this loose organising approach would be buttressed by an understanding of the common general purpose (that is, to bring knowledge and expertise from around the world to bear on development issues) to be served by this interaction despite diverse intellectual, regional and political agendas.

There are several implications for the Global Development Network initiative. Conferences like the one held in Bonn in December 1999 should be held on a regular basis, preceded by a series of regional events. At the same time, however, there is the potential for the creation of issue-based caucuses on different topics that would transcend regional boundaries and build communities of interest on development issues that are not simply regionally based. Separate funding could be secured for the caucuses, and members could organise meetings in advance of GDN conferences, perhaps piggy-backing on the events of other organisations. A state-of-the-art website (with a good search engine) promises to permit the exchange of ideas between the regional and policy caucuses, to give notice of recently published studies and forthcoming conferences and symposia, and to provide hyperlinks to all member organisations and related resources, since the accumulated links promise to be considerable. Generally, these activities can be supported by a small secretariat as well as regional and caucus steering committees that reflect the breadth and diversity of membership.

The goal of the GDN initiative should not be to develop policy positions but rather to facilitate the exchange of ideas and research findings, and to provide manifold opportunities for networking. International organisations and donors could sponsor particular round tables or panels, but there would be many other papers, panels and activities at the conference, regional and caucus events that would include the staff from think tanks, universities, governments, NGOs, and international and donor organisations. Special effort must be made to connect, engage and support policy-oriented academics and university research centres in developing countries. The range of these activities and developments would be reflected in the GDN website. In all cases, the goal should be to maintain a rolling agenda that is broad and stimulating.

Concluding remarks

Governments must be increasingly strategic about their investments in policy inquiry and must have realistic assessments of existing capacities. Investing only in think tanks is insufficient, since the relationship with academic institutions, government research bureaux and other actors is symbiotic: an entire 'ecology' must be nurtured and supported. This suggests that any focus on think tanks *per se* will have limited impact over the longer horizon; a key implication is that international organisations, governments and other donors must support academic institutions by developing stronger, more vibrant disciplines, professional schools and research centres. These are the institutions that will provide the analysts and leaders of tomorrow, as well as the staff and expert knowledge so crucial to the survival of think tanks and, more generally, to the functioning of institutions that comprise healthy policy networks. Attention must also be directed to expanding the 'receptor' capacity of governments in order to increase the chances that policy inquiry from think tanks and academics is reviewed, interpreted and perhaps nurtured.

In addition, donors must have a more elastic view of the many pathways to policy influence, which points to images more like an ongoing 'dance' than a pronounced series of impacts in a short period. Rarely can non-governmental entities, let alone policy units inside bureaucracies, demonstrate definitive impacts on policy outcomes. This does not mean that think tanks are unimportant but rather that the very complexity of policy making augurs for tempered and more subtle expectations about how influence obtains in policy networks. The pathways to influence may be even more indirect and subtle in countries with authoritarian regimes. A longer view suggests that it is essential to develop a sustainable capacity, which includes cultivating trust, building personal and organisational networks inside and outside the country.

It is for these reasons that I have suggested that the GDN would do well to be more circumscribed with respect to identifying its own research priorities and instead focus on facilitating interaction and diffusion of research, and identifying new ideas and initiatives. This approach may seem less 'effective' in conventional terms, but it fits with the dynamics of policy making and knowledge sharing, and it promises to have a greater, if unpredictable, impact on global development.

References

Abelson, D. E. (1996) *American Think Tanks and Their Role in US Foreign Policy*, London and New York: Macmillan.

Baumgartner, F. R. and Jones, B. D. (1993) *Agendas and Instability in American Politics*, Chicago: University of Chicago Press.

Canada, Task Force on Strengthening Policy Capacity (1996a) *Strengthening Our Policy Capacity*. Website: http://www.ccmd-ccg.gc.ca/pdfs/policye.pdf.

Canada, Task Force on Managing Horizontal Policy Issues (1996b) *Managing Horizontal Policy Issues*. Website: http://www.ccmd-ccg.gc.ca/pdfs/horize.pdf.

Canada, Policy Research Secretariat and SSHRC (1999) *The Trends Project Research Papers*, Ottawa: PRS and SSHRC.

Canada, Policy Research Initiative website: http://policyresearch.schoolnet.ca/.

Canadian Environmental Network website: http://www.cen.web.net/.

Caplan, N. (1979) 'The two-communities theory and knowledge utilization', *American Behavioral Scientist* 22(2): 459–70.

Critchlow, D. T. (1985) *The Brookings Institution, 1916–1952: Expertise and the Public Interest in a Democratic Society*, DeKalb: Northern Illinois University Press.

Coleman, W. D. and Skogstad, G. (1990) *Policy Communities and Public Policy in Canada: A Structural Approach*, Mississauga: Copp Clark Pitman.

Heclo, H. (1978) 'Issue Networks and the Executive Establishment', in A. King (ed.) *The New American Political System*, Washington: American Enterprise Institute for Public Policy Research, 87–124.

Jordan, G. (1990) 'Sub-governments, policy communities and networks: re-filling the old bottles?' *Journal of Theoretical Politics* 2(3): 319–38.

Kingdon, J. W. (1995 [1984]) *Agendas, Alternatives, and Public Policies*, second edition, New York, HarperCollins.

Langford, J. W. and Brownsey, K. L. (eds) (1991) *Think Tanks and Governance in the Asia-Pacific Region*, Halifax: Institute for Research on Public Policy.

Lindquist, E. A. (1990) 'The third community, social scientists, and policy inquiry', in S. Brooks and A.-G. Gagnon (eds) *Social Scientists, Policy, and the State*, New York: Praeger.

Lindquist, E. A. (1992) 'Public managers and policy communities: learning to meet new challenges', *Canadian Public Administration* 35(2): 127–59.

Lindquist, E. A. (1993) 'Think tanks or clubs? Assessing the influence and relevance of policy institutes in Canada', *Canadian Public Administration* 36, winter: 547–79.

Lindquist, E. A. (1998) 'The Canadian government, policy research, and network management', report prepared for the Policy Research Secretariat, 8 November.

Lindquist, E. A. and Desveaux, J. A. (1998) *Recruitment and Policy Capacity in Government*, Ottawa: Public Policy Forum.

Lynn, L. E. (ed.) (1978) *Knowledge and Policy: The Uncertain Connection*, Washington: National Academy of Sciences.

March, J. G. and Sevon, G. (1988) 'Gossip, information and decision-making', in J. G. March (ed.) *Decisions and Organizations*, Oxford: Blackwell.

McGann, J. G. and Weaver, R. K. (eds) (2000) *Think Tanks and Civil Societies: Catalysts for Ideas and Action*, Somerset, NJ: Transaction Press.

Pross, P. A. (1986) *Group Politics and Public Policy*, Toronto: Oxford University Press.

Sabatier, P. A. and Jenkins-Smith, H. C. (eds) (1993) *Policy Change and Learning: An Advocacy Coalition Approach*, Boulder, Colo.: Westview Press.

Smith, J. A. (1991) *The Idea Brokers: Think Tanks and the Rise of the New Policy Elite*, New York: Free Press.

Stone, D., Denham, A. and Garnett, M. (eds) (1998) *Think Tanks Across Nations: A Comparative Approach*, Manchester: Manchester University Press.

Weiss, C. H. (1977) 'Research for policy's sake: the enlightenment function of social research', *Policy Analysis* 3(4): 531–45.

Weiss, C. H. (1980) 'Knowledge creep and decision accretion', *Knowledge: Creation, Diffusion, Utilization* 1(3): 381–404.

Conclusion

13 Knowledge, power and policy

Diane Stone

'Knowledge equals power'. This final chapter takes as its starting point this declaration made by the German federal minister for economic cooperation and development, Heidimarie Wiezoreck-Zuel, at GDN99 in Bonn. It is an important political equation and one to keep in mind in the aspiration to 'create and share knowledge'. The significance of knowledge is that it informs, enables and empowers those who possess it and the institutions that are the embodiment of it. Knowledge creation is usually regarded as a good thing for its own sake, but one that may also have unanticipated benefits. Knowledge sharing is viewed as an important route for grappling with complex problems faced by societies and economies of both the developed and developing world. The expansion of state capacities and responsibilities, the rapidity of technological and communications advances, the forces of globalisation, the pressing need for reform, adjustment, and greater uncertainty over policy choices calls forth a requirement for informed decision making. The pace of change creates a dynamic not only for information and analysis but also for intelligent criticism and alternative ideas that is often provided by research.

The chapters that have been included in this volume are drawn primarily from the papers and presentations delivered in the 'Business of Think Tanks' panel sessions at GDN99. Accordingly, the contributions collected here are only one facet of the range of papers and presentations that were prepared for the first conference. The research papers that were delivered in Bonn covered issues as diverse as land reform, privatisation, education, labour standards, financial contagion and regional economic integration. By contrast, the common theme of the papers in the 'Business' panel sessions was an analytical concern with how ideas do or do not influence policy and more specifically, how think tanks and research institutes as organisations and as congregations of scholars and experts might inform policy making and make the critical connections with decision makers. In these panel sessions, there was a recognition that knowledge represents a form of power.

In many respects, the book has been built around the chapter written by Joseph Stiglitz. His presentation in Bonn set out a vision for the future of the network and what could be achieved through sharing global knowledge and reinventing it locally. Accordingly, the remainder of this first section rehearses some of these themes that were adopted by other contributors. However, the following sections draw out in greater detail two particularly strong themes that developed across chapters. One theme concerns influence. Thus the second section addresses the concept of the GDN as a bridge and seeks to connect this experiment to broader themes in the social science literature on the role of ideas in political and economic development. A second theme was the attention given to informal networks and partnerships at both international and national levels to convey ideas and shape consensus. However, relatively little attention has been given to the idea of what makes a network work effectively, efficiently and equitably. The final section ends with a little-discussed matter essential to the longevity and legitimacy of the GDN: the wider issues of network management.

Common themes

Through the GDN, the World Bank gives one representation of its new incarnation as the 'knowledge bank'. In the account given by Stiglitz, the importance of knowledge is cast in at least three ways: a view of knowledge as a global public good; a recognition that knowledge is tacit as well as codified; and an understanding that policy knowledge is grounded in local experience as well as global 'best practice'. On the last score, the gardening metaphor of *nemawashi* is a theme that resonated across some chapters. More prosaically known as policy transfer, it is a process by which societies adapt or synthesise 'global forms' of knowledge to suit local circumstances. It also has a promising reverse effect in the extent to which these organisations are able to feed 'grass-roots knowledge' back into international organisations and donor agencies or what Ivan Krastev referred to as local partners that can provide 'friendly' but 'knowledgeable' criticism. Both Stella Ladi and Simon James recognise the progressive value of moving from a 'one size fits all' approach of development models to one that is more sensitive to local institutions and cultural arrangements, but they also recognise continuing barriers and constraints to the spread and adoption of policy knowledge.

The link between institutions, ideas, power and legitimacy, which Joseph Stiglitz touches upon in Chapter 2, was explored in a number of chapters. Legitimacy in the planning and implementation development programmes or transition reforms is often seen as arising from the participation of civil society actors. Consequently, civil society partners have been sought by multilateral development assistance agencies and other donors. Think tanks tend to be viewed as civil society organisations with the critical capacities to inform the development and/or transition processes as well as to build effective channels of communication between governments and the people. In the shifting stance of the World Bank away from the so-called 'Washington consensus', greater credence is accorded to the idea of 'social capital' and particularly the way in which non-market improvements can impact positively on the market and aid economic development. In this context, with their status as civil society organisations, think tanks represent a form of 'social capital' to be cultivated (Fine 1999); that is, entities that enhance social cohesion and other intangible benefits of civic association.

As Oleg Manaev revealed, in the absence of a healthy or vibrant civil society, the foundations for more constructive and diverse sources of policy advice are often lacking but can be aided by think tanks. The chapters by Ratna Sudarshan on India and Gabriel Ortiz de Zevallos and Alejandro Salas on Peru discuss the productive and fulfilling partnerships for the delivery of public goods and services that can be built by institutes in collaboration with other societal actors. Their potential benefits can be summarised in five points.

- Institutes operate as 'conduits for civic education', helping to improve public understanding of government policies or the impacts of globalisation.
- Institutes 'give voice' to other community bodies and civic associations and help to facilitate their interactions with market actors or governance agencies. This was one of the objectives behind the National Council of Applied Economic Research collaboration with the Self Employed Women's Association in India.
- Think tanks 'fuel debate' by putting forward alternative perspectives, methodologies and proposals for public and official consideration.
- These organisations have the potential to promote 'transparency and accountability' in political life by scrutinising policies, identifying abuses of power and raising questions in public. These latter two functions are particularly pertinent to the Belarusian Association of Think Tanks.
- Institutes can 'promote legitimation', influencing the recognition of respect given (or denied) to public authorities (see Scholte 2000: 190–3).

It is not only in the confines of the nation-state that institutes are active. A number of these organisations seek to address not only their domestic constituency but also regional and global audiences, or what we might refer to as the domain of global civil society (*ibid.*). Many chapters addressed the transnational activities of think tanks or how some are becoming distinctively regional and global in their research focus and their interactions. Sometimes, these research gatherings and dialogues spill over to acquire a governance role such as through informal diplomacy at the regional level, noted by Kao Kim Hourn and by Helen Nesadurai and Diane Stone. Over the past two or three decades, the scale and density of cross-national exchange between think tanks and with other civil society actors such as foundations, universities and training facilities has mounted significantly. Accordingly, the GDN can be regarded both as a forum for global civil society and as a global civil society actor itself.

However, as a couple of papers remind us, neither the status of research institutes and think tanks as 'third-sector' organisations nor their potential benefits can be taken for granted. In particular, Ole Sending and Knut Nustad, along with Ivan Krastev, question the NGO paradigm as one that focuses primarily on formal organisation – a Western transplant of a civil society ideal – to the neglect of informal and traditional relationships that sustain many societies. Within this conceptualisation of civil society, research institutes fit the presumed organisational model. Furthermore, these institutes possess the intellectual and rhetorical skills to 'talk the talk' of development agencies (as Nustad and Sending describe) and present themselves as research NGOs to benefit from the largesse of donor organisations.

While there are fruits from civil engagement, there are also pitfalls (*ibid.*: 194–6). In brief, civic groups can be marred by 'undemocratic processes' in their own internal workings, characterised by 'top-down managerial authoritarianism' and poor transparency with regard to procedures of office, annual reporting and financial accounting. Similarly, 'inadequate representation', a self-selecting leadership and biased access can exaggerate structural inequalities among research communities. These are tendencies against which the GDN needs to be vigilant. Notwithstanding the laudable aims of 'creating and sharing knowledge', a civil society research institute may nonetheless suffer from 'flawed' policy, inadequate standards, distance from other civil society groups or, as stated elsewhere: 'Some research institutes have not got beyond theoretical models to political practicalities' (*ibid.*: 194).

Cross-cutting all chapters was the concern with intellectual reputation and scholarly stature. Both Kao Kim Hourn and Simon James stressed the importance of impartiality in building trust and confidence between think tanks and the government and with the public. Independence and a degree of detachment from power is generally regarded by most of the contributors as necessary to maintaining the credibility and scholarly authority of think tanks. To maintain their reputation and repudiate accusations of politicisation, advocacy and lobbying, or ideological polemic, think tank managers often encourage engagement with academic communities. Those institutes that are most highly regarded also tend to be the institutes that have longstanding interaction with universities and scientific establishments, and those that participate in academic peer review processes. Think tanks adopt the professional norms associated with academia to secure scholarly legitimacy. Furthermore, there is often a considerable degree of mobility between think tanks and university departments, with some think tanks established in universities. Too close an affinity with government, a political party or an NGO can seriously undermine their authority and legitimacy as objective (or at least balanced) knowledge providers and potentially dissolve important distinctions between the research institute and the special interest advocacy group.

The GDN 'bridge'

The proliferation of think tanks around the world over the past two decades has been dramatic. Conservative estimates put the number of think tanks worldwide at between 3,000 and 4,000 (McGann and Weaver 2000). As noted by Stella Ladi, these organisations defy exact definition. Indeed, an electronic discussion convened by the World Bank in November 1999 found little consensus on what is or is not a 'think tank' or 'research institute'.[1] Part of the explanation lies in the remarkable diversity of these organisations.

Institutes and think tanks vary considerably in size, structure, policy ambit and political significance. Some organisations at least aspire to function on a 'non-partisan' or 'non-ideological' basis and claim to adopt a 'scientific' or technical approach to social and economic problems. Some think tanks are 'academic' in style, focusing on research, geared to university interests (and sometimes part of university structures) and building the knowledge base of society. Other organisations are overtly partisan (connected as they may be to political parties or government) or ideologically motivated. Many institutes are routinely engaged in the marketing of ideas, whether in simplified policy-relevant form or in sound bites for the media. Nevertheless, think tank managers and staff tend to be motivated by internalised professional standards similar to those of the university setting. Yet their policy focus differentiates them from university research, which is often more academic, theoretical and less amenable to general consumption. They attempt to inform policy through intellectual argument and analysis rather than lobbying, and many (but not all) think tank directors draw the line at advocacy. This interplay of knowledge and policy is complemented by strategic practices to develop advisory ties to government, industry or the public.

The terms 'think tank' and 'research institute' have been used interchangeably in this volume. As Ratna Sudarshan argues making a distinction between 'research institutes' involved in research and 'think tanks' as advocacy bodies is often a false one. However, for those who do adhere to the distinction it is an important one in that it shapes preconceptions of how knowledge, research or ideas might have an impact on policy makers. The idea of a 'research institute' as a quasi-academic association producing research in a detached, non-partisan, scholarly fashion assumes that knowledge will trickle through into understanding. If this were the case, then there would be no need for associations like the GDN. The best ideas and the most relevant research do not automatically find their way to those in power. It is often necessary to broadcast research results and find other means to make ideas matter.

The greater resort to advocacy and the more pronounced ideological positions of institutes became apparent as their numbers rose in the USA, Britain and other English-speaking nations during the 1980s and as the marketplace for ideas became more congested and competitive. This much-analysed phenomenon (see, *inter alia*, Abelson 2000; Smith 1991; Ricci 1993) reveals that the best ideas do not always capture political attention and that much policy-relevant research would lie fallow without a dialogue with those in power.

This dilemma is encapsulated in the theme of the first GDN conference – 'bridging knowledge and policy'. Scholars have long had difficulty in accounting for the role of ideas in policy and politics, and the lack of analytical attention given to think tanks, academics and experts in the social science literature can be regarded as a more notable manifestation of this problem.

Think tanks are often conceived of as a bridge between academia and decision makers and as having a strategic role of interpreting and communicating the pure and applied research of their colleagues to the wider world. Think tanks bring social science research into the public domain by seeking appointment of their staff to government commissions or industry delegations and by giving evidence to congressional or parliamentary committees. Published research drawing out the policy implications is the most obvious medium of communicating research findings. Seminars, lectures, lunch meetings and conferences are other means of spreading ideas. In this context, the ability of think tank members to establish links with the media, trade unions, pressure groups, political parties, bureaucrats and departments is essential to their networking and coalition building. The links – often informal – create a route of access to decision makers in order to promote ideas and inform public opinion.

The metaphor of 'building bridges' between the research world and the world of politics has become a popular one. It conveys the sense that 'ideas' and 'knowledge' can be put on to a transmission belt into policy deliberations. It has immediate appeal and is a phrase that was frequently adopted at GDN99 in conference plenaries and panels and subsequently in some of the chapters in this volume. For example, in one presentation, 'bridging' was conceptualised in terms of a problem in communication:

> It is the task of academics and research institutes world wide to analyze the complex interrelationships of our times, to describe them and to translate them into a language that will not just be understood by political decision-makers but also by the players of civil society. A great many of the insights that have already been gained and that are important for a more viable future have not been translated into practice so far because there is too little common language between academics and politicians.
>
> (Wiezoreck-Zuel 1999)

The bridge can also be conceptualised as an internal mechanism for the research community to connect individual think tanks and researchers and provide avenues for collaborative or cross-cutting research and other synergies. Another possibility offered by the 'bridge' metaphor is that it offers a unique vantage point. In this sense, the 'GDN bridge' is the opportunity to peruse the passing intellectual currents and eddies of new ideas. Consequently, the 'bridge' metaphor works at a number of levels, in which the GDN functions as a communications bridge, a bridge for research collaboration, a networking bridge for exchanges between individuals and a bridge that connects the scholarly world of researchers with the world of policy and practice.

While this kind of metaphor has strong attractions, it also makes an ontological distinction between power and knowledge. Much of the discussion at the GDN and more generally in the media and scholarly literature about research institutes and think tanks reveals that they are often perceived as occupying not only physical but also cognitive space that is different and apart from that occupied by decision makers. That is, there is a common image of distinct and autonomous communities where researchers, social scientists and experts revolve in the scientific and scholarly realm (or 'ivory tower') providing information, analysis and advice to a separate and politicised domain inhabited by politicians, administrators and civil servants. The spheres are juxtaposed. This is captured in the famous book title *Speaking Truth to Power* (Wildavsky 1979). There is an implicit assumption that there is something rational and pure about 'science' that by 'force of reason' will trickle through into the consciousness and subsequent policy thinking of decision makers, hence their actions. However, as a number of contributors have revealed, the extent to which ideas inform and influence policy is a political process, perhaps more so than it is a rational one.

The public good of knowledge

Knowledge is increasingly cast as a global public good (Kaul *et al* 1999). The role of research institutes producing public goods was raised by Gabriel Ortiz de Zevallos and Alejandro Salas, who recognised that this characteristic often leads to underinvestment in knowledge creation. In this perspective, 'knowledge' is an asset. It is something that can be acquired through education or a knowledge network, or denied through inadequate education provision together with constraints on academic freedom and muzzling of the media.

The main policy problem identified in the public goods framework is not always one of under-provision but often that of inadequate or insufficient access to knowledge (see Stiglitz 1999). The GDN is one mechanism that will help to ameliorate this problem and disseminate development knowledge horizontally between different governance levels (local, national, regional, global) and vertically between network participants – think tanks, foundations, NGOs, donor organisations and government agencies. In short, the GDN could play an essential role in making knowledge more accessible.

The flaw in the public goods framework is that it tends to treat knowledge as homogeneous, free-floating and apolitical. Reference to 'knowledge' does not signify a single body of knowledge that is commonly recognised and ascertainable. On the contrary, it implies a struggle between different 'knowledges' or what are often described as 'discourses', 'world views'[2] and 'regimes of truth'. Accordingly, for many the issue is not simply the creation and dissemination of knowledge but the kind of knowledge that is produced and the kind of knowledge that dominates. As developed in Chapter 3 by Knut Nustad and Ole Sending, the very idea of 'knowledge' cannot be taken for granted. Knowledge takes many different forms, and that form of knowledge which is considered to be relevant is a political process that reflects the 'cognitive interests' of the sources of demand.

This contest of ideas between different discourses or knowledges is not far from the GDN. The struggle over knowledge is manifest in the wider bureaucratic struggles within the World Bank as it changes course away from the Washington consensus towards the Comprehensive Development Framework. The issues crystallised in the electronic discussions and at GDN99. First, some contributors bemoaned the imposition of universal policy models. This was amplified in one of the GDN99 plenary sessions, where the prime minister of Uganda, Apolo Nsibambi, said:

The knowledge of the communities in the South is sometimes deliberately ignored by Northern users who prefer to make their own researchers do short term research on Southern communities and development problems. This has led to situations in which hastily formulated findings are mistaken for knowledge just because they are well-packaged in Northern languages.

(Nsibambi 1999)

Second, others expressed concern that the knowledge, methods and approaches of economics will dominate the GDN to the marginalisation of other disciplines and practitioner insights. Interventions by representatives of the European Association of Development Research and Training Institutes (EADI) at the Bonn conference and in the electronic discussion groups have drawn attention to one set of 'cognitive interest' deemed to be dominating the GDN process at a formative stage of its institutionalisation.

The (funding) incentive policy of the World Bank and deliberate choice to almost exclusively support Economic (!) Research Institutions to participate was considered to be too narrow, as many existing Research Institutes of a broader orientation could feel by-passed. Multi-disciplinary approaches come closer to the reality of the people in the countries of the South (and the North) than exclusive (economistic) ways at [sic] looking toward development phenomena.[3]

In another context an even stronger criticism of the role of economists in international financial institutions comes from Joseph Stiglitz (2000):

When the IMF decides to assist a country, it dispatches a 'mission' of economists. These economists frequently lack extensive experience in the country; they are more likely to have firsthand knowledge of its five-star hotels than of the villages that dot its countryside. They work hard, poring over numbers deep into the night. But their task is impossible. In a period of days or, at most, weeks, they are charged with developing a coherent program sensitive to the needs of the country. Needless to say, a little number-crunching rarely provides adequate insights into the development strategy for an entire nation. Even worse, the number-crunching isn't always that good. The mathematical models the IMF uses are frequently flawed or out-of-date. Critics accuse the institution of taking a cookie-cutter approach to economics, and they're right. ...

The great strength, and the ultimate weakness, of the economic doctrines upon which they relied is that the doctrines are – or are supposed to be – universal. Institutions, history, or even the distribution of income simply do not matter. Good economists know the universal truths and can look beyond the array of facts and details that obscure these truths.

Although the rebuke from IMF economists towards Stiglitz' portrayal of them is understandable, economics has hegemonic tendencies in the social sciences and has been intellectually imperialistic by imposing its 'parsimonious models' and 'substantive rationality' within many international organisations (Higgott 2000).

The preceding quotes offer at least two possible readings for the future of the GDN given that the working group on governance proposed that 'GDN will have a strong economics core but will draw on all social sciences'. On the one hand, the GDN can be perceived as a vehicle to entrench and resource the cognitive interests of economic knowledge. In such a case, the views and insights coming from other disciplinary sources on development are not excluded but are exploited not simply to bolster the legitimacy of the GDN but as a means for economics to 'socialise' other disciplines. On the other hand, if it is accepted that hegemony is never complete in either inspiration or execution, then the GDN is also a medium through which other disciplinary and practitioner perspectives can 'house train' economists. However, the latter is unlikely to occur unless other disciplines are well represented in GDN structures.

It is not the intention here to suggest that other social science knowledge is 'better' than that provided by economics. The concern is to indicate that it is a particular knowledge that is institutionalised in the major international financial institutions to a degree that other forms of knowledge are not. A similar point is raised by Gabriel Ortiz de Zevallos and Alejandro Salas, who note that constitutional reform in Peru is dominated by the law profession to the detriment, on occasion, of other professional insights. To recognise some of these power differentials between experts and disciplines embedded in institutions would go some way towards making the GDN an interdisciplinary policy bridge rather than an uneven multi-disciplinary research forum.

Finally, a few have expressed reservations about the structural power of the World Bank in promoting its policy preferences founded on market liberalism through the network. Without labouring the point, the continuance of divisive debate over the 'Washington consensus' symbolises the power of ideas.[4] These conflicts are not merely intellectual differences but are part of a wider contest over the terms of policy debate and in the conceptualisation of 'development' that forms social realities.

The elusiveness of influence

The 'bridge' metaphor is not the only means by which to conceive of knowledge meeting power. A more organic and interdependent view of the relationship between knowledge and power can be found. In Chapter 12, for example, Evert Lindquist developed the idea of 'three communities' and stressed the interdependencies and broader 'ecology' of knowledge.

The question of knowledge having wider policy relevance, impact and influence is a difficult one and is subject to numerous interpretations. The preceding chapters addressed this issue in different ways. Ivan Krastev made the distinction between direct and indirect influence. In a similar fashion, Simon James built a tripartite typology of 'atmospheric', 'short- to medium-term agendas' and 'micro-policy' realms of influence. Policy research institutes are not solely engaged in disinterested research but also seek, in some degree over the immediate to medium term, impact on the content of legislation or character of decision making. They often have long-term objectives of shaping our understanding of socio-political realities. While most institutes are not consistently or even often successful in these endeavours, they have nevertheless become recognisable features of the policy landscape in many countries.

The routes to influence are also numerous, but very rarely direct or unobstructed. Ideas are embedded in institutions, and institutions shape our interactions. The weight of 'conventional wisdom' or pre-existing institutionalised knowledge sets agendas and creates path dependencies that can be highly resistant to the new insights and knowledge created by research. Nevertheless, as the chapters by both Joseph Stiglitz and Helen Nesadurai and Diane Stone outline, 'social learning' is a process that can promote progressive change. Learning is conceived of in two senses: by Stiglitz as 'learning by doing' through the local reappropriation, synthesis and adaptation of knowledge that promotes self-confidence, self-esteem and self-efficacy in local communities; and by Nesadurai and Stone as reinterpretations of interests that allow new collective identities and opportunities for collaboration such as through regional cooperation. In both cases, the impact or influence of institutes as agents of learning is not observable or amenable to the standards of falsifiable scientific inquiry.

While Knut Nustad and Ole Sending asked 'whose knowledge?' was shaping the GDN and development practices more generally, Evert Lindquist cautioned to ask 'influence with whom?' In this regard, both Oleg Manaev and Kao Kim Hourn indicated that those they sought to impress could be the general public and civil society groups just as much as it could be government or the political process. Indeed, Oleg Manaev clearly brought home the point that ideas have influence or, at the very least, that attracting government attention can have negative consequences. Informed policy debates and expertise can represent a challenge to power. In contrast to the observable use of power by those in authority to impose tax, to declare war (or the illegitimate exercise of power by the Mafia), this form of influence has been labelled 'soft power'. It is a more subtle and unseen process, where knowledge has a role in 'shaping policy agendas, in challenging the language and terminology of public debate, in redefining the mental maps of policy-makers' (Wallace 1998: 224).

Networking is also posited as one route to policy influence and means of making knowledge accessible. Networks are an organisational form with extraordinary capacities for innovation, managing risk, building trust, facilitating joint action and gathering information in a manner that flows around and between geographical, legal and institutional barriers. When networks include the active participation and involvement of decision makers they have the potential to influence policy (Coleman and Perl 1999). Even without such political involvement, the norms, values and aspirations of networks can have a significant impact on the climate of elite opinion and the culture of public debate with 'atmospheric' impact.

Global network development

A network is a medium through which a shared sense of obligation and common cause can be cultivated. Shared values, a sense of obligation and recognition of the value of cooperation can act as either a complement or counter to rationally bounded self-interested activity. It provides one basis for the creation of public goods.

Many of the chapters in this volume discuss the various kinds of network in which research institutes and think tanks interact. While the term 'network' was not adopted, the 'partnerships' and emerging 'linkages' inside the Peruvian government and Congress outlined by Gabriel Ortiz de Zevallos and Alejandro Salas have some network features. In similar fashion, Ratna Sudarshan identifies a medley of networks – research networks, NGO networks, local and global networks – in which Indian think tanks participate. The chapters on Central and Eastern Europe and Southeast Asia take a different focus to address regional networks, while Stella Ladi argues that 'policy transfer networks' have become apparent in an era of globalisation.

The GDN is not the first global network, nor will it be the last. However, it represents an important initiative and may be symptomatic of wider global trends towards network forms of governance. The boundary between the international and the national or local has shifted dramatically, with various policy initiatives cross-cutting these three levels of governance. As Joseph Stiglitz notes, the world is still a long way from any form of global governance; however, in the absence of global institutions, networks are filling much of the void (see Reinicke and Deng 2000).

Policy networks

The social science literature is replete with competing and complementary 'policy network' concepts. Four frameworks have been mentioned in some of the preceding chapters – policy communities, advocacy coalitions, epistemic communities and discourse coalitions. These are briefly outlined again, and a new network concept – 'transnational advocacy networks' – is introduced in order to draw together some common themes across chapters.

The idea of 'discourse' as the primary medium through which research institutes and think tanks act is found in Chapter 10, where Helen Nesadurai and Diane Stone write of a think tank 'habit of dialogue' helping to create regional identities. This is also found in Chapter 8, where Ivan Krastev argues that 'It is the management of expert discourse and not in-depth research that has empowered think tanks'. Ratna Sudarshan suggests that the MIMAP (Micro Impact of Macro and Adjustment Policies) network can be classed as a 'discourse coalition' of Southern researchers who seek to define a policy problem in a certain way and to create a common set of ideas, concepts and categories through which policy problems can be understood.

For many, discourse is the mode through which our social realities are constructed. First, discourse is an essential part of the process known as the 'mobilisation of bias'. In this view, discourse is a set of 'ideas, concepts and categories through which meaning is given to phenomena' (Hajer 1993: 45). Accordingly, the focus is on how a policy problem is defined and the discourse through which the problem is understood. Policy arguments and recommendations (such as those advocated by think tanks) are selective and involve interpretative struggles. Second, within a coalition, the discourse is amplified and carried beyond intellectual domains. The technocratic policy expertise of think tank policy experts is aligned with the interests of political and economic elites. Consequently, think tank contributions represent part of a wider struggle to control the terms of debate. Discourse coalitions seek to impose their 'discourse' in policy domains. If their discourse shapes the way in which society conceptualises the world or a particular problem, then the coalition has achieved 'discourse structuration', and agendas are likely to be restricted to a limited spectrum of possibilities. If a discourse becomes entrenched in the minds of many as the dominant mode of perception, it can become distilled in institutions and organisational practices as the conventional mode of reasoning. This latter process is 'discourse institutionalisation' (*ibid.*: 47).

An example of this process where think tanks act as discourse managers was most forcefully put by Ivan Krastev in Chapter 8:

> Think tanks were major agents in the rhetorical revolution that took place in Central and Eastern Europe at the beginning of the 1990s. They were instrumental in cleaning up the ruins of the Marxist paradigm and in overcoming suspicion about the market and private property. Think tanks found the right arguments to convince the public of the failure of the old system. The strange disappearance of the economic and political ideas behind the 'human face of socialism' can be explained only if we underline the radical change in policy language that was promoted by the IMF, the World Bank and think tanks. In order to be heard, the opponents of the reforms were forced to speak the language of the Washington consensus.

In this framework, discourse is the object of analysis to the neglect of individuals or organisations as carriers of discourse. In other words, in this 'interpretativist tradition', the discourse or policy narratives give meaning to actors and determine their relations. Consequently, discourse coalitions are bound by the power of the 'storyline', which is open to a multitude of interpretations. These coalitions have an open structure (where actors can continue to differ) and are relatively unstable. By contrast, the following network concepts give greater credence to the material and ideational interests of actors and more coordinated activity (Busch 2000).

'Policy communities' are stable networks of policy actors both inside and outside government that are highly integrated with the policy-making process. Think tanks and researchers are likely to be accorded 'insider' status if they share the central values and attitudes of the policy community (see Coleman and Perl 1999; Ladi in this volume, Chapter 11). However, actors invest in these communities to pursue material interests, and their interactions are shaped by resource dependencies and constant bargaining. There are some similarities with the 'advocacy coalition' framework.

Like a policy community, an advocacy coalition can include journalists, researchers and policy analysts as well as elected officials and bureaucratic leaders: that is, people who share a common set of basic values, causal assumptions and problem perceptions and who show a non-trivial degree of coordinated activity over time (Sabatier and Jenkins-Smith 1993). However, unlike policy communities, where joint action is founded on interest, the glue that holds advocacy coalitions together are 'deep core beliefs' – the normative and ontological axioms that form an individual's basic personal philosophy and that are relatively impermeable to change (Bennett and Howlett 1992: 284).[5] It is a radical reordering of policy analysis from interests to belief systems (Busch 2000: 18). As Evert Lindquist notes (Chapter 12), the presence of competing coalitions can result in situations where expertise is not seen as 'objective knowledge' but as 'contested information'. Policy thus becomes a battle of ideas.

Yet again, some analysts have identified think tanks as participating in more expert 'epistemic communities' (Haas 1992). These consist primarily of knowledge actors – professionals, researchers, scientists – who share common ideas about policy and seek privileged access to decision-making forums on the basis of their scientific expertise and scholarly knowledge. Epistemic communities may be in possession of expert technical knowledge, but when they are entrenched in international institutions they occupy positions of power and are able to embed their ideas. For example, an epistemic community of neo-classical economists is said to have entrenched itself in the World Bank (Deacon *et al.* 1998). Yet the dominance of epistemic communities comes under challenge both externally from other such communities and networks and from internal implosion if the core values and consensual knowledge are found wanting. Such questioning and reassessment can be found in the move from the intellectual underpinnings of first-generation reforms to the second-generation reforms to which Stiglitz alludes. It has brought new cohorts of specialists into the World Bank with expertise in public sector reform, civil society development or regulation diluting the old consensus. This parallels the views of Ivan Krastev, who has coined the phrase 'Washington confusion' as symptomatic of the absence of new consensus.

Think tanks are sometimes identified as participating in broad 'transnational issue networks' that accommodate a range of non-governmental organisations (NGOs) and activists (Keck and Sikkink 1998). These coalitions seek to shape the climate of public debate and influence global policy agendas and are often less integrated into policy making than policy community actors. These networks are bound together by shared values, dense exchanges of information and services, and in common with the idea of 'discourse coalitions' a shared discourse. Where epistemic communities are more exclusive and 'scientific' in composition, founded on 'codified' forms of knowledge, a transnational issue network is more amenable to incorporating 'tacit' and 'grass-roots' varieties of knowledge. Unlike the policy community and advocacy coalition models, this approach also places a much stronger emphasis on the techniques and strategies of networking as a transnational activity through which ideas and norms are spread internationally.

These different understandings of networks provide conceptual tools to address the global and regional interactions of think tanks and their relations with international organisations and other actors. Each framework emphasises different features of the way in which policy thinking may be shaped through network participation. It is not necessary to view these approaches as contradictory. Instead, they highlight the multi-dimensional manner in which networks might accord influence – through discourse, through bargaining or through transnational coalition building. Similarly, they highlight the different environments in which they operate. Thus policy communities and advocacy coalitions tend to evolve in relatively stable and predictable policy environments. By contrast, epistemic communities and transnational advocacy networks emerge in more ambiguous environments where new issues or policy problems are poorly understood or not yet politically recognised.

Moreover, these kinds of network present many advantages for amplifying, filtering, feeding or transmitting research to other network participants and beyond. The collective action of networks is a source of legitimacy and an enhancement of potential policy impact that is unlikely to be achieved through individual organisational activity. In varying degrees, these approaches regard knowledge as an independent source of power and knowledge actors with a capacity, in some circumstances, to influence policy.

It is *not* the case that the GDN can simply be labelled a particular kind of policy network. The GDN is new, evolving and composed of disparate actors. As such, it cannot be categorised as an epistemic community. There is no consensus in the GDN regarding the best path to promote sustainable development or alleviate poverty. Nor is such a consensus sought. It is more appropriate to portray the GDN as a public forum within which epistemic communities and transnational advocacy networks or discourse coalitions might intersect and interact. However, some of these networks may come to dominate the GDN (particularly when their position is formalised) and exercise greater power or 'voice' to shape the destiny of the network and embed a particular mode of policy-relevant knowledge.

Network life

Relatively little attention has been paid to the idea of what makes a network 'tick'. It is not the case that once a collection of individuals and organisations has been brought together they will work collectively and cooperatively in harmony. Networks fail as often as they succeed. Rivalry, lack of common purpose, the absence of a shared vision, squabbles over the distribution of resources, complaints about denied inclusion or access and feuding over who controls the network are all sources of division that can fracture a network.

Within the GDN, powerful political, managerial and professional interests need to be managed and negotiated. Effective coordination requires a clear idea of the 'basis of mutuality' on which the network is founded. In other words, why is coordination required? What are the strategic benefits? What is the added value (Jackson and Stainsby 2000)?

A valid question is whether networking between think tanks on research production has the desired outcomes or, indeed, whether there may be unanticipated costs. Networking is an activity that requires resources, time and personnel. Many institutes may not be able to contribute or participate to the extent that they may wish. Alternatively, the executive of an institute may consider it more appropriate to concentrate research efforts on domestic issues and audiences rather than investing in global elite gatherings. Additionally, potential actors may be dubious of what can be achieved through the GDN. Despite the external recognition and credibility that the network may confer on its participants, many governments may simply continue to ignore research insights.

Nevertheless, think tanks can often find domestic reasons to explain why they might want to interact with institutes in other countries. Schemes to promote democracy in the developing world show the potential of think tanks to feature at both ends of this form of political cooperation. They are resources feeding the promotion of democratic institutions, and as recipients of international assistance they gain renewed capability to play an important part in the policy process of emerging democracies. For example, Australian (Uhr 2000), German (Thunert 2000) and American (Carrothers 1999) think tanks have become key players in democracy assistance in other countries by responding to the policy objectives of their own governments.

Nevertheless, there need to be real incentives for collective action in the design of a common purpose. Knowledge creation and knowledge sharing are the basis of mutuality in the network. Coordination is required to overcome market failure and underinvestment in research. The strategic benefits for GDN participants are access to research partners, mentoring and short-cuts to donors. The added value – as Stiglitz writes – is the release of localised forms of knowledge.

Ironically, in seeking to stimulate the production of a public good – knowledge – the GDN itself may be suffering from the same problem of underinvestment. In short, the GDN has aspects of a public good itself. As a network, the GDN is composed of 'social capital': that is, 'a glue that holds societies together' based on common identification, a sense of belonging or common purpose and shared behavioural norms (Serageldin and Groontaert 2000: 44). Achieving cooperation and reaping its benefits are plagued by the problem of collective action. There will be free-riding. It also suggests that the cohesiveness of collective action built on ideas and value-oriented behaviour is unstable if the interest struggle for material returns is not resolved in a network (Busch 2000: 18).

Even so, network life is not simply about the coordination of planning and budgeting, or launching new products from which network participants may benefit. Coordination is necessary, but so is coherence. A network is a society in and of itself. As Gabriel Ortiz de Zavallos and Alejandro Salas remind us, 'trust' is of great importance in a network.

> Lack of trust will undermine any alliance relationship. While a strong sense of common purpose (collective goals) is the source of coherence, trust is the essential bonding agent.
>
> (Jackson and Stainsby 2000: 13)

In addition, network coherence requires the effective exchange of information, open channels of communication and a sense of the future that guides network participants' behaviour towards joint benefits. A consequence is that effective network management is crucial.

Network management is no easy feat given that networks are made up of a myriad of connections and evolving entities characterised by shifting relationships and power arrangements. Network managers need many skills: a sensitivity to conditions of ambiguity and uncertainty; tact and diplomacy in identifying and resolving conflicts of interest and disputes; determination to weed out 'free-riders'; and communications skills in sustaining dialogues 'to build up a better understanding of the nature of common problems facing the network as a whole and to search for consensus about how best to solve them' (*ibid.*: 14). Network management is more 'artistry' than 'techne'. It involves charisma and leadership from key individuals who can create a vision and inspire trust, commitment and a sense of obligation within a network.

To date, the GDN secretariat at the World Bank has played the role of network manager in building the architecture of the GDN (and in absorbing most of the transaction costs). However, as noted above, the GDN is also an encapsulation of social capital. 'Social capital comes through changes in the relations among persons that facilitate action' (Coleman 2000: 19). Accordingly, the relations, resources and rules of the GDN are likely to change constantly with the shifting culture, perceptions and behaviours of network participants. These intricacies and social relations cannot be understood or appreciated simply by reference to the governance structures, to www.gdnet.org or to participant institutes of the GDN. Instead, the social norms and power relations of networking for knowledge creation and knowledge sharing will define the GDN over the long run.

Notes

1   See http://www.worldbank.org/devforum/forum_gdn.html.
2   The notion of 'world views' comes from the sociologist Max Weber ('*Weltenschauungen*')
3   Thomas Lawo, 19 April 2000, in the GDN web strategy discussion. See http://www.worldbank.org/devforum/forum_gdn.html.
4   Although there has been a movement away from the 'Washington consensus', as reflected in the Comprehensive Development Framework, some analysts are now referring to the 'post-Washington consensus' (Higgott 2000).

5   Advocacy coalitions can be distinguished from one another by their beliefs and resources. In most policy subsystems the number of politically significant coalitions is quite small, yet a dominant advocacy coalition is unlikely to be unseated merely by analytical debate. In periods of relative stability, routine and incremental decision patterns, policy makers prefer information that does not question the underlying consensus of a policy programme. It is external events (political turnover, war, policy crises) that change the terms of debate significantly, create uncertainty and undermine consensus.

References

Abelson, D. E. (2000*) Do Think Tanks Matter? A Comparative Analysis of the USA and UK*, Canada, McGill/Queens University Press.

Bennett, C. J. and Howlett, M. (1992) 'The lessons of learning: reconciling theories of policy learning and policy change', *Policy Sciences* 25(3): 275–94.

Busch, A. (2000) 'Interests or ideas: an overview of ideational concepts in public policy research', in D. Braun and A. Busch (eds) *Public Policy and Political Ideas*, Cheltenham: Edward Elgar.

Carrothers, T. (1999) *Aiding Democracy Abroad: The Learning Curve*, Washington: Carnegie Endowment for International Peace.

Coleman, J. (2000) 'Social capital in the creation of human capital', in P. Dasgupta and I. Serageldin (eds) *Social Capital: A Multifaceted Perspective*, Washington: World Bank.

Coleman, W. and Perl, A. (1999) 'Internationalized policy environments and policy network analysis', *Political Studies* 47(4): 691–709.

Deacon, B., Koivusalo, M. and Stubbs, P. (1998) *Aspects of Global Social Policy Analysis*, Helsinki: STAKES.

Fine, B. (1999) 'The developmental state is dead – long live social capital?' *Development and Change* 30(1): 1–19.

Haas, P. (1992) 'Introduction: epistemic communities and international policy coordination', *International Organization* 46(1): 1–35.

Hajer, M. (1993) 'Discourse coalitions and institutionalisation of practice: the case of acid rain in Great Britain', in F. Fischer and J. Forester (eds) *The Argumentative Turn in Policy Analysis and Planning*, London: UCL Press.

Higgott, R. (2000) 'Taming economics, emboldening international relations: the theory and practice of international political economy in an era of globalisation', in S. Lawson (ed.) *The New Agenda for International Relations: Ten Years After the Wall*, Cambridge: Polity Press.

Jackson, P. M. and Stainsby, L. (2000) 'Managing public sector networked organizations', *Public Money and Management* 20(1): 11–16.

Kaul, I., Grunberg, I. and Stern, M. A. (eds) (1999) *Global Public Goods: International Cooperation in the 21st Century*, New York: Oxford University Press and the United Nations Development Programme.

Keck, M. and Sikkink, K. (1998) *Transnational Issue Networks in International Politics*, Ithaca, NY: Cornell University Press.

McGann, J. and Weaver, R. K. (eds) (2000) *Think Tanks and Civil Societies: Catalysts for Ideas and Action*, Somerset, NJ: Transaction Press.

Nsibambi, A. (1999) 'The role of knowledge in development: perspectives from Uganda', plenary, Global Development Network Conference, Bonn, 5 December.

Reinicke, W. and Deng, F. (2000) 'Critical choices: the United Nations, networks and the future of global governance', executive summary. Accessed 8 June 2000 and available at www.globalpublicpolicy.net/.

Ricci, D. (1993) *The Transformation of American Politics: The New Washington and the Rise of American Politics*, New Haven, Conn.: Yale University Press.

Sabatier, P. A. and Jenkins-Smith, H. C. (eds) (1993), *Policy Change and Learning: An Advocacy Coalition Approach*, Boulder, Colo.: Westview Press.

Scholte, J.-A. (2000) 'Global civil society', in N. Woods (ed.) *The Political Economy of Globalization*, London: Macmillan.

Serageldin, I. and Groontaert, C. (2000) 'Defining social capital: an integrating view', in P. Dasgupta and I. Serageldin (eds) *Social Capital: A Multifaceted Perspective*, Washington: World Bank.

Smith, J. A. (1991) *The Idea Brokers: Think Tanks and the Rise of the New Policy Elite*, New York: Free Press.

Stiglitz, J. (1999) 'Knowledge as a global public good', in I. Kaul, I. Grunberg and M. A. Stern (eds) *Global Public Goods: International Cooperation in the 21st Century*, New York: Oxford University Press and the United Nations Development Programme.

Stiglitz, J. (2000) 'What I learned at the world economic crisis', *The New Republic*, 14 April, accessed 9 June 2000 at http://www.tnr.com/041700/stiglitz041700.html.

Thunert, M. (2000) 'Players beyond borders? German think tanks as catalysts of internationalisation', *Global Society* 14(2): 191–211.

Uhr, J. (2000) 'Think tanks and the policy-making community in Australia', *NIRA Review* 7(2): 35–40.

Wallace, W. (1998) 'Ideas and influence', in D. Stone., A. Denham and M. Garnett (eds) *Think Tanks Across Nations: A Comparative Approach*, Manchester: Manchester University Press.

Wildavsky, A. (1979) *Speaking Truth to Power: the Art and Craft of Policy Analysis*, Boston, Mass.: Little, Brown.

Wiezoreck-Zuel, H. (1999) 'Bridging the gap between knowledge and policy', plenary speech, Global Development Network Conference, 5 December.

Index